D0761015

The Materiality of Learning

The field of educational research lacks a methodology for the study of learning that does not begin with humans, their aims, and their interests. *The Materiality of Learning* seeks to overcome this human-centered mentality by developing a novel spatial approach to the materiality of learning. Drawing on science and technology studies (STS), Estrid Sørensen compares an Internet-based 3D virtual environment project in a fourth-grade class with the class's work with traditional learning materials, including blackboards, textbooks, notebooks, pencils, and rulers. Taking into account pupils' and teachers' physical bodies, Professor Sørensen analyzes the multiple forms of technology, knowledge, and presence that are enacted with the materials. Featuring detailed ethnographic descriptions and useful end-of-chapter summaries, this book is an important reference for professionals and graduate or postgraduate students interested in a variety of fields, including educational studies, educational psychology, social anthropology, and STS.

Estrid Sørensen is currently a Research Associate in the Department of European Ethnology at Humboldt University in Berlin. She is also Associate Professor in the Department of Learning at the School of Education at Aarhus University, Denmark. She holds a Ph.D. from the University of Copenhagen, where she was a research leader in the EU-funded project "5D – Local Learning Communities in a Global World." Previously, she was a visiting scholar at the Centre for Science Studies at Lancaster University, and she has held various other research and teaching positions at universities in Berlin and Denmark. She also worked on research projects concerning protection of children from harmful media content as well as on computer game health information. Moreover, she has been a member of the Danish film classification board. In 2006 Professor Sørensen was granted the Alexander von Humboldt Fellowship. She has contributed to several edited volumes and to many peer-reviewed journals, including *Comparative Sociology*, *Forum Qualitative Social Research*, *Nordisk Psykologi*, *Nordiske Udkast – Tidsskrift for kritisk samfundsforskning*, *Outlines – Critical Social Studies*, and *Psyke og Logos*.

LEARNING IN DOING: SOCIAL, COGNITIVE, AND
COMPUTATIONAL PERSPECTIVES

SERIES EDITOR *EMERITUS*
John Seely Brown, *Xerox Palo Alto Research Center*

GENERAL EDITORS
Roy Pea, *Professor of Education and the Learning Sciences and Director, Stanford Center for Innovations in Learning, Stanford University*
Christian Heath, *The Management Centre, King's College, London*
Lucy A. Suchman, *Centre for Science Studies and Department of Sociology, Lancaster University, UK*

Plans and Situated Actions: The Problem of Human-Machine Communication
Lucy A. Suchman

The Construction Zone: Working for Cognitive Change in Schools
Denis Newman, Peg Griffin, and Michael Cole

Situated Learning: Legitimate Peripheral Participation
Jean Lave and Etienne Wenger

Street Mathematics and School Mathematics
Terezinha Nunes, David William Carraher, and Analucia Dias Schliemann

Understanding Practice: Perspectives on Activity and Context
Seth Chaiklin and Jean Lave, Editors

Distributed Cognitions: Psychological and Educational Considerations
Gavriel Salomon, Editor

The Computer as Medium
Peter Bogh Anderson, Berit Holmqvist, and Jens F. Jensen, Editors

Sociocultural Studies of Mind
James V. Wertsch, Pablo Del Rio, and Jens F. Jensen, Editors

Sociocultural Psychology: Theory and Practice of Doing and Knowing
Laura M. W. Martin, Katherine Nelson, and Ethel Tobach, Editors

Continued after the index

The Materiality of Learning

Technology and Knowledge in Educational Practice

ESTRID SØRENSEN
Humboldt University

CAMBRIDGE
UNIVERSITY PRESS

CAMBRIDGE UNIVERSITY PRESS
Cambridge, New York, Melbourne, Madrid, Cape Town, Singapore, São Paulo, Delhi

Cambridge University Press
32 Avenue of the Americas, New York, NY 10013-2473, USA

www.cambridge.org
Information on this title: www.cambridge.org/9780521882088

First published 2009

Printed in the United States of America

A catalog record for this publication is available from the British Library.

Library of Congress Cataloging in Publication Data
Estrid Sørensen, 1967–
   The materiality of learning: technology and knowledge in educational
   practice / Estrid, Sørensen
      p.   cm. – (Learning in doing)
   Includes bibliographical references.
   ISBN 978-0-521-88208-8 (hardback)
   1. Education, Primary – Computer-assisted instruction.   2. Internet in
   education.   3. Educational technology.   I. Title.   II. Series.
   LB 1028.5.S688 2009
   372.133′4 – dc22
   2008031159

ISBN 978-0-521-88208-8 hardback

Contents

Series Foreword   *page* ix
Acknowledgments   xi

1 A Minimal Methodology   1

   The Study of Materials in Educational Research   5
   Book Overview: Methodology and Empirical Work   10
   Spatial Imaginaries   26
   The Methodology of the Materiality of Learning –
   Lesson 1: Minimal Methodology   27

2 Components and Opponents   30

   Constructing the Research Object and Research Field   32
   Femtedit as an Enrollment of Heterogeneous Components   34
   Association of Otherwise Disparate Parts   36
   Trials of Strength in the Femtedit Design   39
   Classic-ANT and the Network   52
   Conclusion: The Construction of a Stable Technology   58
   The Methodology of the Materiality of Learning –
   Lesson 2: Defining Materiality   60

3 Forms of Technology   62

   A Second Examination of Femtedit   62
   Critiques of the Network Metaphor   66
   Relations and Spaces   69
   Fluid Patterns of Relations   77
   Multiplicity   81
   Conclusion: Spatial Formations and Flexible, Multiple Technology   85
   The Methodology of the Materiality of Learning –
   Lesson 3: Spatiality   87

4 Forms of Knowledge   89

   The Quest for Resemblance   92
   Classroom Jumping Demonstration: The Standard
   Measurement and Resemblance   94
   Regional Space   97
   Boyle's Experiment: The Material Technology   100
   Representational Knowledge   102
   The Bed-Loft Inaugural Ceremony: Resonance Space   104
   Boyle's Experiment: Literary and Social Technologies   107
   Communal Knowledge   108
   Tvia's Twin Towers: Fluid Space in Femtedit   112
   The Pakistani Song: What Form of Knowledge?   118
   Liquid Knowledge   125
   Conclusion: Knowledge and Learning   130
   The Methodology of the Materiality of Learning –
   Lesson 4: Knowledge   135

5 Forms of Presence   137

   Blackboard and Songs, Regions and Collectives   140
   Regional Presence in the Classroom   144
   Authority and Subjects   148
   Restlessness and One-to-One Relationships in the
   Virtual Environment   154
   Separating with Discontinuities   161
   Fluid Authority   166
   The Power of Interactivity, the Power of Fluidity   168
   Conclusion: Posthumanist Presence   170
   The Methodology of the Materiality of Learning –
   Lesson 5: Presence   175

6 The Materiality of Learning   177

   PISA and the Multiplicity of Educational Practice   182
   Comparing Technologies   189
   The Reality, Reimagining, and Rearranging of
   Educational Practice   191
   The Methodology of the Materiality of Learning –
   Lesson 6: The Materiality of Learning   193

   Reference List   195
   Index   207

Series Foreword

This series for Cambridge University Press is widely known as an international forum for studies of situated learning and cognition.

Innovative contributions are being made by anthropology; by cognitive, developmental, and cultural psychology; by computer science; by education; and by social theory. These contributions are providing the basis for new ways of understanding the social, historical, and contextual nature of learning, thinking, and practice that emerges from human activity. The empirical settings of these research inquiries range from the classroom to the workplace, to the high-technology office, and to learning in the streets and in other communities of practice. The situated nature of learning and remembering through activity is a central fact. It may appear obvious that human minds develop in social situations and extend their sphere of activity and communicative competencies. But cognitive theories of knowledge representation and learning alone have not provided sufficient insight into these relationships.

This series was born of the conviction that new exciting interdisciplinary syntheses are underway as scholars and practitioners from diverse fields seek to develop theory and empirical investigations adequate for characterizing the complex relations of social and mental life, and for understanding successful learning wherever it occurs. The series invites contributions that advance our understanding of these seminal issues.

Roy Pea
Christian Heath
Lucy Suchman

Acknowledgments

Collaboration with colleagues and friends in the Fifth Dimension Copenhagen group has been crucial for the realization of the research project discussed in this book. I am especially thankful to Nina Armand, Agnete Husted-Andersen, Kenneth Jensen, Tine Jensen, and Morten Jack for their inspiring and rewarding teamwork. I am also grateful to the Fifth Dimension groups in Ronneby and Barcelona for fruitful discussions and collaboration in the EU-funded "School of Tomorrow" project.

A special thank-you goes to St. Marc Street School[1] – its teachers, pupils, headmaster, and parents – for contributing to my research. Ole Dreier has been a great help through the years, and his sharp analyses have been crucial in driving this work ahead. His persistent encouragement to pursue my points and believe in my work has been of great value to me. During my stay at Lancaster University's Centre for Science Studies I experienced a deeply inspiring intellectual environment. Warm thanks go to Lucy Suchman, John Law, Vera Menegon, Dixi Strand, Jeannette Pols, Rita Struhkamp, and Thomas Scheffer. Lucy Suchman has especially been a great support in the writing of this book.

I am grateful to friends and colleagues across institutions in Copenhagen, with whom I have had great pleasure in discussing my work: Brit Ross Winthereik, Tine Jensen, Dorte Kousholt, and Eva Silberschmidt Viala. The actor-network theory (ANT) community in Copenhagen and the Danish Association of Science and Technology Studies has furthermore continuously inspired my intellectual development. Thanks to Georg Breidenstein for commenting on parts of the book. The feedback from my dissertation committee was furthermore crucial to my

---

[1] As any other names of places, institutions, and persons directly related to the informants of the research presented in this study, this name is a pseudonym.

motivation to write this book. For this I am sincerely grateful to Vinciane Despret, Nick Lee, and Morten Nissen.

Finally, my deepest gratitude goes to Thomas Scheffer and to Nanna, Karla, and Gulliver Scheffer Sørensen, who keep doing the marvelous and vital invisible work of keeping me in a good mood. This is probably the most important single contribution to this work.

1   A Minimal Methodology

Yet school officials here and in several other places said laptops had been abused by students, did not fit into lesson plans, and showed little, if any, measurable effect on grades and test scores at a time of increased pressure to meet state standards. Districts have dropped laptop programs after resistance from teachers, logistical and technical problems, and escalating maintenance costs.

Such disappointments are the latest example of how technology is often embraced by philanthropists and political leaders as a quick fix, only to leave teachers flummoxed about how best to integrate the new gadgets into curriculums. Last month, the United States Department of Education released a study showing no difference in academic achievement between students who used educational software programs for math and reading and those who did not.

Hu Winnie, *New York Times*, 4 May 2007

In 2006 public schools in the United States had on average one computer per 4.2 pupils, which is equivalent to a total of more than 53 million computers (U.S. Census Bureau 2007, table 248). In 2006 Danish schools provided a new computer[1] for every 4.9 pupils (UNI-C 2007). Converted to monetary value, this amounts to an investment, in the United States, of more than $30 billion, which is almost $240 per American household. In addition to this amount is the cost of software, maintenance, training, Internet access, and so on. What has all this money been invested into? We know that it has been invested into materials, and according to the *New York Times* these materials failed to deliver the expected result. But what, then, did they deliver? What can we say about the educational practices that have been invested into? Which educational practices have come about? Not the ones imagined, obviously, but what then? After having invested so much money and so much effort into technology in schools, it is upsetting that the question of what practices these bring about is widely

---

[1] A "new" computer is defined as being less than four years old.

1

neglected. Such questions – and their answers – could teach us a lot, not only about the ways in which materials contribute to educational practice, but also about what was wrong with our initial expectations.

It may seem absurd that such questions are so rarely asked. However, these omissions are quite understandable. The blindness toward the question of how educational practice is affected by materials, beyond the expected results, can be found in the widespread humanist approach to education. I characterize as humanist approaches that start from understandings of the human, of human development, learning, and needs, and that typically ask how the world can be arranged to support one or another desired dimension of human life. Consequently, materials are typically conceived as instruments for educational practice, and the questions asked concern how such instruments can advance educational performances and well-being.

The concept of materials as instruments for humans distinguishes sharply between the human and the instrument the human is using. If the instrument does not deliver the expected result, it makes no sense to further scrutinize the educational practice into which it was introduced. We could however also take a posthumanist stance – which this book does – and place the human not above materials (as the creator or user) but *among* materials. These materials may be used by humans, but they may also use the humans and influence and change the educational practice, which then is no longer particularly human; instead it is *socio-material*. From this point of departure, the question of whether a technology meets human aims becomes overshadowed by questions of what practice takes place when a particular arrangement of social and material components is established. It makes us ask what practice is constituted through this socio-material arrangement, what knowledge comes about, what kinds of pupils and teachers are created, and what learning is achieved. This stance can provide us with some idea of what we received from our enormous investments into educational technology. And it may teach us about the *materiality of learning*.

This book is an attempt to suggest an alternative to humanist studies of education. It studies school practices, but its starting point is neither in pupils nor in teachers, and neither in goals nor in needs. Instead it begins with a focus on materials and is fueled by the observation that humans are not entirely in control of school practices, that what happens in schools is not only due to the pedagogy, authority or style of teachers, children's motivations and abilities, modes of interactions, planning and structuring of school practices, educational culture, or the societal function of education. This book is supported by the assumption that new as well as already established technologies take part in and contribute to forming school practices, and from this point of departure it asks what practices occur and how they are formed.

The question of what and how such technologies contribute to school practice is, however, only secondary to the investigations presented in this book. Due to its humanist tradition, educational research lacks a methodology for the study of learning that does not begin with humans, their aims, and their interests. The question I therefore seek to answer through this book concerns how to account for how materials participate in school practices and for what is performed through this participation. In other words, this book addresses how to account for the materiality of learning from a posthumanist stance.

To this end, I compare how newly implemented technologies participate in school practice with the way in which established technologies do so, using ethnography. Ethnography is a suitable method for studying practice, and for finding answers to open questions about the nature and formation of these practices. Doing an ethnography of new and established technologies means studying them in practice (Hine 2000, 2005; Miller & Slater 2000). The established technologies we encounter in this study include a blackboard, chalk, a chalk-holder, a one-meter ruler, songs, bodies, notebooks, a bed-loft, sheets of paper, chairs, and a bell. The new technologies include an online 3D[2] virtual environment, a weblog[3] (more commonly know as a "blog"), and a conference system. An online 3D virtual environment is a computer program that can be accessed on the Internet. It creates the illusion of a landscape in which the user can move around a graphic character – called an avatar – and create graphic scenarios. The user can meet other people online in the virtual environment, and she can communicate with them electronically through chat and by way of the avatar's gestures. Figure 1 shows the interface of the Active Worlds virtual environment that I discuss throughout the book.[4] A blog is

---

[2] Commonly, virtual environment technology such as Active Worlds is described as "three dimensional," even though it is based not on 3D graphics but on the so-called 2½D images, which are digital images that appear to be three dimensional and that can be rotated on the screen.

[3] http://www.blogger.com.

[4] Other online 3D virtual environments available at the time of my research – 2000 to 2001 – include Blaxxun Contact (http://www.blaxxun.de) and Onlive! Traveler (http://www.onlive.com). The latter allows users to speak to each other when a microphone and speakers are connected to the computer. Active Worlds was one of the most used and most promising graphic virtual environments. It however never succeeded in achieving

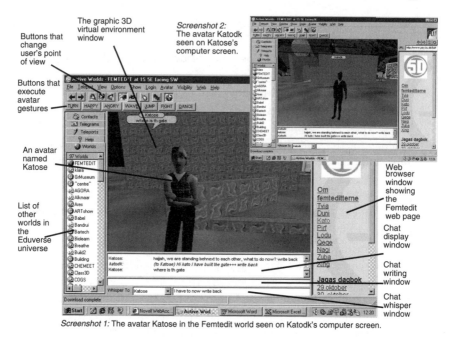

Screenshot 1: The avatar Katose in the Femtedit world seen on Katodk's computer screen.

Figure 1. Screenshots of the Active Worlds interface, showing two avatars (named Katose and Katodk) confronting each other in the virtual world, called Femtedit, discussed throughout this book.

a journal-style interface on the Internet in which users can enter messages that are automatically organized chronologically, so the latest message is on the top of the page while older messages move down one place each time a new message is entered. In the study we used an online discussion forum system that was similar to a blog. Unlike a blog, however, it was a closed user group, and it was set up such that users could organize messages in a string system whereby discussions could take place in separate spaces. By opening a new string, a user would open a new discussion separated from the one taking place in the source string.

broad popularity. After three years in beta, Adobe launched new graphic virtual environment Atmosphere (http://www.adobe.com/products/atmosphere) in February 2004, accompanied by great expectations. Ten months later the program was discontinued due to "market conditions, customer feedback and research done by Adobe," according to their website. Linden Lab's Second Life graphical virtual environment was launched in 2003. It was not until 2006, however, that a sudden rise in the popularity of Second Life (from 100,000 residents in January 2006 to more than 4 million residents a year later) gave rise to a broader use and especially to a broader public awareness of virtual environments. In 2005 a separate teenage world was launched by Linden Lab.

My ethnographic studies of these new and established technologies took place in a Danish fourth-grade class. The book discusses how the materials and technologies took part in the school practice, and through these discussions it answers step-by-step the question of how to account for the materiality of learning.

I answer this question by doing it, by accounting for the materiality of learning. What is the materiality of learning, what is materiality, and what is learning? I reach a definition of materiality in Chapter 2. We however have to wait until Chapter 4 for a definition of learning, and until Chapter 6 for a definition of the materiality of learning. In most educational research, there is a strong preconception of learning as an individual achievement. Such a conception cannot be adopted by a posthumanist approach because it predefines learning as realized by humans, not as a result of a symmetric interplay of humans and materials. Many scholars have done important work to re-conceptualize learning as a social achievement (e.g., Lave 1988; Lave & Wenger 1991; Nielsen & Kvale 1999; Salomon 1993), but, as I argue in Chapters 4 and 5, the concept of materiality in these approaches is rather weak. On the basis of insights gained through approaches to learning as a social achievement I develop in this book a methodology to study learning as not social but socio-material. The endeavor of introducing a new dimension – social or material – into learning theory is not only a matter of taking an additional element into account. From the development of approaches to learning as a social achievement we have learned that such a step changes the whole methodology of learning and the understanding of learning as a whole. Consequently it is a crucial principle of this book to define learning not in advance of the empirical study but instead as a result of the study and the accompanying discussions on how to account for the materiality of learning.

The Study of Materials in Educational Research

Going Beyond Technology as a Means to an End

It would be wrong to say that materials are entirely neglected in educational research. There is a large body of literature on educational technology, which, in addition to studying humans in school practice, is concerned with technology. Some of the central questions of research in educational technology concern how technology makes learning more efficient and more meaningful and how collaboration can be supported by technology (e.g., Koschmann 1996; Koschmann et al. 2002). These are good questions, and they are indeed important questions. But note how they limit the study of technology: When the focus is on learning efficiency, on motivation, on collaboration, and on other human or social phenomena, the only part technology is able to play in the research accounts is that of a means to social, psychological, or pedagogic ends. The answers tell us about the ways in which the technologies in question are or are not suitable for serving human aims. The diverse other ways in which materials take part in social interaction remain under-theorized and little examined. Human aims, interests, or consciousness play the leading part, and technology is relegated to the secondary part. In this book I let technology play the leading role, or at least I place it on the same footing as humans.

Consider this story from the history of technology: In the 1870s Graham Bell made public demonstrations of the telephone in which audiences would listen to Bell's assistant, Thomas Watson, reading the news in a nearby city. This early use of the telephone for broadcasting is very different from the two-way one-to-one communication that later became its primary function. There are several examples in the history of technology showing that the designer's original expectation of how a device would be used largely diverged from how the device eventually came to be used. Most often, this is explained with reference to social needs, organizational structures, culture, competencies, or economy and market forces. In other words, explanations point to social circumstances surrounding the technology, and less frequently to how the technology took part in the practices in question. For example, Larry Cuban (1986) lists the main obstacles for increased film use in the classroom:

- Teachers' lack of skills in using equipment and film
- Cost of films, equipment and upkeep
- Inaccessibility of equipment when it is needed
- Finding and fitting the right film to the class (p. 18)

These obstacles are all primarily social in the sense that they can be remedied by social rearrangements such as training, different economic prioritization, better organization, and more information. There is nothing in these four points that has to do with the specificities of film, that is, with the material in question. Cuban has not considered in which ways film may contribute to a different form of knowledge than textbooks do, for instance, or whether the use of film gave rise to new problematic forms of interaction between the pupils and the teacher. Furthermore, he does not consider whether the form of learning to which films may contribute could in any way be an obstacle to increased use of film in the classroom. The way in which materials take part in interactions in educational practice is rarely considered in the literature.

Researchers in educational technology can learn from the observation made by scholars of science and technology (STS) that technologies often are unfaithful (Akrich 1992; Latour 1988) to their designers, users, and researchers. The fact that educational technologies may contribute to educational practice in ways that are different from the expectations of their creators, implementers, users, and investigators is generally neglected. We find descriptions of technologies failing to deliver the expected educational outcome (e.g., Boyd 2002), but researchers rarely ask what was performed by and through the technologies in place of the expected outcome. Some may consider that an irrelevant question. They may maintain that if technologies do not achieve what is desired, then these technologies are of no interest, and consequently further inquiry is irrelevant. There are at least three reasons why I do not subscribe to this position.

First, it makes sense to ask how specific technologies contribute to practice without focusing on what we would like them to do, because they might contribute to performing forms of learning and collaborating that are unexpected but that may be fruitful if developed further.

Second, studying technology beyond the focus of educational aims makes us aware that even when technologies do support our educational aims, they also always produce other effects. When technology is treated as an instrument, questions about the exact role of technology remain unanswered, as does the question of whether changes in the design of technology or modifications in the interaction with technology could turn the practice in other (more desirable) directions.

Finally, the emphasis on technology as a means to educational aims establishes an intellectual division of labor, which puts educational theory and conceptualization of educational aims above the understanding of technology in educational practice. Researchers first consider how children learn and develop and what characterizes good interaction, and only after that they ask how technology can be applied to create these conditions. Researchers rarely consider that it may be the other way around: that we theorize about learning the way we do because we have certain learning materials in mind when we account for learning, or at least that the learning materials in use influence the formation of learning and affect our thinking and theorizing about education in general. I argue that this is the case and consequently that we should place a stronger emphasis on materiality in educational theory in general.

Through empirical analyses of the school practice of a Danish fourth-grade class in the classroom and in a computer lab working with a 3D virtual environment, this book shows how digital and traditional learning materials influence educational practice in general, and how they contribute in particular to shaping different forms of knowledge and varieties of presence.

Paths Toward the Study of the Materiality of Learning

As a consequence of my previously mentioned disagreements with the human-centered approach to research in education, I have found inspiration for the work presented in this book outside the field of educational theory. My analyses are mainly inspired by STS, which is an interdisciplinary approach that has not yet been given much attention by the educational research field.

STS originates in studies of the sociology of science (e.g., Merton 1973), the history of science (e.g., Kuhn 1970), the philosophy of science (e.g., Popper 1963), and the anthropology of science (e.g., Traweek 1988). These disciplines all focus on the study of science and the production of knowledge. As a result of empirical studies of science, science studies scholars started to see technology as an intrinsic aspect of science and knowledge production (e.g., Knorr Cetina 1999; Latour & Woolgar 1986; Traweek 1988). Consequently, some scholars started referring to their work as studies of science, technology, and society,[5] and STS was born. STS scholars seek to understand the relationships among technology, science, political systems, social relations, and human values and to describe how these relationships are influenced by science and technology and, in turn, how these relationships affect science and technology (e.g., Sismondo 2004). Because technologies – and materials in general – have been (and still are) broadly neglected as part of the constitution of

---

[5] There is no consensus about whether STS refers to "studies of science, technology, and society" or to "science and technology studies." Some scholars insist on the first option, emphasizing that we study science and technology not as isolated areas but as crucial and influential aspects of society. I subscribe to the view that society is a crucial aspect of STS, but, like many others, I use the phrase "science and technology studies" in everyday communication simply because it is linguistically less clumsy than the former. I think it is more important to show the presence of an awareness of society in the work we do than to use the right labels.

knowledge in particular, and of social processes in general, materiality came to be a central theme of one of the most theoretically sophisticated approaches to STS, namely actor-network theory (ANT). Over the past decade ANT has expanded the discussion of what is called socio-material practice from a narrow focus on science and the study of scientific (including medical) and engineering practices to a broad examination of other empirical fields such as financial markets (Knorr Cetina & Preda 2004), legal practices (Jasanoff 2007; Latour 2004b), the multiple identity of aircraft technology (Law 2002a), and the study of organizations (Elgaard Jensen 2001). From the perspective of STS this book is a contribution that expands its approach to yet another field: educational practice. Like science, school practices produce knowledge, and, like in science, materials are core participants in educational practice, or such is my claim.

There are other paths toward the focus on materiality in educational research. My journey to this field of study was also a personal one. In 1992 I went to college to study psychology. I had read Freud's *Interpretations of Dreams* (Freud 1994), and I found his attempt to explain the inner psychological life fascinating. I quickly learned that there is much more to academic psychology than psychoanalysis. I was particularly thrilled by the challenge of understanding the individual as socially embedded. I studied George Herbert Mead (1934) and ethnomethodology (Garfinkle 1967). I learned to criticize the way in which these interactional approaches bracket the societal dimensions of human life, and I turned to activity theory (Leontiev 1978; Vygotsky 1978) and critical psychology (Dreier 1993; Holzkamp 1995). I read the book *Situated Learning* (Lave & Wenger 1991), and I found its account of the person-in-the-world and of learning as a movement toward the (non-existing) center of a social culture very convincing, as did many other scholars. The book became a landmark for a new approach to learning as social. The more I studied and did empirical work, the more I realized that there was an absence of materials in these approaches' empirical analyses and that they had difficulty approaching materiality empirically. This was what turned me toward STS and especially toward ANT. Over the years, I have met many scholars whose stories are similar to mine. Many of these excellent researchers have a background in psychology, but only few of them work in psychology departments. They primarily work in more or less interdisciplinary departments and with interdisciplinary projects. Many call themselves "social scientists" or "STS scholars" because the "psychologist" label gives rise to associations that these scholars for years have worked to overcome. The discussion of materiality is a discussion on the boundary of the discipline of psychology, just as it is a discussion on and of the boundaries of educational research. My personal story is far from private. Just as the person is embedded in a social and material world, my story – and this book – is the story of contemporary movements in social, psychological, and educational research.

Book Overview: Methodology and Empirical Work

The Chapters

The book is divided into six chapters. Chapters 2 and 3 concern materials, materiality, and how to study them. I investigate the question of how to account for materials in practice by studying the way in which the virtual environment technology became a subject of research, which, as I show, was a result of a process of a contingent practice. Methods books tend to be written from a management perspective, focusing on how the research process as a whole can be managed and directed toward an intended goal. This is indeed a common perspective when conducting a research process, but it is far from the only one. During the research project the researcher finds himself in the midst of data, appointments, documents, method guidelines, deadlines, informants, literature, colleagues, and institutional and disciplinary entanglements. In this position his attention is not only, and not foremost, on the research process as a whole, but very much directed toward how to attend to the variety of here-and-now practicalities with which he is confronted. Chapter 2 describes the initial phase of the method I applied from the perspective of being entangled in a complex research practice. It presents the method as contingent, which notably is different from being incidental. I account for the virtual environment by describing how it was constructed as a research object, and thus the discussion of how to account for a material melts into a discussion of the research method. I conclude Chapter 2 with a definition of material and of materiality.

Chapter 3 opens a Pandora's Box of sorts; a number of components are drawn in that undermine the description of the virtual environment in Chapter 2. This leads to a conclusion about the *multiplicity* of materials, and, more important, it leads to the conclusion that describing materials and other components as elements is misleading when accounting for the materiality of learning. I unfold instead a *spatial* approach that asks not about elements or relations but about the patterns of relations that social and material participants perform in practice. The spatial approach developed in Chapter 3 constitutes the methodology for the analyses in Chapters 4 and 5. These two chapters deal with what is performed through the participation of the technologies in school practice. Two sets of performative effects of the way in which the technology participated in practice are explored: *forms of knowledge* and *forms of presence*.

Whereas Chapters 2 and 3 focus on the 3D virtual environment platform, Chapters 4 and 5 compare this digital technology with the traditional learning materials that I observed in a fourth-grade classroom. The decision to make this comparison was just as contingent as many of the other steps in this research process. It was however a crucial and fortunate step. The idea arose out of the field itself – I repeatedly heard the children, the teachers, my colleagues, and myself comparing digital technology with what happened in traditional classrooms. I made an arrangement with a fourth-grade teacher to observe her class, but I considered this a minor side step in my project. However, comparing classroom observation field notes with the data from the virtual environment project turned out to be highly profitable for understanding the materiality of learning, and these comparisons became central to the analyses I present in this book.

Chapter 4 concerns forms of knowledge. Starting with the assumption that materials take part in and contribute to forming school practices, we must expect that different materials play different parts and thus contribute to different forms of knowledge. Chapter 5 follows the same scheme but asks about the forms of presence performed with different materials. The question of presence refers to the ways in which the humans involved came to participate in different ways due to the involvement of different technologies. Knowledge and presence – or person or subjectivity, as the latter is more often labeled – are both central aspects of the literature on learning, and throughout Chapters 4 and 5 I get closer to a discussion of learning and of the materiality of learning. A definition of the materiality of learning is however saved for the concluding chapter.

Beyond Conceptual Confrontation

I often encounter scholars of situated learning and activity theory who claim that my commitment to develop a socio-material approach to educational practice is far from new, and that they have been doing this for decades. These comments seem correct; I frequently find in the literature formulations of these approaches that are similar to what I would write from an ANT approach. For instance, Sasha Barab and Jonathan A. Plucker (2002) write that "ability and talent arise in the dynamic transaction among the individual, the physical environment, and the sociocultural context" (p. 174) and thus demonstrate sensitivity to human capacities as socio-material achievements. When I reach the empirical discussions, however, extensive and decisive differences appear. Apparent theoretical agreement often leads to very different kinds of empirical analyses. I have therefore decided to minimize purely theoretical discussions of the ways in which materials contribute to school practice. The logical meaning and coherence of the concepts we use is less important; what is crucial is how they help us do empirical studies and analyses and the kinds of studies and analyses in which they result. I therefore develop and discuss theoretical notions through empirical studies and analyses, and the book is formed by the research process and the accounts of it. It is written not as an account of an already completed project, as is most often the case in the scientific literature, but as a sequence of insights established throughout the course of the book. This form is a consequence of the principle of not defining concepts a priori, but developing them in interaction with the empirical material. Accordingly, this first chapter introduces just what is necessary to start from: a few methodological terms.

Theoretical Technologies and Imaginaries

The principle of defining concepts through discussions of the empirical data has given rise to two types of critique of my work. Some scholars comment that my analyses are empiricist and lack any form of theory, and others state that the empirical data only illustrate an a priori theory presented parallel to the analyses. In other words, we can say that some critics categorize my work as inductive, while others classify it as deductive. I do not think any of these labels are appropriate for the analyses in this book. The notions of induction and deduction imply that there is a gap between theorizing and the world that is theorized: the world is "out there," and the task of the researcher is either to describe the world according to her theory "in here" or to form a theory "in here" on the basis of what she observes "out there." Pragmatist philosopher John Dewey (1929) suggests a quite different relationship between the theory and the world. He describes scientific concepts and approaches as *theoretical technology* in the sense that, depending on the concepts and the relations they have to other concepts and to practice, concepts contribute to making particular empirical studies possible. Understanding concepts not as the building blocks of a theory (either prior to or as result of empirical work) but as theoretical technologies, my goal is not to provide explanations for why the practices I study are as they are, even though my descriptions may lead to a greater insight into how humans and nonhumans relate and which effects this may generate. My aim is to develop theoretical technologies that may help us study the materiality of learning. It is neither theoretical nor empirical, neither inductive nor deductive; instead it is *methodological*. Working in a methodological mode is of little use if one strives for certainty. It is however attractive if one wishes to imagine how practice could be different and how to reconfigure (Haraway 1997) or rearrange humans and things to allow new forms of technology, knowledge, presence, and learning to emerge.

Another way of describing the ambitions of this book is to label it ontological, which positions it at a distance from the epistemological endeavor of deduction and induction. I do not deal with ontology as do essentialists, who focus on the inherent qualities of objects. On the contrary, my curiosity concerns how humans and things come to be – how they *become* – as effects of the arrangements in which they are entangled. Looking at philosopher of science Helen Verran's (1998) notion of the *imaginary* helps clarify how a methodological commitment differs from an inductive or deductive approach in the relationship implied between theoretical and empirical work. Verran unfolds her understanding of the imaginary through an analytical comparison between Aboriginal and pastoral ways of knowing land. The latter – in consonance with Western thinking – knows land by quantifying it. Lengths and widths constitute a logic that translates qualities that are understood to be *in* the land. But where do the qualities we express through quantification come from? According to Kant these qualities are synthetic a priori concepts. Numbers provide us with a structure that makes us synthesize notions of qualities as infinite extensions when related to a perceptual entity. Knowing land is a cognitive maneuver – it is purely epistemic.

Aborigines know land not through quantification but through kinship relations. Kin relations translate qualities of the land in the same way that the logic of numbers does. Whereas the inherent qualities of the land are neglected or even denied by the application of Kant's quantification to a priori concepts and cognition, Aboriginals live and celebrate these qualities. The Yolngu (indigenous inhabitants of eastern Arnhem Land in Australia) acknowledge that it is through stories about and traffic across the boundaries between different "time-spaces" that the qualities of the land are maintained. Traversing boundaries is an overt participation in public ceremony. Thus, Aboriginal knowing is a mix of ontic and epistemic commitments. Verran calls these ontic/epistemic.

Performing songs and stories that come up with metaphoric insights that map the land on which they live is valued as Yolngu intellectual work. These songs and stories form a correct map that everyone knows – or lives – in varying degrees of detail. Pastoralists, however, know there are no metaphors or images involved in knowing the actual land. There are just the rigid facts of quantifying and surveying the land. Implicit in the pastoralists' knowing is the idea that various individuals might imagine and use all sorts of metaphors to represent the land, but that is the domain of art and emotion, which has no place in the knowing of the actual land.

Verran emphasizes that the main difference between the two ways of knowing has to do with how they treat images. Whereas images are central for the Aboriginal knowing, they are denied by the Westerners. Aboriginal land titles are performed through songs and stories, whereas pastoralists' land titles are understood as texts on maps that neutrally represent the land, independent of human imaginaries. Imaginaries, people, and the land, Verran emphasizes, come into being together, and thus are deeply implicated in and by one another. This is the case not only for Aborigines but also for Westerners. However, Westerners deny the role of imaginaries in knowing, Verran (1998) notes. They deny that "[m]aps are a particular way of living space and encode a complex set of conventions and standards that only hold because they continue to be enacted as people make and use maps, and because a great deal of work is put into making them hold" (p. 250). Maps and other quantitative measures of land are not simply a cognitive operation belonging to the human and distant from the land. They are procedures contributing to making the land. By denying the agency of representations and imaginaries – maps, land titles, quantification – in knowing, Westerners are incapable of reimagining their ontic commitment to the land and are thus unable to negotiate a cohabitation (see Haraway 1991, 2003, 2008) of and with the land. Instead they retain (while denying) Kant's imaginary of world elements as accessed through cognitive, and thus individual, operations. In her discussion of human-machine reconfigurations, anthropologist of technology Lucy Suchman (2007) emphasizes that the notion of imaginaries

> references the way in which how we see and what we imagine the world to be is shaped not only by our individual experiences but also by the specific cultural and historical resources that the world makes available to us, based on our particular location within it. And perhaps most importantly for my purposes here, cultural imaginaries are realized in material ways. (p. 1, n. 1)

As it is for Suchman, it is important for the purpose of this book that imaginaries are constituted materially. Furthermore, I apply the notion of imaginaries in the following analysis of the materiality of learning in order to attempt to know materiality of learning differently from the dominant Western epistemic way. The aim of the ontic/epistemic commitment of imaginaries is to know – and to reimagine – the materiality of learning in ways that make available new connections among people, materials, and places. This may enable an artful integration (Suchman 1999) of technology and practice.

Performativity

Including imaginaries in our thinking lends us kinship with Aboriginals. It makes a performative or enacting mode of knowing primary. Verran (1998) emphasizes:

> This is to engage a notion of knowledge [and a practice of knowing] which is not representationalist but which asserts that all knowledge derives from particular practical contexts and is an embodiment rather than a representation. The idea that there is a "natural world" for knowledge to be about, entirely distinct from the ways human and non-humans as knowers and/or agents interact, must be abandoned. (p. 254, n. 15, my insertion)

Dealing with the text of this book as *performative* is a way of thinking about it in a non-representationalist way. According to *Webster's New World Dictionary and Thesaurus* (1997).

SYN. – perform, often a mere formal equivalent for *do*, is usually used of a more or less involved process rather than a single act [to perform an experiment]; *execute* implies a putting into effect or completing that which has been planned or ordered [to execute a law]; *accomplish* suggests effort and perseverance in carrying out a plan or purpose [to accomplish a mission]; . . . *fulfill*, in strict discrimination, implies the full realization of what is expected or demanded [to fulfill a promise].

I would like to emphasize the equivalence of performing and doing. Talking about the text in this book as performative emphasizes what it *does*. This is a crucial posthumanist and material attitude because it highlights not what some human may intend with the text or how he may interpret the text but what the text does. What it does, like what the concepts and theoretical technologies suggested in this book do, is continue my empirical fieldwork and observations. As Dewey (1938) noted, concepts are related to other concepts and to practice. This practice could be the practice of investigating a field, just as it could be the practice investigated. I thus understand the text of this book as a discursive continuance or prolonging of the empirical practice in the forth-grade class in which I took part (Sørensen 2001). As Verran (1998) put it in the preceding quote, knowledge "derives from particular practical contexts and is an embodiment [of that context] rather than a representation."

Whereas notions of induction and deduction imply that theories are abstract representations of the real world, we can say that a performance prolongs (Despret 2004a) a preexisting reality, which does not make the performance more or less real or abstract than the preexisting reality. This is one of the crucial moves in the performative turn: the attempt to "make matter matter" (Barad 1998, 2007) by staying on the level of socio-material reality and by not turning our theorizing or knowing into perspectives, interpretations, or representations. A performance and its preexisting reality are different *versions* (Despret 2004a; Mol 1999) of the real, of which there is no original, but only such different versions (see also Latour 1999c).

As Verran emphasized about Aboriginal knowing, performativity implies that a text is not isolated from the reality it prolongs or embodies. The embodiment of reality is a particular embodiment that becomes the way it becomes due to the concepts and approaches – the theoretical technologies – of which the text consists. As Dewey said, different theoretical technologies contribute to making specific empirical studies possible. When for instance, in Chapter 5, I describe the human presence of a certain spatial formation as that of an agent, we may understand this as a particular translation – and thus change – of the preexisting reality that is made possible through the approach I develop in this book. It is due to this blending of theoretical technologies and the (now) preexisting reality – of theoretical and empirical components – that I call the approach methodological rather than either theoretical or empiricist. Describing a form of presence as that of an agent is thus a methodological move that allows the reader to take this concept and apply it to another text, to a practice in which it may help her rearrange the pattern of relations (another theoretical technology that I develop in this book; see Chapter 3) she encounters here.

Let me return once more to *Webster's New World Dictionary and The-saurus*. It emphasizes that performance is an involved process rather than a single act. This is important. Whereas action is a process with a temporal extension from its beginning to its end (Hirschauer 2004), "performance" describes the involvement of a variety of related components: the preexisting reality, the text, and the approach, together forming a socio-material *assemblage.* Contrary to the notion of action, which implies a human rationality – or at least knowledgeable humans (Giddens 1984) – performance describes an effect of the socio-material assemblage (Law 2002a).

Performance has come to be a quite popular term in the social and human sciences. It is applied in many different ways, but common among them is an attempt to reach beyond the linguistic turn and its understanding of knowledge as especially related to language and verbal and visual representations. "This turn has too often cut us off from much that is most interesting about human practices, most especially their embodied and situated nature" geographer and spatial theorist Nigel Thrift (1996, p. 7) emphasizes. The notion of performance applied in this book has as its main source of inspiration the previously mentioned authors, as well as, in feminist and science studies, scholar Karen Barad (1998, 2007) and feminist and technoscientist Donna Haraway (1997; see also Gane & Haraway 2006).

In this context, performance has nothing to do with theater or with staging in everyday life, as it is used in micro-sociologist Erving Goffman's work (1959). Goffman distinguishes between presentations of self on the one hand and self as a hidden reality lying behind and producing those presentations on the other. This is quite different from the notion of performativity applied in this book. Here, the presentation of self can be seen as a performance, but so can whatever might be lying behind. One might ask, In what ways is it made to lie behind? In what ways is this behindness performed? What does the pattern of relations that put some presentations on the front stage and some behind look like?

Because the notion of performance in Goffman's use has inappropriate connotations, empirical philosopher Annemarie Mol suggests we instead talk about *enactment* (Mol 2002). However, STS scholar Torben Elgaard Jensen (2001) notes that organizational theorist Karl Weick uses this term to describe human sense making, which is a just as inappropriate connotation of performance. Systems design analyst Dixi Henriksen (2003) notes that organization and information technology scholar Wanda J. Orlikowski uses the term "enactment" in a structuration approach (Giddens 1984). So, Elgaard Jensen continues, "the dream of a relatively 'unspoiled' concept is scattered once again" (2001, p. 89). I will follow Elgaard Jensen's suggestion and stick to the notion of performance.

Participation

The notion of performance is related to the question of what is performed. What about the question of how it is performed? How does technology take part in a practice? The notion of participation can help us ask this question. The notion of participation is primarily disseminated in educational research, thanks to anthropologist and learning theorist Jean Lave and social learning theorist Etienne Wenger (Lave & Wenger 1991). Like almost all other researchers, they apply the notion exclusively with reference to humans. Psychologist and scholar of subject research Ole Dreier (1999) has developed and specified the notion of *personal participation*, which he identifies using the following features:

- It indicates that a participant is always already involved in practice.
- It emphasizes the particularity and practical nature of the participant.
- It points to the partial aspect of practice.
- It indicates that a participant is always part of practice, even when not re-producing but disagreeing with or changing it.

For Dreier the participant is always a person (Dreier 1993, 2003). Because my aim is to study the participation of technology and not personal participation, I depart from Dreier's theory, and, applying the ANT's principle of *symmetry* (e.g., Callon & Law 1997; Johnson 1995; Latour 1999a), I apply "participant" and "participation" to nonhumans as well as to humans. This altered notion of participation invites us to study a computer program as one of the participants entangled in the practical accomplishment of practices, knowledge, presence, and learning. Stefan Hirschauer is a sociologist with special interest in the study of bodies. He remarks that

> [a]rtefacts (a. o.) are not actors but *participants* of social processes. Suggesting this notion does not point to a set of situated participants as in symbolic interactionism nor the partakers in a democratic process (participation) as in political theory[6], but to all entities that are involved in accomplishing practices in a way that is specific for them. The talk of participants lies "on the linguistic level" of the talk of *doing culture*. Notably, the English *doing* is grammatically a present participle. It belongs to the so-called infinite verb forms that contrary to the finite forms are undefined in person and numbers. The actor is unimportant for the infinite verbs: Something stays "smoking" – even if it is human, Colt, chimney or volcano. (Hirschauer 2004, pp. 74–75, my translation)

---

[6] Nor, I would like to add, does it point to a partaker of a democratic design process, as in participatory design.

Whereas Dreier's four points emphasize the human's doings in practice, Hirschauer uses the notion to turn any component into a participant of practice, independently of person and number. As was the case for the notion of performance, Hirschauer underlines the relation between participation and doing. Doing is an effect of the assemblage, and, when talking about the participation of a computer program, we find that instead of studying the computer program as a more or less well-delimited object or actor, our description becomes focused on the software as the assemblage of parts involved in accomplishing technological practices. Discussing virtual environments in terms of participation is a way of creating sensitivity to questions concerning how this application participates in practice in different, sometimes surprising, and unforeseen ways.

Data Collection Methods

A methodology for accounting for the materiality of learning is developed in this book by actually doing this: accounting for the materiality of learning. In order to investigate the participation of the online software and what it performed, I designed in collaboration with my research group[7] two versions of an online 3D virtual environment, which will be discussed throughout the book. We called the first version FEMTEDIM. It participated in a ten-month after-school project (September 2000–June 2001) with nine- to twelve-year-old children who met once a week to work with the virtual environment. The second version, called Femtedit, was involved in an in-school project that ran through seven weeks (October–December 2001) in two fourth-grade classes. Because the software was located on the Internet, users did not need to be in the same physical room. Some of the children who participated in FEMTEDIM and Femtedit were situated in the southern Swedish town of Ronneby[8], while others logged on from a school in Copenhagen, Denmark. I did my ethnographic fieldwork on the two projects in the Copenhagen St. Marc Street School.

We got permission to carry out the FEMTEDIM project in the computer lab of St. Marc Street School from the headmaster. St. Marc

---

[7] Many students and researchers were involved for varying periods of time in the research projects discussed in this book. The following persons took part in the empirical studies I discuss and constitute the "research team" I refer to several times: Michael Aagaard, Nina Armand, Agnete Husted-Andersen, Erik Axel, Kenneth H. Jensen, and Tine Jensen.

[8] Rosita Anderson and Carina Anderson at the Blekinge Institute of Technology were the leading researchers in the Swedish team.

Street School is located in a lower-middle-class area of Copenhagen with a high concentration of immigrants (for Denmark). The school has been proactive in creating a progressive pedagogic profile. This has attracted many ethnic Danish parents and has positioned St. Marc Street School as one of the "white" schools of the area – only approximately 35 percent of the pupils are children of immigrants. St. Marc Street School is a small school with only one class at each grade level. Denmark has a "unified school system," which means that pupils remain with the same group of children from the voluntary preschool (five- to six-year-olds) or first grade to ninth grade – the last year of elementary school – at which point the pupils are fifteen to sixteen years of age.

In order to enroll children to take part in FEMTEDIM, I presented the project at a morning gathering for the whole school, and my research team hung posters in the school about the project. Furthermore, we visited each of the fourth-, fifth-, and sixth-grade classes once during the school day and told them briefly about the FEMTEDIM project. This was all done in agreement with the headmaster and with the teachers of each class. We distributed a project description on a sheet of paper for each pupil to take home. The sheet also included an enrollment form on which children were asked to fill in their name and their parents' names, their grade, and whether they agreed to take part in a research project that involved being filmed and anonymously described in research reports. The form was to be signed by the child and by a parent and returned to the teachers, from whom one of my colleagues collected them a few days later.

Twenty-eight nine- to twelve-year-old children signed up for the FEMTEDIM project. Several of these only came the first few times, other children enrolled later, and many children came on and off. We appreciated when children attended continuously, but we did not require regular attendance, and although we let children who had been missing know that we welcomed their return, we never questioned their absence. A total of thirty-eight children attended the FEMTEDIM afternoon activity, which took place every Monday afternoon from 1:30 to 3:00 pm. A group of seventeen children were more or less regular attendees, of whom eleven were boys and six were girls. In this book, all children's and teachers' names are pseudonyms, whereas the researchers' and avatars' names are not.

I treat the FEMTEDIM project as a pilot study. Femtedit was a follow-up to the FEMTEDIM project. We gained access to the fourth-grade class within which the Femtedit project took place through its two teachers, who approached my colleagues when they presented the FEMTEDIM project at a staff meeting at St. Marc Street School. The teachers at

St. Marc Street School were organized into teams, which meant that each class had only two teachers, who collaborated closely and shared all the teaching, except for physical education. The fourth-grade teachers became involved in the preparation of the Femtedit project through three planning meetings. During the project they split the class in half and took turns bringing one half to work on the Femtedit project while one teacher stayed in the classroom with the other half of the class.

There were twenty-four nine- to ten-year-old children in the fourth-grade class. Of these, twelve were girls and sixteen were of an ethnic Danish background. Each child and his parent signed a form consenting to take part in a research project, to be filmed, and to be described anonymously in research reports. During the FEMTEDIM and Femtedit projects, the involved researchers were observing participants (Hammersley & Atkinson 1995). We planned the sessions and functioned as teachers of a sort during the sessions, taking on the role of "encouragers." We helped the children whenever they needed it but also supported and encouraged them to go on with whatever they were doing. (For more detailed discussions on our research positions, see Jensen [2005a, 2005b].) The different forms of presence this created are discussed further in Chapter 5.

Assisting the children in this way and thereby being engaged participants of the FEMTEDIM and Femtedit projects contributed to the "everydayness" of the research, compared to the stylized atmosphere of laboratory experiments. But it also entailed some difficulties for doing research. When a researcher acts as an observing participant, her distance as an observer decreases, and she gains the immersed engagement of a participant (Amit 2000). Distance is important for making ethnographic observations, and the observing participant needs to maintain a delicate balance between participating and observing. It is however not only up to the researcher to maintain this balance. As discussed in more detail in Chapter 5, the online 3D virtual environment contributed to establishing a pattern of relations in which an overview of the whole online application or the whole class was not available. This made each researcher's perspective quite narrow, concerning mainly the particular participation he engaged in. This was especially the case in Femtedit. Whereas the researchers in FEMTEDIM moved around in the computer lab, attending to different children and different computers, our positions in the Femtedit project were strongly regulated. We divided the children among us so that each of us was mainly engaged with two children at a time, who were working individually or in a pair. Because only half of the class was attending the Femtedit at a time, each researcher engaged with four to eight children in total (for further discussion of the reasons for these divisions, see Chapter 2). My participant observations of Femtedit concerned six children.

The observations we made during both FEMTEDIM and Femtedit were collected in field notes that each researcher wrote after each session. I typically wrote eight to ten pages on my computer, which often took most of the day. I made as detailed, as thick, descriptions as possible of how the practice had unfolded, without any specific focus. I tried to register as much as possible in the field notes by starting at the beginning of the session – often from when the researchers met – and thoroughly describing all I remembered about what had taken place: the actions, utterances, responses, and the social or material entities entangled in these occurrences, be they humans, objects, or displays on computer screens. I was careful to write the field notes as accounts of processes that created stories of continuous streams of interaction. Contrary to postmodern grounded theory scholar Adele Clarke (2005), who starts with the question of who and what were present in the empirical setting and then creates a "messy map" that randomly places these elements on paper, it was important for my work never to focus on elements but always to describe relations. As much as possible, any sequence in my ethnographic writing began with something *happening*, contrary to elements or to something being. Something happening can be anything that can be described with verbs. Focusing on what happens rather than on the elements doing and saying is, in my view, an imperative principle of studying practice. When we want to learn about materials in education and how to account for them, such a practice approach is crucial, because it is only through a careful study of practice that we can realize what materials become through the process of interacting with other parts, among these, humans. In my field notes I registered the feelings and thoughts I had during the fieldwork, along with what happened "around" me. I tried to describe the present as I had experienced it. This meant that whenever my writing of field notes inspired other thoughts, understandings, or analyses of what had taken place – of what I was writing about – I noted these in separate memos. I tried not to collect too many of such "afterthoughts"; I tried not to reflect on what I was writing. This was difficult. It required that I, as much as possible, ignore my embodied presence of writing field notes and mentally immerse myself in the presence of the FEMTEDIM or Femtedit sessions of that day.

Apart from the FEMTEDIM and Femtedit sessions, I collected data on the design process before the projects started and, when the projects were running, between sessions. The processes of designing FEMTEDIM and Femtedit was an interplay between individual work and meetings with my research team. I wrote several outlines of frame stories that were discussed in the group and subsequently rewritten mainly by me, discussed in the group again, and once again rewritten. As during the sessions with the children, my position as a researcher was that of an observing participant. During the FEMTEDIM and Femtedit sessions, I focused on what was going on there – giving the children and the virtual environment the most attention – but during the design process before the projects started and between the individual sessions I observed my and my research team's design practices. This division between sessions and design processes, however, was not total. During the sessions, and in my field notes, I also focused on describing the design and the ways in which I had experienced how it worked. This awareness was necessary for the continuous process of designing.

During the Femtedit project we shared and discussed our field notes and experiences among Danish and Swedish researchers and teachers in an online discussion forum, which we set up specifically for the project (see Chapter 2). The data collected during the sessions and during the design processes are listed in Table 1.

The partial view of each researcher's field notes contrasted strongly with the mosaic or pin board (Law 2002a) that all the researchers' field notes, and other materials, formed together. My field notes were the prime source of data for the analyses in the following chapters. After completing the data collection, I read and looked through all data and added memos (Clarke 2005) to my field notes when I felt that they were relevant to the analysis of the materiality of learning. These memos contained supplementations to and questions about the field notes. Of all the field notes, my notes kept their position as the central material on which I based my analyses. Sometimes, however, the descriptions in my field notes were not sufficient for completing an analysis, or it became clear that my field notes lacked descriptions of certain parts that could be found in, for instance, the video recordings. In these cases I used these other sources as the central material for my analyses, as the following chapters show.

As mentioned previously, I also carried out an ethnographic classroom observation (Klette 1998; Lindblad & Sahlström 1998) in the fourth-grade class at St. Marc Street School that later took part in Femtedit project. I had observed that during FEMTEDIM and during the planning of Femtedit researchers, children, and teachers recurrently compared the activities related to the digital technologies with non-digital

Table 1. *Data collected during the studies of FEMTEDIM and Femtedit sessions and during the design process.*

Data	FEMTEDIM	Femtedit
My field notes	x	x
Colleagues' field notes	x	x
The graphic design of the virtual environment	x	x
Screenshots taken after each session of what was built in the virtual environment	x	x
Chat logs	x	x
Video recordings of the whole room	x	x
Video recordings of individual children and computer screens	x	x
Children's/Femteditians' blogs		x
Web pages associated with the virtual environment	x	x
Outlines of frame stories	x	x
Weekly plans	x	x
Notes from researchers' meetings	x	x
Emails circulating among researchers in which plans and manuscripts were discussed	x	
Written communication in the discussion forum		x

classroom activities. After presenting the teachers with this observation, they invited me into their classroom to observe the ways in which learning and other materials took part in classroom practice, and they let me sit quietly at the back of the classroom with a notebook and allowed a video camera to run in the corner of the classroom, recording a wide-angle view of the classroom. From my position at the back of the classroom I had a good view of the class. I wanted to study what went on with and around learning and other materials in the classroom. This was why I decided on a *nomadic* form of observation; that is, one that does not dwell too long on any material or interaction. I needed to observe the material long enough to get a sense of what it was involved in, but I wanted to be careful not to give any materials priority over others. I expected that some materials would be more conspicuous than others. I expected that I, like the other humans in the classroom, would be absorbed by the unfolding of the practice, which would bring some materials into focus and make others disappear. And I expected, furthermore, that the materials that the teachers focused on would be the ones I would have a tendency to focus on, even though they might not be more important for the performance of classroom activities than the inconspicuous ones. The nomadic gaze forced me to let the focus of my observation travel the classroom from material to material to experience conspicuous as well as inconspicuous materials.

My blue notebook, my pen, my position at the back of the classroom, and my nomadic gaze were my devices for producing field notes during my classroom study. I was a *participant observer* (Hammersley & Atkinson 1995; Hastrup & Ovesen 1985), taking part neither in the learning nor in the teaching. I was so busy with noting what I saw and heard that I often was quite incapable of attending to the teaching. My way of participating was different from any other participant in the room. But I was nonetheless a participant. By my sheer presence I was drawn into the practice as a participant. Pupils, for instance, were interested in what I did; they asked what I was writing and sometimes acted in front of me in order to enter my notes. Similarly, one teacher would often provide me with a kind of stage direction, occasionally commenting on what was going on while teaching. During one lesson, for instance, she looked at me and said, "This is when it can be a bit difficult to proceed as planned." This is a comment she obviously would not have given had I not been present. Furthermore, by the end of my stay in the classroom, I noted:

> I'm happy my field work is soon over. The teacher more and more often reprimands or corrects the children that I am or just have been observing, even though they sometimes just play a bit with what to me looks like legitimate materials. I feel like I am her radar that directs her attention to where something is happening. (Field note 2909_93)

I collected 102 pages of handwritten notes and 16 hours of video recordings from my classroom observation. As was the case for the data collection in the computer lab, the field notes constituted the main source for the analyses of the classroom practice in Chapters 4 and 5, but I also looked through the video material several times, and it became a crucial background for my interpretation of the field notes.

Due to the seeming "intelligence" of interactive technology, humanists may be willing to accept it as not only a tool serving human aims but also as a participant of socio-material practice. However, one may find it more difficult to accept that this may also be the case for analog technologies such as a blackboard, a ruler, or an exercise book. In this book I treat new and established, analog and digital technologies symmetrically, describing them in the same way and with the same vocabulary.

Spatial Imaginaries

> [I]t is the general cleanliness of the room which strikes the incoming pupil. He may not comment; he may only be half consciously aware, but he will notice the floor, the ledges, and the desk. It will affect his attitude and behaviour if they are messy and if there is litter about. Make sure that the room is always tidy. (Marland 1993, p. 35)

In this account from the classroom management literature, the consciousness of the child is influenced by material things and by the room. In order to account for how materials take part in school practice on the basis of the data collected, I needed to be careful not to create descriptions like Michael Marland's, which follow Kant's imaginary, that is, implying that there is a gap between perceived materials and the perception thereof and that cognitive operations establish perception. In Chapter 4 we see that among other forms of knowledge there were indeed constellations in which the pupils were performed as separate from the world that they perceived, but in order to come to this conclusion as an empirical result, it is necessary not to take such an arrangement for granted, as Marland does. Marland takes for granted that the relationship between the material and the child is that of the child noticing the material. How does he know? Did he analyze this? The analyses presented in this book attempt to do precisely that: instead of predefining the specific ways in which humans and materials relate to one another, I analyze the particular forms of technology, knowledge, and presence that are performed out of particular socio-material arrangements. The question of how parts relate to one another is an empirical question.

Relations always entail at least two components that are close to, far from, above, or in other ways in relation to each other. Depicted this way, a relation can be described as an extension or a formation in space. Using a minimal methodology, which applies the theoretical technologies of imaginaries, performance, and participation, as my point of departure, the following four chapters analyze the data by describing them in terms of *spatial imaginaries*. The focus on space and spatiality is more or less explicit in ANT and poststructuralist literature (see Crang & Thrift 2000; Thrift 1996). In Chapter 3 I develop the notion of spatial imaginaries as a sensitivity to describing how participants relate and what spatial formation is thereby created. The spatial imaginary of a socio-material arrangement describes the pattern, landscape, or shape that is formed spatially by and through relations and the parts they connect. Spatial imaginaries are formal descriptions that depict the characteristics of the form of the patterns of relations among parts that are shaped by and through the relations in particular practices. In this book the analytical task of spatial imaginaries is to characterize the different forms of technology, knowledge, presence, and learning that are shaped through the different spaces to which different materials contribute.

The spatial imaginaries presented in this book draw extensively on the *spatial metaphors* suggested by Mol and sociologist and STS scholar John Law: network, fluid, and region (de Laet & Mol 2000; Law 1999, 2002b; Law & Mol 2001; Law & Singleton 2005; Mol & Law 1994). I use these as metaphors to characterize the different patterns of relation in which the computer program and other materials participated in practice. The three spatial metaphors form different spatial imaginaries of the materials. The metaphor of network indicates the connectedness; fluid, the varying character of the ways in which components are related; and region, the grouping of elements in containers. One of the particularly helpful aspects of spatial imaginaries is that they enable us to describe how one technology participates in different ways, forming different patterns of relations.

Whereas I apply spatial imaginaries to describe different forms of technology in Chapters 2 and 3, this theoretical technology helps me in Chapters 4 and 5 to describe different forms of knowledge and forms of presence. Even though we do not reach a definition of the materiality of learning until the concluding chapter, I describe the steps toward formulating a methodology for accounting for the materiality of learning in six "lessons" on the materiality of learning, which are present at the end of each chapter.

The Methodology of the Materiality of Learning
Lesson 1: Minimal Methodology
This book is about the materiality of learning, about how materials participate in educational practice. More importantly, it is about how to account for this participation. Because we are used to talking about technology as something we design or use or in other ways do something *with*, the words and phrases available create an imaginary of humans and technology as clearly separate elements – humans are active and technologies are passive, humans do and technologies have things done to them. When we start approaching materials as part of practice, just as humans are, our verbal repertoire starts sounding out of tune with our approach. This is how creating a methodology for

accounting for materiality becomes an issue in its own right: We need a new vocabulary.

The first step in the methodology of studying the materiality of learning has to do with loosening ourselves from our humanist inheritance. In order to study materiality we must avoid starting from a humanist focus on learning, development, interpersonal relations, intentions, and meaning. Only by forgetting about human aspiration is it possible to start dealing seriously with materiality. Instead of beginning with the question of whether technology does what humans want it to do, we should ask how materials participate in practice and what is thereby performed.

This implies a *minimal methodology*, which does not a priori define the role of technology in practice – and consequently defines neither the role of humans nor the ontology of knowledge, presence, or learning. It is a methodology that attempts to know as little as possible in advance. Definitions are results, not beginnings. Three methodological concepts are crucial for initiating the research process. These are the concepts that allow us to ask the questions of how and what without overlooking the fact that these questions are themselves materials that contribute to doing theory.

Participation is the concept that allows us to ask how materials and other participants participate in practice. It is a concept that guides us to observe and account for what happens, what is done in a practice. We should not focus on participants; instead we should follow participation, which is the way in which components take part in practice. We think we know what the components of practice are, and what they do: "he notices the cleanliness of the room." But the task of science is not to repeat what we think we already know. The task of a study of the materiality of learning is to hesitate and analyze in detail which participations are taking place. Is the relationship between the pupil and the room really "noticing"? Describe how materials and other participants participate in practice.

Performance allows us to ask what is achieved through an arrangement of interrelating parts, of participations. If the relationship between the boy and the room is that of "noticing," we may say that through this relationship he is performed as an "observer," and his knowledge of the room is performed as "impression."

The concept of the *imaginary* helps us understand the inter-relations among and the performance of the practical endeavors of our experiences in the empirical field and the sorting and classifying efforts of the research practice. It suggests a commitment to a performative form of theorizing that prolongs the empirical work and embodies it through the theoretical technologies of concepts and approaches. Concepts and sensitivities are thus developed in the course of the research process, not as representational knowledge about the empirical practice but as methodological concepts that embody and translate the empirical experiences. Studying the materiality of learning implies an appreciation for the materiality of doing research.

2 Components and Opponents

The study of technology is a central aspect of the study of the materiality of learning – whether it is new or old, digital or non-digital. However, like most others who devote their research to the understanding of educational technology, my point of departure is digital technology. I take the issue of how to define technology as an empirical question. We start with the specific digital software that is the focus of this study: Active Worlds. How to account for this program and for technology in general is the focus of this and the following chapter. Consider the following two descriptions of Active Worlds:

> Activeworlds is one of a number of Internet-based systems which allows users to interact with each other in virtual environments as avatars . . . Activeworlds is the only one of these systems which has allowed users to build in the environment, and thus hundreds of thousands of users have been shaping the emerging physical and human geographies of this set of virtual worlds. Activeworlds consists of hundreds of worlds (more than 500 at the time of writing), including Alphaworld, which is the largest, most highly developed, and most populated of these worlds. (Schroeder et al. 2001, p. 570)

> The main feature of ActiveWorlds is that users can claim land and build, building is carried out using a selection of predefined objects from windows, doors and walls to trees, shrubs, and paving tiles. These objects can be cloned and placed on virtual land to create what is essentially a large virtual "Lego" set. (Hudson-Smith 2001, p. 78)

These accounts shift between describing software functionalities and users' application of these functions. This is how technology is typically accounted for within the structure of single sentences but also in the composition of accounts of technology: first technological features are described and then their application. In other words, the material aspect and the social aspect of technological practice are systematically separated. Accounts of technology most often refer to technology in singular and as having intrinsic properties: "[it] allows users to interact" (Schroeder et al. 2001, p. 570), "it allows participants to use an avatar" (Barab et al. 2006, p. 62), "the 3D nature of this software makes" (Ligorio & van Veen 2006, p. 107), "these objects can be cloned and placed" (Hudson-Smith 2001, p. 78). Accordingly, they establish a generalized "user": "users can walk through, navigate, and fly" (Ligorio & van Veen 2006, p. 107), "users can 'enter' spaces" (ibid.), "users can claim land and build" (Hudson-Smith 2001, p. 78). These accounts of technology as robust and unchangeable and of ways of using technology as universal and de-contextualized are rarely explicitly questioned.

Accounts of Active Worlds in educational contexts usually present theoretical educational goals prior to the presentation of the software, which again is followed by reports on the application of Active Worlds and is sometimes concluded with a theoretical discussion of whether the social use of the technology fulfilled the theoretical goals (e.g., Barab et al. 2006; Ligorio & van Veen 2006). The sequence of discussions of theory, technology, and use varies among accounts of Active Worlds, but such accounts rarely diverge from the pattern of describing these aspects separately. Descriptions of technology also seldom provide any account of the interrelations among the technology, the application, and the theory. Formulations such as "in accordance with the theory" or "following the conceptual framework" are usually applied to create a connection between the theory and the technological design, but they do not succeed in providing any thorough understanding of how the relation between theory and technology is shaped. Likewise, we learn that one technological feature of Active Worlds is the ability to build in the environment *and* that hundreds of thousands of users have been doing so, but such *and*s do not make up for a description of how a technological feature in practical reality relates to human activity.

Whereas descriptions of Active Worlds as a well-delimited object separate from the just-as-well-delimited user subject are evident in practically all accounts of the technology, it is noteworthy that the technological and the social are at times described as intimately entangled and as contingently situated in space and time: "users have been shaping the emerging physical and human geographies" (Schroeder et al. 2001, p. 570) and "[Active Worlds] currently consists of over 700 worlds" (Hudson-Smith 2001, p. 78). The image of a purified technology is disturbed by such empirical descriptions of Active Worlds as interactively created by users and as changing over time. The logical inconsistencies of purification and entanglement inspire many questions: If the application changes over time, would not its properties change as well? If the technology changes due to users' particular interaction with the software, how can we account for users in general terms? Even though accounts of Active Worlds describe in different ways the intrinsic properties of the computer program, they are also always saturated with accounts of "users." If the software really was separate from the user and applied according to her will, why does no one seem to be able to describe the digital program without extensively referring to users?

Such questions destabilize the widespread account of technology as stable singular tools separate from and under the control of human beings. They also display the difficulties we have in accounting for technologies and for materials in general. This chapter and the following chapter ask what technology is and how to describe and characterize it. In order to get to an empirically founded understanding of technology, materiality, and the material that is contrary to the a priori definition of technology as ontologically different from human users, I describe in this chapter the construction of Active Worlds through a report of the process of turning it into the research object Femtedit. In relation to the empirical descriptions I discuss in this and the following chapter, three core notions of a methodology of the materiality of learning will be introduced: materiality, multiplicity, and spatiality.

Constructing the Research Object and Research Field

I start my account at a point at which the technology under discussion had yet to become a research object. Qualitative research studies are usually introduced by presenting the research object and research field as phenomena chosen by the researcher prior to the study. Reasons for picking exactly this object or precisely that field are often given with reference to the researcher's interests and questions, which again are situated in current discussions in a particular scientific field. Put otherwise: The researcher's rationality and his scientific embeddedness are presented as the background for examining precisely this object and this field. Sometimes, problems with enlisting informants and getting access to research fields are discussed as issues requiring certain ethical, behavioral, and theoretical precautions (e.g., Spradley 1979). Other researchers emphasize that their initial interactions with the research field and research objects may eventually lead them to look at entirely different domains than expected, which again changes the research field and object (Hammersley & Atkinson 1995; Winthereik et al. 2002). These interactions, it is emphasized, are not just preparation measures prior to the actual study but also data informing the researcher about the characteristics of the field and object. Such studies show that the researchers' choice of object and field are not autonomous; they are influenced by his interaction with the field.

I attempt to twist this imaginary. I show that we are dealing not with a researcher's choice or rationality influenced by interaction but with researchers, objects, humans, and other things, each contributing to forming the research object and field through their mutual interaction. The chapter deals with the making of a technology and of a research object and research field. Their making involved more than adjusting foci and sensitivities, modifying research questions, and changing ways of inter-acting. It involved more than human adaptation. It was also a matter of changing a virtual environment into a research object. The software was an object of art when I first encountered it. In other circumstances the virtual environment technology was an educational object, a technological object, an administrative object, an object of edutainment, or a game.

The virtual environment had to be designed in order to become a research object, and it had to be situated in an appropriate research field. The way in which scientists turn objects into research objects is a well-researched topic in STS (e.g., Knorr Cetina 1999; Latour & Woolgar 1986; Pickering 1995). STS scholars Casper Bruun Jensen and Peter Lauritsen (Jensen & Lauritsen 2005) note that their fellow STS scholars often discuss how scientists make entities cohere through their scientific practice, but they rarely address how the same process unfolds in their own work. As an attempt to place the knowledge process of the research endeavor on par with the knowledge process that unfolds – symmetrically (Bloor 1976) – in the field of study, this chapter addresses the process through which components of the research process came to cohere.

The chapter has a double aim – on the one hand it presents the research object and field and the technologies, humans, processes, and activities involved; on the other hand it introduces a vocabulary developed within ANT for describing the construction of socio-technical realities. I do this through empirical description and analysis, as my performative approach requests. Through a narrative of the early stages in the formation of the research project, the chapter shows step-by-step how a computer program became entangled in relations with other components, which eventually turned it into a research object. Even more components became involved, and the research field – a school setting – came into being.

The description of the Femtedit design follows Law's (1989) notion of *heterogeneous engineering*, which he uses to describe how Portuguese vessels in the thirteenth to fifteenth centuries were prepared for trade journeys to India – by engineering them to withstand the strength of the Atlantic, the winds, the Muslims, and other social and material components that they might encounter on their way. Law is interested in showing how objects and technical practices become stabilized through a heterogeneous inter-mingling of social and material parts. His aim is especially to argue that the social should not be privileged in explanations of such processes: "Other factors – natural, economic, or technical – may be more obdurate than the social and may resist the best efforts of the system builder to reshape them. Other factors may, therefore, explain better the shape of artefacts" (Law 1989, p. 113).

In the following text, I describe in a similar way the heterogeneous engineering of a 3D virtual environment. Law's line of argument consists of three points: heterogeneous engineering is about 1) enrolling hetero-geneous components, 2) associating otherwise disparate parts, and 3) dealing with trials of strength. First, I describe Femtedit as an enrollment of a number of heterogeneous (socio and material) components. Enroll-ment was however not enough to build up a research project. It was only by associating a large number of otherwise disparate parts that a research object and research field could be formed. This is the second point I describe about heterogeneous engineering. Third, I show how designing Femtedit as my research object was about more than associating parts. Femtedit had opponents, and it came to be the way it did through trials of strength (Latour 1988; Law 1989) against the forces that threatened to undermine the design.

Femtedit as an Enrollment of Heterogeneous Components

I first came to know Active Worlds when I took part in a series of online TV broadcastings in collaboration with the Danish artist group Superflex.[1] Superflex used Active Worlds to create the town Karlskrona2 (later also Wolfsburg2)[2] on the Internet as a community platform for the citizens of the Swedish town Karlskrona to discuss and model city planning. Active Worlds caught my interest. Philosopher Isabelle Stengers (1997) writes that the word "interest" stems from the Latin "inter-esse," which means

---

[1] http://www.superflex.dk. For discussions of the online TV broadcastings, see Brewster (2001), Ejlskov et al. (2001), and Steiner (2003).

[2] See http://www.superflex.net/tools/supercity/karlskrona2 and http://www.superflex.net/tools/supercity/wolfsburg2.

"situated between," and thus catching interest is about creating relations. Hitherto, my research and Active Worlds had nothing in common. In philosopher and anthropologist of science Bruno Latour's (1987) vocabulary, they were *disinterested*. Then Active Worlds caught my interest.[3] It is banal, yet seductive: accepting this means accepting the agency of technology to create relations with the human. Establishing the interest, the link, between my research project and Active Worlds was possible due to particular characteristics of both that allowed them to be connected.

Among these connection points was the community character of Karlskrona2. It enabled an approach to technology that goes beyond an account of a tool used by an individual. It furthermore fit the request of scholars of computer-supported collaborative learning (CSCL) for a move from individually oriented software tools toward multi-user applications (Hoppe 2007). The collaborative construction of the virtual world Karlskrona2 also constituted a connecting point between the notion of participation and a study of technology as procedurally constituted, rather than stable, with intrinsic properties. The Karlskrona citizens made hyperlinks from objects in Karlskrona2 that opened web pages in an integrated browser. This enabled a study of the technology not as enclosed in the situation of use but as potentially able to reach out beyond it.

Because of these ways in which Karlskrona2 and my research project were able to connect, the virtual environment was a good candidate for becoming the focal component of my study of the materiality of learning. Note that it was so only due to the enrollment of social and material components. This is Law's first point about heterogeneous engineering (1989): It is about enrolling *heterogeneous* components, about engineering and connecting technological features and social interests and activities. Heterogeneity is a central term in ANT, referring to associations of social and material components. In my case it was about associating a computer program with methodological concepts.

The description of the technology and research object as heterogeneous suggests an alternative to accounting for the researcher as a central, rational agent of the formation of the research object. As the description shows, heterogeneous engineering is contingent but not arbitrary. It is

---

[3] Obviously, the "I" that is speaking in this text is not a "whole person" (if ever such exists) but a particular voice that is constituted through the assemblage accounted for in this book in coordination with the genre and format of the rhetoric device of this book. This "I" changes, and at the point at which Active Worlds caught "my" interest, "I" was the virtuality, the desire, the becoming of this book. In other words, the "I" whose interest was caught can be understood synonymously as "my research project."

dependent on the materiality of the components that are being entangled, on their ability to connect to one another. I have emphasized – in a way that is more pronounced than Law's – that it is necessary for the partaking components to be able to connect to one another in order for the heterogeneous engineering to be completed. These capacities for connecting were achieved on the one hand through the way in which components were already formed – through literature, discussions, and the epistemic cultures (Knorr Cetina 1999) in which the research process was entangled – as well as through the specific shape of Karlskrona2. On the other hand, they were achieved in the encounter between Karlskrona2 and my research project. The technology and the research project took their form by and through their interlinkages. And it was as an effect of these contingent interlinkages that the components enrolled were heterogeneous.

It is a common misunderstanding that the claim that objects are contingent implies that their ontology is arbitrary. Stengers (2000a) writes that "whoever doubts the existence of the Sun would have stacked against him or her not only the witness of astronomers and our everyday experience, but also the witness of our retinas, invented to detect light, and the chlorophyll of plants, invented to capture its energy" (pp. 97–98). Just as it would be highly impossible to doubt the existence of the sun due to the enormously extended heterogeneous network in which it is entangled, there is no need to doubt the real existence of a research object only because it is described as contingently constructed. Contingency is highly consequential, material, and real.

Association of Otherwise Disparate Parts

The heterogeneous components had to be able to relate to one another. I have described how a computer software and a methodological concept became interrelated. However, heterogeneous engineering also has to take into account how objects relate to social factors and material infrastructures and to local matters and distant components, Law notes (1989). These are crucial for the heterogeneous components to achieve the ability to interrelate and to stay connected. Accordingly, heterogeneous engineering is about the building of systems. With this insight, it is appropriate to move from talking about components to talking about participants – or parts, to avoid anthropomorphism – even though Law sticks to the notion of component. This notion conveys the image of rather stable entities put together. Parts and participants, on the other hand, have a share in practices; they have histories that allow them to connect to practices in different ways. They do not only contribute to composing practices; they are also formed through the way in which they take part of this composition.

Research fields provide social factors and material infrastructures that help heterogeneous components build systems. Together with research groups at Blekinge Institute of Technology[4] and Universitàt Autònoma de Barcelona,[5] my research group applied for and was granted funding from the EU's Fifth Frame Program funding scheme "School of Tomorrow." The Fifth Dimension network connected these researchers. Fifth Dimension is a concept for a combined research field and after-school computer activity for children, originally founded on activity theory by literacy scholar Peg Griffin and cultural psychologist Michael Cole in California in the mid-1980s. Since then it has spread to several other places, mainly in the United States but also in Europe, Australia, and South America (e.g., Cole 1996; Griffin & Cole 1984). Under the title "Local Learning in a Global World," the aim of our EU research project was to study the possibility of introducing the principles developed through research in Fifth Dimension after-school activities in the United States into in-school activities in Europe.[6] A first step in this direction was the establishment of a Fifth Dimension after-school activity every Monday afternoon at the inner-city St. Marc Street School in Copenhagen.

These afternoon activities formed the educational field required in order to continue the EU project. Furthermore, it was a site in which the research object could be situated. However, Karlskrona2 lacked crucial aspects that would enable it to connect to the Fifth Dimension and to the educational context, and hence to be the research object of my study. The art project allowed people to play with the layout of their city and involved activities to which elementary school children could not be expected to relate. In order to become situated in the research field, the technology had to be *dissociated* (Law 1989) from the art context. I described previously that the first step of heterogeneous engineering consisted of associating the technology with methodological concepts. In this second step, the

---

[4] This group included, among others, Berthel Sutter, School of Management; Monica Nilsson, School of Health Science; and Carina Anderson and Rosita Anderson, Learning Lab.

[5] This group included, among others, José Luis Lalueza Sazatornil and Sònia Sanchez Busquès, Department of Basic, Developmental and Educational Psychology and Marc Bria Ramirez, DEHISI.

[6] This book is not directly part of the EU project, which is why I do not discuss its aims, methods, and theories. For further literature on this EU project, see Jensen et al. (2005), Nocon (2005), Sørensen (2003), and http://www.5D.org.

technology and methodological concepts were adjusted. The Karlskrona2 identity had to be cut (Strathern 1996) off of the computer program, leaving us with only the purified 3D virtual environment concept, which allowed new connections to be made to the educational field and to the Fifth Dimension research program. New heterogeneous hybrids could be constructed (Latour 1993).

When related to the Fifth Dimension project, several facets of the technology surfaced that had hitherto been absent. Active Worlds had an educational department, called Eduverse,[7] which offered virtual worlds free of charge for educational research purposes. Being free of charge and easy to use, Active Worlds could be enrolled in schools, which in general had virtually no money for software and whose teachers and children were only moderately trained in digital technology. These connection points were again contingent but crucial for connecting the online application together with the research project in an educational field.

We were granted a virtual world[8] called FEMTEDIM. After working with FEMTEDIM for a year, the fourth-grade teachers of St. Marc Street School approached us and asked if we would make a similar project for their class. In addition to the Danish fourth grade class, a Swedish class from Ronneby was enrolled into this new project. A second virtual world was added to the first: the Femtedit world, which is the focus of this book (FEMTEDIM can be considered a beta version of Femtedit).

Law (1989) underlines that individual components are nothing on their own. Technology is not made up simply by juxtaposing heterogeneous components. The enrollment of the heterogeneous components of methodological concepts and Karlskrona2, as described in the preceding section, did not make a research project. It was through careful associations of otherwise disparate parts – a local school, an EU funding program, distant research groups, and an educational virtual environment – that the 3D virtual environment technology could be turned into a research object and that an educational research field could take shape.

---

[7] http://www.activeworlds.com/edu.

[8] A "universe" in Active Worlds contains a number of virtual "worlds" (see Figure 1). When logging on to Active Worlds, the user must choose which universe to log on to. Although the user cannot jump from one universe to another, it is possible to move between worlds within a universe. All universes are built on the Active Worlds platform. The Active Worlds universe is one of these universes, and it consists mainly of virtual worlds made for entertainment purposes. The Eduverse universe contains worlds with educational or research aims. Karlskrona2 and Wolfsburg2 were both universes with only one world (which means that the user does not notice the difference between universe and world).

Trials of Strength in the Femtedit Design

Whereas the heterogeneous engineering approach shares with a systems-building perspective (e.g., Hughes 1989) the understanding that technology enrolls heterogeneous components and that these are associated, Law departs from the systems approach on a third point: the emphasis on *trials of strength*. Law (1989) discusses the struggle between the Atlantic Ocean and the brave Vivaldi brothers' galley, which disappeared on the way to India. The galley lost the trial of strength against the Altantic. Three types of technological innovation had to be introduced before Europeans could pass to Cape Bojador. One of these was the development of sailing ships in the place of rower-driven boats. Sailing ships reduced the need for manpower, and thus it became possible to carry onboard enough stores of food to maintain the crew. I will not discuss the two other innovations but only emphasize Law's point: he describes this advancement in shipping engineering as a trial of strength between galleys and the Atlantic, and he points out that the Portuguese had to add lines of force – like the sailing ship – in order to prevail over the power of the Atlantic. In other words, we can say that the powers of the Atlantic became entangled with the sailing ship. In the process of constructing the mixed-rigged sailing vessel, the forces of the Atlantic and the attempt to conquer these forces were decisive components. Thus, Law's analytical strategy is to treat the environment within which a design is created as hostile and the environment's parts as opponents to the design.

There were many opponents and trials of strength involved in designing Femtedit. Several of them were crucial for the formation of the design. In the following discussion, I present three trials of strength through which Femtedit was constructed. There is an important difference between accounting for technology by describing trials of strength and by applying the more generalizing formulations used by the authors discussing Active Worlds in the introduction to this chapter. Trials of strength are always described as interactions among specific human or nonhuman objects. They show that technology is a practical, contingent, and heterogeneous interplay, a view that is quite different from the account of technology as stable, robust, and well-delimited.

Capturing and Keeping the Children's Attention

In their field notes, the researchers working with FEMTEDIM expressed much concern about children showing signs of boredom; they worried that, for many, the online 3D virtual environment did not inspire much activity. In FEMTEDIM the children were assigned the task of building up villages in the virtual environment. The creation myth presented to the children at the start of the project involved the avatar Avafar, who had been living in the virtual world FEMTEDIM all his life. He was now getting old and loosing his vision, and mysteriously the virtual environment was disappearing at the same rate as Avafar's vision loss. Avafar was unable to maintain the virtual environment and asked the children to take over (see Sørensen 2005). This creation myth provided a history, a background, for the FEMTEDIM activities that was intended to set the activity in motion and assign identity to the FEMTEDIM virtual environment. But, like Avafar's vision, his importance in the creation myth vanished.

During the first FEMTEDIM session the children were engaged and thrilled about taking over the responsibility for the virtual world. They were eager to solve the location-finding tasks Avafar had set. They stormed the computer lab and the virtual environment, ready to invest their impressive energy into whatever was offered. During this first session the creation myth had succeeded in allying itself with the children's attention. But it did not last. After a few sessions the creation myth was more or less forgotten. It lost the trial of strength with the children's attention, which drifted in several directions, some involving FEMTE-DIM, others not. This challenged the coherence of the technology. As an educational technology FEMTEDIM had to be part of an organized practice.[9] We could not continue the after-school practice if the children were engaged in too many different activities, simply because it is impossible in an educational practice for a small number of educators to provide educational support to a large number of children when the educational practice is not organized to be focused on a (more or less) common activity. FEMTEDIM did not satisfactorily succeed in connecting the attention of the children to the virtual environment. Too many other features of the world attracted children's attention, and these other features constituted a trial of strength with FEMTEDIM, as they competed for the children's attention.

---

[9] We were sympathetic to approaches emphasizing that learning does not take place only in formal learning situations (Cole 1996; Dreier 2003, 2008; Lave 1988; Lave & Wenger 1991; McCormick & Paechter 1999; Rogoff & Wertsch 1984), but we also acknowledged research emphasizing the mix of informal and formal learning (Colley et al. 2002), which supports facilitating learning through organized activities.

In the planning of Femtedit, we prepared for this trial of strength by writing a frame story that was more persistent than the FEMTEDIM creation myth had been:

> The citizens of Femtedit, the Femteditians, come into being as a result of program errors on the server hosting their virtual world. When they arrive in Femtedit, they are curious, but empty. Soon they start building a home and surfing the Internet, and from their homes they make links to web pages they have visited. This begins to fill them up. As a result of building their homes and linking to web pages, they build up their identities. A Femteditian's identity corresponds to the complete content of the web pages to which they have linked.
>
> Everything was fine in Femtedit until the day a virus attacked the server. Slowly but unmistakably, the buildings in Femtedit disappeared and with them the links. The Femteditians' identities were deleted. Eventually the virus was cleaned away. But Femtedit had already almost vanished and the Femteditians had become empty like zombies, unable to do anything at all, including saving their own world. Just in time, however, the youngest of the Femteditians, Jaga, managed to write to the researchers, asking for their help in saving Femtedit by building up new homes and by reanimating the Femteditians by making hyperlinks from their homes. The researchers realized that this was a major task, so they gathered together a Danish and a Swedish fourth-grade class, explained the whole story, and entrusted to them the rescue operation: Operation Femtedit.

The FEMTEDIM creation myth had been historical, forming a past that should have made Avafar absent present (Law and Mol 2001) in the sense that even though he had died and was absent, he still had an influence on the virtual world. However, instead of becoming absent present, Avafar only became absent, without any influence on FEMTEDIM. In order to avoid the risk of the Femtedit frame story becoming absent, we created the Femteditians as becomings in the virtual world that developed together with the project to the end, at which point they would be reanimated in the Femtedit world. However, the frame story would only be realized if the children's attention was translated into rebuilding the Femteditians' homes.

Because Active Worlds involves the option of linking to Internet web pages, it became possible to construct the task of reanimating Femteditians. Linking involved more than writing a URL in a dialogue box in Active Worlds. The URLs had to be brought into Femtedit, which required that the children watch out for them in their everyday surroundings. In 2001, when the project took place, URLs already were everywhere in public life: in supermarkets, on plastic bags, on clothes and sweets, on toys, in newspapers and magazines, on busses, on TV, and in everyday conversations. In order for the linking function to work, activities beyond the digital components had to be enrolled: watching for URLs to record, finding paper on which to write the URLs, putting the notes in their pockets to carry them back to the school – including all the communication and interactions these procedures might involve. Because of the enormously varied content of the Internet, we could expect there to be content available that would relate to any of the children's varied interests and that would thereby draw attention invested elsewhere into the platform. For the same reason, the task of linking to web pages on the Internet made it possible to establish a connection between the individual child's world and Femtedit, even though we did not know any of the children in advance. The linking option was at the same time undefined, as it allowed for a very precise adaptation of the content of Femtedit to each individual child.

The Femteditians' enervated condition functioned as a connection point that made it possible to bind the children's attention to the activity. As zombies the Femteditians were too weak to interact and communicate synchronously with the children in the Femtedit virtual environment. They could only communicate asynchronously, through the blog. Children received messages in the blog every week from their Femteditian, with comments on what they had been doing and questions about the chosen links – questions that challenged and encouraged the children to continue constructing links and buildings. The messages were ordered chronologically; the most recent message was posted at the top of the page, while the older messages were moved down (see Figure 2). The blog continuously manifested the presence of the Femteditians and encouraged the children to continuously direct their attention to the focal activity of the project. Hewitt (2001) writes that, unlike face-to-face conversation, which is transitory, computer-mediated conversation preserves discourse, allowing pupils to return to their ideas. We can even say that the blog constructs discourse as storage. This formulation indicates that the ontology of discourse emerges through its material mediation and not simply that children act differently when equipped with the blog as a tool.

FEMTEDIM had taught us that sustaining the investment of children's attention into the technology required variation. Such variation was built into Femtedit through a feedback plan, which outlined the progression of the comments that the Femteditians posted in the blog (see Table 2). The feedback plan increased the complexity of the activities over

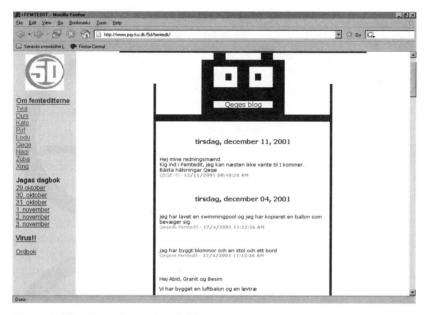

Figure 2. The Femteditian Qeqe's blog.

the seven sessions through four steps: First, the Femteditians commented on an unambiguous task. They then gave feedback in the form of inquiries into any of the individual links. Third, they reacted on how the given links related to one another – for instance, how a child would feel about the identity of their Femteditian, who was made up of links to mobile phone ringtones and to Cartoon Network's web page. The fourth step consisted of feedback on relations among different Femteditian's links – for example, "how does it work to be a mobile phone fanatic, when I live next to a Femteditian with links to U.S. web pages of satiric political content?" This way, the feedback continuously pushed activities in the Femtedit world. The children's own building and linking, as well as the relations between what different children were doing, were turned back on them as fuel for further building and linking, but each round of feedback varied slightly from the last round.

In order for the Femteditian to be able to write to the children about what they had built, a system had to be established that provided the teacher or researcher who typed the Femteditians' comments with knowledge about what the children had been building. We allocated two Femteditians to each researcher, who would be in charge of observing during the Femtedit sessions what the children in charge of that Femteditian were doing. Consequently, there was always a Danish and a Swedish

Table 2. *Plan for the sequence of the Femteditians' feedback to the children.*

	Femteditian's Comment (Examples to Guide the Formation of Comments)	Femteditian's Inquiry (Examples to Guide the Formation of Inquiries)	Children's Activities
Session 1		I cannot get into Femtedit. Please, open my gate!	Gate is opened.
Session 2	Thanks for opening my gate, I'm back in Femtedit.	I am homeless, please build me a home.	Building begins.
Session 3	Oh, I am getting a home, what a wonderful feeling.	I feel so empty, please give me links.	Building continues, linking begins.
Session 4	Being filled up is nice. I feel I am becoming an x (depending on content of web pages linked to) person.	I wonder if having an x identity is good for my life, is that all I need?	Links and buildings are added and adjusted.
Session 5	My identity is evolving. Thanks!	I am confused. I am both x and y (depending on content of web pages linked to). Does that give me a split identity?	Links and buildings are added and adjusted.
Session 6	Thanks to you, it becomes clearer to me who I am, and I am gaining strength to look around.	I realize my neighbor has a z identity. Does that fit with me being an x? How will we coexist?	Links and buildings are added and adjusted.
Session 7	Hurray, you have filled me up, I can move, I'm alive!		Children interact with the Femteditians.

researcher or teacher responsible for formulating each Femteditian's feedback. Every week researchers wrote field notes and posted them on an online researcher-teacher discussion forum set up for the project. After sharing their field notes, the researchers discussed the notes with one another in the forum and together they formulated a feedback comment for each Femteditian and posted them in the blogs for the children to read Tuesday morning.

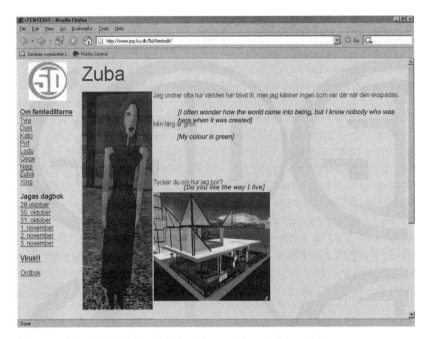

Figure 3. The Femteditian Zuba's web page (translation added).

Another material that helped bind the children's attention to Femtedit was the Femtedit web page.[10] The FEMTEDIM creation myth had been presented to the children only once and only orally. Oral communication is flighty, and without any continuous oral repetition or translation of the creation myth into writing, it had been too weak to bind children's attention to FEMTEDIM. Due to this experience, we strengthened the frame story of Femtedit to be more persistent in the trial of strength with the other aspects of the world attracting the children's attention. By presenting the frame story not only orally but also on the Femtedit web page, it could continuously feed into the building activities. Each Femteditian had its own web page with pictures and a few sentences about its former life (see Figure 3), which persistently provided fixed materials for reanimating the Femteditian and rebuilding its home. Due to the permanence of the web page and its continuous availability, the children could at any time visit this page to draw on its materials; as a consequence, the web pages kept the frame story alive in Femtedit. Because they were allied with the blogs, the feedback plan, and the researcher-teacher discussion forum, the

[10] http://materiality-of-learning.net.

web pages contributed to sustaining the frame story's ability to keep the children's attention bound to Femtedit.

Face-to-Face Localism Versus Online Technology

In the FEMTEDIM project, collaboration between the Danish and Swedish children had been scarce. The Danish children could communicate with other Danes in their own language, and they could mix online chat with face-to-face talk in the computer lab. Furthermore, the children at St. Marc Street School had many more resources for expanding and exploring relationships with the Danish participants outside FEMTEDIM. Relationships with the children at Blekinge Institute of Technology, in Sweden, could only develop online, away from the children's rich and wide-ranging repertoire of face-to-face communication skills. This difference between face-to-face and online communication was crucial; for instance, it affected the friendships and love relations that were built up or attempted through FEMTEDIM. Through a mix of offline and online communication, one girl enthusiastically built relations with her schoolmates. She however told me she would not know what to do with a friend she only knew online. I call the tendency to prioritize communication with schoolmates (online or offline) *face-to-face localism*. Face-to-face localism was an opponent to one of the critical qualities that should connect the computer program with the children: the online communication facilities.

Some components are more malleable than others. We could not make the Danish and Swedish children speak the same language in order to make online communication easier. And we could not contend with the challenge from the local practices, which had many more resources for sustaining and expanding relationships than the purely online relations. But we could facilitate and organize online collaboration better. We approached the trial of strength between the online communication facilities and face-to-face localism by forming Danish-Swedish couples, who were assigned the common task of reanimating one Femteditian and rebuilding its home. The names of their avatars were identified with the name of their Femteditian and a country code suffix. For example, the name of the avatar belonging to the Danish children working with the Femteditian Duni was Duni*dk*, whereas their Swedish avatar partner was Duni*se*. This strategy answered the question of what to do with an online friend: They had joint missions to fulfill. This was the first force added to the Femtedit design in order to withstand the trial of strength with face-to-face localism.

The second force brought into this trial of strength was a virtual localism. Even though it is possible to chat with other users whose avatars are not in the visual field of the user's avatar, children generally followed the face-to-face genre of communicating, requiring that their communication partner's avatar was in visual contact with their own. Look at this chat log[11] from Femtedit:

Katose: Annika it is Kajsa who is katose

Katose: write back annika, kajsa

Katodk: *(to Katose)*[12] *Hi Kajsa, where ere you.*[13]

---

[11] This chat has been "cleaned," which means that all other communication that does not involve Katose and Katodk is left out. A chat room works like a cocktail party – a lot of people all speak at once. However, in the chat room one cannot distinguish the voices by their physical proximity. All written "voices" have the same "volume," the same appearance. This means that various discussions are going on at the same time, and each message is shown in the display in the temporal order in which it is posted; the messages are not distinguished by which discussion they are part of. For example:

Katose:	Annika it is Kajsa who is katose
Pirfdk:	hi pirfse I am Tasleema is it going ok with femtedit
Jagadk:	
Dunise:	Hi
Ludose:	HI LUDODK
Jagadk:	what shall we build
Katose:	write back annika, kajsa
Nagidk:	hi Nagise
Zubadk:	hi Zubase
Pirfse:	
Xingse:	Xing where are you
Qeqese:	do you have any suggestion
Katodk:	*(to Katose) Hi Kajsa, where ere you.*

In order to focus on the discussion that goes on between Katose and Katodk, I have cleaned the chat of the messages that do not come from Katose and Katodk. It is, however, worthwhile to bear in mind that this simplified conversation is much easier to follow than it was for the participants in Femtedit.

[12] The parentheses and italics indicate an exception to the principle that all "voices" in a chat room have the same "volume." Katodk is using the "whispering" function, which makes the messages appear only in Katose's display. To make it clear to Katose that this is a message particularly addressed to her, the system adds "(to Katose)" in parentheses, as well as coloring the message blue and italicizing it. I have included the parenthetical note and kept the italics in my re-creations of Femtedit conversations, although the messages are not colored blue. Whispering is a way to make it easier for the addressee to notice the message; it is also a way of creating private conversations that other chat room participants cannot access.

[13] The chat logs and, later, blogs are translated from Danish and Swedish into English, thus the differences in the languages are lost. I have translated spelling errors into

> *Katose*: I am at our house, come here, 0N 6E
>
> *Katose*: write back then
>
> *Katose*: what shall we build
>
> *Katodk*: *(to Katose) Hi you are standing just opposite annika.*
>
> *Katose*: we have to buil write back
>
> *Katodk*: *(to Katose) We have to make the gate pink.*
>
> *Katose*: where did you go
>
> *Katodk*: *(to Katose) Back to our gates.*
>
> *Katodk*: Hi katose. I have colored the gate pink.
>
> *Katose*: good, now I have to write in the blog, see you (Chat log 011113)

Five of these thirteen turns are related to localizing the avatar of the communication partner in the virtual environment. This sequence illustrates that the children found it mandatory to locate each others' avatars in order to collaborate and communicate. Graphic "ruins" of the Femteditians' former homes were built in Femtedit as geographic markers that localized where children could find their Femteditian's home to rebuild, and – more important – where to find their online collaborators. Because they were the remains of the destroyed Femtedit as described in the frame story, the ruins made the frame story tangibly present in the virtual world. The ruins furthermore related to the part of the frame story that anticipated the reconstruction of Femtedit, for they constituted the foundations for the new buildings that were to be created. Through these ruins a new *virtual localism* was created that rendered face-to-face localism less imperative. As the chat excerpt shows, it did not prevent problems with finding each other, but it did provide fixed geographical places that the children could refer to when communicating their locations: "at our house," "at our gate."

Technical Limitations Versus Smooth Operation

In order to work, the Femtedit virtual environment required that the Active Worlds application run on the school computers. These computers and Internet connections were obviously not only there for the Femtedit

---

similar spelling errors in English, just as I have translated the punctuation and structure of sentences into similar formal, informal, correct, or incorrect punctuation and sentence structures in order to remain faithful to the children's writing style.

project; they were used for all the computer activities of the two schools. They had the strength and bandwidth appropriate for the general needs of the schools, as much as the schools' budgets allowed. Due to the quite limited bandwidth of the Internet connection from the library of Pine Valley School, where the Swedish part of the Femtedit project was going to take place, the quality of the graphics decreased when the number of computers online simultaneously increased. In the computer lab of St. Marc Street School, only ten computers met the technical requirements for running Active Worlds. Needless to say, neither of the fourth-grade classes involved had been established for the sake of the Femtedit project. As a consequence of many other networks in which the classes were enrolled, there were twenty-four children in the fourth-grade class at St. Marc Street School and twenty in the Pine Valley School fourth-grade class.

The bandwidth and the quality of the computers caused complications when they interacted with the combination of the technical requirements of the online 3D virtual environment and the number of children in the classes. A trial of strength occurred. The combination of limited bandwidth and a relatively large number of children was an opponent to the Femtedit design. If we did not fight this opponent, Femtedit would never be able to run. It would be undermined by children competing for the computers of acceptable quality and by computers obstructing the building activities due to their inability to render the graphics of the virtual environment. We needed to associate more and different forces with the Femtedit design in order to defeat those opponents.

The force added to the design was an organization of the children. We divided the children in two groups. Half of the class would be in the computer lab from 9:45 to 10:30, and the other half from 10:30 to 11:15. We called the early Femtedit group Agents945 and the late one Detectives1030. On those Tuesday mornings, one group worked with Femtedit while the other half of the class stayed in the classroom with one of the teachers. This time schedule, however, was insensitive to the differences in the number of children in the two classes. The fourth-grade class at Pine Valley School had only twenty children, which meant that when the Danish class was divided in half (two groups of twelve), there would be two children left over in each group when forming couples with the Swedish children (two groups of ten). Some of the Danish children had to pair up. Each individual child or pair of Danish children was coupled with a Swedish partner. Together they were in charge of reanimating one appointed Femteditian.

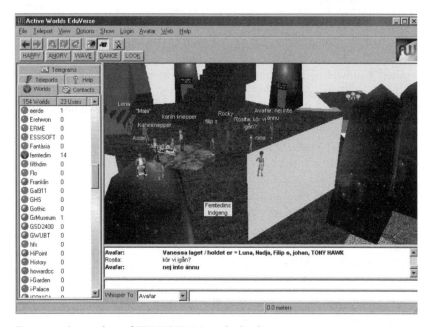

Figure 4. Screenshot of FEMTEDIM in the bird's-eye view.

The organization of children in groups and the time schedule dividing them were added to the design in the trial of strength with the limited bandwidth and the poor-quality computers. The Femtedit design won the trial in the sense that the project was able to carry through to the end. But the organization was not a sovereign opponent to the poor-quality computers and limited bandwidth. Several times the computers froze due to overworked graphics cards, and sometimes the children at Pine Valley School could not use the "bird's-eye view" function (see Figure 4), because it required a quicker rendering of graphics than the bandwidth allowed. In these cases researchers had to stop doing research and instead solve these technical problems and help the children communicate with their online partners.

Characteristics of Trials of Strength

There were other trials of strength besides the ones described. For instance, there was a trial of strength with the teachers, who wanted the Femtedit project to be about building a Viking village. This is discussed in Chapter 4. Table 3 summarizes the three different strategies taken when dealing with the three previously mentioned trials of strength that contributed to forming Femtedit.

Table 3. *The different versions of the Femtedit trials of strength and how they were addressed.*

Opponent	Character of Opponent	Part of Femtedit That Is Challenged	Components Added to Challenge Opponent	Trial of Strength Strategy
The drifting of children's attention	Human	Continuity of Femtedit	Extended frame story narrating Femteditians as becomings, feature linking Femtedit to potentially all Internet content, researcher forum, blogs, avatar web pages, sequential feedback plan	Opponents turned into allies by adding materials to attract and focus children's attention
Face-to-face localism	Mix of human and nonhuman	Online character of virtual environment	Graphic ruins and common tasks	Opponent kept intact but neutralized by adding a virtual localism that replaced the opponent
Technical limitations	Nonhuman	Smooth operation of Femtedit	Organization of children and time schedule	Opponent kept intact but neutralized by adding components that turned technical limitations into technical adequacy

In the first trial of strength I presented, the opponent was human; in the second, it was a mix of human and nonhuman qualities; and, in the last, the opponent was nonhuman. In each case the trial of strength was about adding components to and reorganizing components of a network already in shape. Accordingly, I find it more appropriate to understand trials of strength as rearmaments and reorganizations that change the balance of power, rather than as Law (1989) describes them – as opponents fighting a battle.

No matter how a trial of strength appears, it shows that the technology is constructed not only from the components that are "inside" the software, but also through opponents that challenge the technology from "outside." Thereby these outside components become part of the inside of the technology, and talking about inside and outside ceases to make sense. In Law's words, we can say that building a technology is about "how to juxtapose and relate heterogeneous elements together such that they stay in place and are not dissociated by other actors in the environment in the course of the inevitable struggles – whether these are social or physical or mix of the two" (Law 1989, p. 117).

It was through associations of a large number of human and nonhuman components, which I have described in this section, that the energy of forty-four children could be drawn together with a technology that, by switching on the computers, allowed the teacher to make her class engage with a variety of topics and people, work with them in different creative ways, and come into contact with diverse experiences from remote places and diverse materials during school hours as well as beyond. By way of all these parts and interlinkages, a network was constructed that associated crucial components in the study of materiality of learning.

I give Law the last words about understanding designing as a trial of strength, which is his third and last point about heterogeneous engineering:

> [Designers] seek to create a network of heterogeneous but mutually sustaining elements. They seek to dissociate hostile forces and to associate them with their enterprise by transforming them. The crucial point, however, is that the structure of the network reflects the power and the nature of both the forces available and the forces with which the network collides. To say, then, that an artifact is well adapted to its environment is to say that it forms a part of a system or network that is able to assimilate (or turn away) potentially hostile external forces. It is, consequently, to note that the network in question is relatively stable. (Law 1989, p. 121, my insertion)

Classic-ANT and the Network

I have described how objects were separated and connected in order to turn Active Worlds into the research object Femtedit, and in order to establish a school practice as the research field for studying the materiality of learning. Understanding this process as heterogeneous engineering implies understanding the design of the research object and field as a network. "Network" is obviously one of the central terms in ANT (Latour 1987, 1999d). In what I term *classic-ANT*, to be precise. In the context of this book network is the first spatial imaginary I present.

The ANT vocabulary is developed through STS analyses of how scientific facts and technologies come to be (e.g., Latour 1987, 1988; Latour & Woolgar 1986). Technologies – like an analogue camera, for instance – are often taken as automatons that work by themselves. "Clic, clac, merci Kodak," they say in France (Latour 1987, p. 115), indicating that one simply pushes the button and the camera does the rest. STS studies have shown that technologies are far from autonomous. They work only because they are intimately entangled (e.g., Callon 1998) in larger assemblages. They are constructed not only by welding metal and connecting electrical circuits, but also by establishing infrastructures (e.g., Star 2002).

The analogue camera does only a minor part of the work necessary for one to take a picture. The rest of the work is done by humans and things circulating through an infrastructure of photo-developing laboratories (which include machinery, staff, security measures, and systems for the regular delivery of chemicals and so on); a system for collecting film and returning pictures; arrangements for transporting film and pictures between the laboratory and shop; people interested in photography who make available mass production of cameras and photo developing; legal regulations of markets; and economic systems. In digital photography, the infrastructure is arranged differently. More work is allocated to the photographer, computer, and printer, who are collectively in charge of printing the photos. The sum of the efforts invested into establishing such an infrastructure of tightly bound socio-material objects, which allows entities to circulate, is what Latour calls a network (Latour 1987, 1999a, 1999d). Let me clarify six core aspects of a network.

First, the network metaphor describes an assemblage of heterogeneous components (Callon 1986; Latour 1999a). They are heterogeneous in the sense that they may be of different kinds: human, nonhuman, technical, and social. The position of a component in a network is not due to its "ontological kind." Rather, it is the other way around: The ontology of a component is established by its relations in the network.

Second, from this it follows that spatial terms like "proximity" and "distance" get a new meaning. Through the frame story, a URL on the back of a bus, which Hajjah took home from school, came to be next to the digital building blocks of the Femtedit virtual environment. In a network imaginary, what is written on the back of a bus can be the neighbor of what is built in a virtual environment, even though they are distant in Euclidian terms. The network is defined by the interrelations among the components.

Third, all parts in the network contribute to making up the network – the building blocks, the chat function, the blogs, the feedback plan, the computers, the number of children in the classes, the class organization, the online discussion forum, the children's desire for variation, and so on. All of these do their work to constitute the network.

Fourth, as soon as relations change and components stop providing their part of the work to keep the network together, the network starts dissolving. I described how the freezing of the computers and the bored children threatened the projects. Children as well as computers each did their job in the overall network, and as soon as any of them started doing something else or nothing at all, the network was in danger of dissolving.

As long as objects in a network stay in place and do their jobs, the network stays intact. The fifth point is that when this is the case, the network can move without changing shape. Law (1989) describes how the Portuguese vessels could travel from Lisbon to Calicut and back again because each plank, each sail, each sailor, each translator, and all the other components each did their piece of work and stayed in place. The Femtedit virtual world needed to move through the seven sessions planned for the project. If the Internet, the number of children in the class, the blogs, the ruins in the Femtedit world, and the researchers' discussion forum each stayed in place and did their work, then the technology could stay intact until the Femteditians had been reanimated. Latour calls a network that stays intact and that does not change when moving an *immutable mobile* (Latour 1990).

Sixth, it is not magic that makes the network stay immutable when moving; it is materiality. The network components keep one another in place. For example, the graphic ruins gathered children in a local place in the Femtedit virtual environment that, thanks to the Internet connection and sufficient bandwidth, supported the communication and collaboration between children at St. Marc Street School and at Pine Valley School. The sufficient bandwidth was made possible by the organization of children in time and space, and the resulting communication and collaboration allowed the children to reanimate the Femteditians and rebuild their homes. Thereby and with support from the Femtedit website, the frame story was re-enacted. Because the frame story was re-enacted during the Femtedit sessions, the researchers could write their field notes, which they could share and discuss thanks to the online researcher forum. Only because these components stayed in place could the researchers write blog comments to the children from the Femteditians. The children then could connect the comments to their work, and this could be converted into fuel for further building and linking. In this way, each component of the network was tightly connected to the others, and through this material bundling they kept one another in place and kept the network intact. Table 4 summarizes some of the central points of the network. The patterns described in the other three columns will be introduced throughout the book.

Table 4. *Comparison the of four spatial imaginaries discussed throughout the book.*

	Network	Resonance	Fluidity	Region
General Description	Web of components with well-defined relationships.	Field extended from a center.	Pattern of continuous transformation.	Homogenous areas divided by boundaries.
Defining Feature	Stable relations.	Stable relations, a center, closure.	Invariant (gradual) mutation.	Boundaries surrounding regions/objects.
Elements	Heterogeneous components that receive their identity through their relations in the network.	Heterogeneous components that receive their identity through the way in which they resonate with the center.	Parts that are amorphous; bonds that are flexible. A world of mixtures; components 1) may or may not be separated; 2) inform one another, but the way in which they do so may vary over time.	Homogenous elements clustered together, enclosed by boundaries. Defined by closure.
Relations among Elements	Relations are defined by proximity in identity. Components that go together depend on one another.	Relations are defined by the harmony among components.	Relations are constantly changing.	Elements are related in terms of similarity due to their common location.
Stability	Components hold one another and the network in place.	Stability is dependent on the ability of components to resonate with the center and create closure.	Stability is achieved through ongoing mutation and continuity.	Stability is in terms of homogeneity. Boundaries suppress the differences among the elements inside.
Dissolution	Occurs when linkages start to vary.	Occurs when connections within or to the center break, when there is no closure.	Occurs when the fluid space no longer absorbs its surroundings.	Occurs when differences within the region start to emerge.

(*continued*)

Table 4. (*continued*)

	Network	Resonance	Fluidity	Region
Displacement	The whole network moves as one.	The space is extended when new components are integrated.	Fluid patterns cut across places by absorbing parts from different places, whereby the shape changes.	Regions are immobile.
Demarcation	No demarcation. The network is infinite.	Reach of center.	Discontinuity.	Boundaries.
Mutation	Enlargement. Once constructed, the network is immutable. (See, however, "Temporality")	The identity of the space changes with the participation of individual components.	Fluid patterns mutate from one arrangement into another without discontinuity.	Immutable. The region does not change.
Temporality	Linear progression of time toward an end. Once constructed, time is folded into the network. (See, however, "Mutation")	Progression.	Continuous, invariant time of becoming.	Timeless. Regions are forever.
Differences	The network's opponents are dissociated or turned into allies.	Differences are caused by gradual variation in relation to center.	Differences and similarities come in varying shades and colors – they go together.	Differences exist across regions.
Similarities	Allies are integrated into the network.	Components share their (however varying) relation to the center.	It is not possible to 1) determine inside from outside; 2) determine identities neatly or conclusively.	Similarities lie within the space. Variables inside regions are averaged and fixed.
Norms	Different norms may remain within the network as long as they keep one another in place.	Different norms may remain within the resonance as long as they keep one another and the center in place.	Normality is a gradient rather than a cutoff point.	Each region has its norm. Different norms exist across regions.

Latour (1987) advises us to study technologies by describing the process through which they are constructed or by looking at them in a state of crisis. At these points, he states, the network is fragile and the objects involved in making it come into view. Latour's technique of studying technologies in their making makes use of detailed descriptions of how objects come to be, of their career (Scheffer 2003) toward being settled. Nick Bingham and Nigel Thrift (2000) describe how ANT concentrates "on movement, on process, on the constant hum of the world as the different elements of it are brought into relation with one another, often in new styles and unconsidered combinations" (p. 281).

The vocabulary suggested by Latour is introduced to create such descriptions. Apart from the notion of networks, Latour introduces, among others, the notions of disinterest, interest, enrollment, and black boxing to make processual descriptions of how things come to be. First, objects are *disinterested*, without any mutual influence. Then, they develop new goals to make one another *interested* in joining forces. This enables both to *enroll* in a common network that will eventually be *black boxed*. Through this process the objects come to take the shape of one thing, making invisible the assemblage of heterogeneous objects and the process through which the assemblage has been composed. Like a research object, cameras and other technologies usually take the shape of black boxed autonomous things with essential properties that can be approached and studied or used in and of themselves. The network metaphor invites us to open up these black boxes of essentialist descriptions and to focus on the networks of which they are made up. The vocabulary emphasizes relationality. Objects become what they are as a result of socio-material relations.

Using this vocabulary, STS teaches us that to describe a technology one has to *decenter*[14] from the object one wants to learn about and study the socio-material network in which it is entangled. I described Active Worlds as a research object by decentering from the object "itself" and looking at the relations in association with which it came to be.

---

[14] From another theoretical standpoint, Ole Dreier (1993, 2003) has suggested this notion in his studies of psychological treatment, emphasizing the need to zoom out (decenter) from the narrow focus on the individual and the psychotherapeutic practice to look at the psychosocial life in which personal problems are situated. In 2002 the notion of decentering appears in STS, as a central notion in Law's book *Aircraft Stories* (2002a), suggesting a decentering of the object in science studies. One of the crucial differences between the two is that Dreier emphasizes the decentered subject whereas Law's endeavor is to decenter the object.

Conclusion: The Construction of a Stable Technology

I have presented the construction of an online 3D virtual environment as the research object of my investigations and school practice as the research field. I have introduced the vocabulary of classic-ANT for describing the construction of technologies, and I applied that vocabulary to the construction of the research object as a network. The network metaphor changed the imaginary of research object and research field to an understanding of the technology – as a network – entangling both what was hitherto called "object" and what we used to know as "field." Object and field merged in the network description. Following this object-field symmetrical account of technology, we can, with Law, define technology as follows:

> Let me, then, define technology as a family of methods for associating and channelling other entities and forces, both human and non-human. It is a method . . . for the construction of a relatively stable system of related bits and pieces with emergent properties in a hostile or indifferent environment. When I say this, I do not mean that the methods are somehow different from the forces that they channel. Technology does not act as a kind of traffic policeman that is distinct in nature from the traffic it directs. It is itself nothing other than a set of channelled forces or associated entities. (Law 1989, pp. 115–116)

The descriptions of Active Worlds in the introduction to this chapter centered on what humans can do with the technology, or what the technology is in and of itself, as a purified entity. Describing Femtedit as a result of heterogeneous engineering shows that this technology is not a well-defined uniform thing to be identified by its function or by its component parts in general or in abstract. It shows that it is not only material but also social. The point that technology should be studied as heterogeneous is usually referred to as the principle of general symmetry in ANT.

Furthermore, it is important to notice that the account of Femtedit as a network treated discursive and material components symmetrically. The categorical division of thinking and practice and of theory and empirical work in Western scientific tradition (St. Pierre 1997; Thrift 1996; Verran 1998) has created a habit of jumping between empirical observation and discursive categorization. Accepting the Kantian gap between perceptual elements and perception, only few account empirically for the relation between discourse and materials. The account of how Femtedit became a research object showed how words and concepts were connected to the material parts of Femtedit. Theory was neither applied, inscribed, materialized, nor implemented into the technology. Instead theory participated in performing the technology, whereby the object became a research object, connecting research aims and communities with software functionalities. As a result, we can talk synonymously of technology and research object.

These three points of symmetry (between object and field, human and nonhuman, and material and discursive [e.g., Callon & Law 1997; Johnson 1995; Latour 1999a]), stated throughout the account of technology as a network, all have to do with the process of components coming together to make up Femtedit. When the technology eventually is constructed, we may encounter a unified object, and the component parts become invisible. In the construction process, however, it is crucial to take a detailed look at the way in which individual components succeed in relating to one another through dissociation and association. As my account shows, the path from Karlskrona2 to Femtedit was long and involved a great number of people, plans, concepts, digital applications, and organizations. Without these components, the Femtedit could not possibly be a working technology. Karlskrona2 worked in one particular practice, and making Femtedit out of it required subtraction and addition of a vast number of components. To do something with a technology, one must add and subtract components to such an extent that the technology that is finally applied is in effect a different technology.

Finally, accounting for technology in terms of network involves the description of trials of strength. Trials of strength are processes. Technologies do not simply exist; they *become*. The stability we imply when we talk about what a technology *is* is an achieved stability. This insight leads us from an understanding of technology as a product to accounting for technology as a process.

By describing Femtedit in terms of network, its socio-material parts have achieved a much more important role than we usually see in accounts of educational technology (Hoppe 2007). This shows the particularities of the technology and makes clear why, for example, paper, a shadow play, or other material would not have been involved. The online characteristics, the linking options, and the frame story that came to be by combining as many of the program functions as possible were all material components that were crucial to the Femtedit design's final form. When, in Chapters 4 and 5, I compare the Femtedit project with classroom practices, we see in greater detail the differences the materials made.

The Methodology of the Materiality of Learning
Lesson 2: Defining Materiality

This chapter has taught us about the notion of materiality without explicitly defining it. That will be the task of this lesson. I have shown how the virtual environment, situated in a learning context, is more than a technology situated in a social setting. The virtual environment came to be by connecting linking features, a sequential feedback plan, virtual ruins, theoretical concepts, research interests, class sizes, a researcher forum, a time schedule, avatar names, and much more. It was formed through the interaction of social and material components to such an extent that at some point defining any component as either material or social ceased to make sense. The social and the material were woven into each other in complex, yet concrete, practical networks. This is a classic point in ANT literature. Scholars use the notions of heterogeneities, hybrids, and cyborgs (Haraway, 1991) to refer to the ambiguous ontology of any human or thing, because they are inescapably constructed out of social as well as material components. Although these insights are original and important, they present us with an aching double bind: They insist that nothing is either material or social, yet they talk about the socio-material and about mixes of the social and material. Even the terms "heterogeneity," "hybrid," and "cyborg" imply that somewhere inside these amalgams are entities that are ontologically social or material. Real double-binds cannot be resolved. ANT rarely provides clear definitions of the material or of materiality. This can be justified by arguing that defining materials and materiality is counterproductive and only emphasizes differences between the social and the material, which we avoid by insisting on the notion of heterogeneity.

I will however argue that we need the term "material" as well as "materiality." The first, material, may become superfluous in the future, if postsocial understandings spread and make everyone think, talk, and act in terms of cyborgs, hybrids, and socio-material relations and if everyone forgets the time when some things were conceptualized as social while others were understood as material. At the present time in history we are far from such a condition, and we need the notion of material to describe assemblages that are tangible and purified and thus appear as isolated entities at the service of human sociality. I let material stand for an entity that has achieved a purified nonhuman character, and I let materiality refer to the achieved quality of a hybrid that allows it to relate to other parts. Thus, the notion of materiality applies to social as well as material parts. It allows us to talk about the materiality of a person, of laughter, of a gun, and of a virtual environment. When talking about a partaker's materiality, I refer to its achieved ability to relate to other specific partakers (Sørensen 2007). The notion of materiality creates a new double bind, but this time it is a productive one, I hope. I use the term materiality – which is semantically related to material – even though I let it refer to material as well as social relations. This is because I believe we in educational research are more in need of words that draw our attention to what we used to call "things" than we are in need of words that remind us of accounting for what through the processes of purification are called social or human relations.

In the pursuit of the materiality of learning, these notions on the one hand lead us to think about tangible, material things that surround us in learning and educational practices, which we traditionally do not take into account in theoretical work. On the other hand, we are sensitized to accounting for how relations that allow different parts to connect came into being.

3 Forms of Technology

The previous chapter introduced descriptions and formulations that at a second examination did not quite fit[1] the network characteristics. There were components that did not stay in place. There was mutation instead of stability. And there was collaboration in the place of trials of strength. In this chapter, I discuss these failing, mutating, and collaborating relations and the patterns they contributed to performing. I explain that describing Femtedit as a network presents only one form of the technology, out of the multiple forms that existed. The network metaphor is not sufficient. It is even partly misleading.

Law and Mol (Law 2002b; Law & Mol 2001; Mol & Law 1994) provide us with additional ways of describing technological practice. They suggest the metaphor of fluid space, which helps account for different performances of the technology. This chapter moves from the *relational* imaginary of the network to a *spatial* imaginary of patterns of relations, of which the network is only one among multiple performances of the technology.

A Second Examination of Femtedit

Optional Components

In the network pattern of relations, each component does its job and stays in place. In the Femtedit network, the children's connection to the online feature of the virtual environment was maintained through common tasks given to mixed groups of children from the two schools and through the graphic ruins of the Femteditians' homes, which were built in the online 3D virtual environment and provided the children with a location for online collaboration. These components were ammunition in the trial of strength with face-to-face localism. However, I did not mention in Chapter 2 that the

---

[1] I have borrowed this inspiring wording from "Things That Don't Quite Fit," the title of the first of a series of just as inspiring workshops arranged by John Law at the Centre for Science Studies, Lancaster University.

graphic ruins and common tasks lost the trial of strength against face-to-face localism. There was not much online collaboration between the children at St. Marc Street School and those at Pine Valley School.

Contrary to what the network metaphor let us expect, these "irregularities" did not make the technology dissolve, even though its components did not stay in place and did not do their jobs. The Femtedit technology stayed intact – the Danish and Swedish children built and linked next to each other, but without much collaboration. The Femteditians became composite but poorly coordinated products of the building blocks and links that each side of the team added to the Femtedit world. Femtedit did not dissolve; it varied.

The Portuguese vessels Law (1989) describes would not have stayed intact had the association of planks, mast, sails, oarsmen, storage capacity, and supply of fresh water not won the trial of strength against the strong current from the Canaries, persistent mists, and the depths of the sea. This was the tragic fate of the Vivaldi brothers' trip to the Indies in 1291: "[T]hey sailed their galleys past the pillars of Hercules and out of recorded history" (ibid., p. 117). The assemblage of human and nonhuman objects making up this trip was dissolved into its component parts – a tragic fate. The fate of Femtedit was not tragic. Even though the common tasks and graphic ruins lost the trial of strength against face-to-face localism, Femtedit did not dissociate into its component parts.

The trials of strength Law presents are dramatic. They are about life and death. My descriptions are not. Irregularities did not evoke disruptions. Instead of breaking apart, Femtedit varied. It became a technology to which two classes on each side of Oresund were connected, but without the planned intimate collaboration. Component parts slipped out of the network without it dissociating. The components did not act in the pattern that network components do.

A raft might be an appropriate allegory to think of when characterizing what happened:[2] The only way to rebuild a floating raft without falling into the water is to do the reconstruction bit by bit. If everything is taken apart at the same time, the result is dissolution. The raft is not a network. Its component parts are not obligatory. They can be left out without the assemblage dissolving. One can pull out a plank and the raft will not sink, just as one can exclude online collaboration from the Femtedit design and the project will still continue.

---

[2] In an earlier unpublished version of his article "Objects and Spaces" (2002b), Law suggested the allegory of Duhem's raft.

This, however, did not mean that the common tasks, the graphic ruins, or the infrequent online collaboration were redundant. Many of the component parts of Femtedit could be left out. The building function could stop working, and the Femteditians would then be reanimated only through hyperlinks. The blogs could stop working, and the Femteditians' feedback would have been distributed via email. One can never know in advance which component will fall short or be excluded. Therefore, each component part was necessary in case any of the others stopped working. If one component broke off, the rest could continue without it. Compare this to Law's (1989) description of heterogeneous engineering, in which he notes that "to say that an artifact is well adapted to its environment is . . . to note that the network in question is relatively *stable*" (p. 121, emphasis added). Being well adapted and relatively stable was not equivalent in the case of Femtedit, at least not in terms of components staying in place. The departure of some of the components did not make Femtedit less well adopted. The network imaginary does not fit. Or, at least, not quite. Obviously, if all component parts were removed at the same time, Femtedit would dissolve, just as the raft would. But a few components at a time could stop doing their work without Femtedit dissolving. Stability was not created through all components staying in place. On the contrary, the components of Femtedit floated in and out; they were optional and exchangeable. Femtedit was fluid.

Ongoing Trials

Many of the trials of strength making up Femtedit were won by the Femtedit design. The one described previously – between graphic ruins and common tasks on the one hand and face-to-face localism on the other – was lost. In the network metaphor, trials of strength, whether they were won or lost, were almost always concluded. There was an end result to the trials of strength. Other trials were different. They went on and on. In Chapter 2 I described how the organization of children in groups and a time schedule were inserted into the trial of strength with the limited bandwidth and poor-quality computers. But I also noted that the organization was not a sovereign opponent, because the computers kept freezing and the digital functions recurrently stopped working. Researchers engaged in whatever repair work was necessary, re-booting computers, changing program settings, and helping communicate to the team members in the other country that temporary breakdowns were taking place. This allowed Femtedit to continue, even though the problem was not solved. The limited bandwidth and poor-quality computers kept challenging Femtedit, and the conflicts kept reappearing. The trial of strength was not settled. The limited bandwidth and poor-quality computers did not triumph over Femtedit, putting an end to the technology. Nor did the organization of children in groups and the time schedule overcome the opposition from the limited bandwidth and poor-quality computers. It was not a zero-sum game like the one described by the network metaphor, in which there is always one winner and one loser. It was an ongoing trial.

In addition, Femtedit differed from the characteristic of a network as a pattern of relations proceeding toward stability, which is obtained when the trails end. Instead, stability was obtained by the flexible and changing efforts of the researchers, who helped when the limited bandwidth and poor-quality computers threatened to destroy the technology. Settings were changed; children were relocated to other computers; messages were sent. These brief, temporary interventions did not become permanent components of the assemblage. But they were necessary for the continuity of the technology. Indeed, Femtedit proceeded because of the ongoing repair work and recurring struggle with the limited bandwidth and poor-quality computers. Thus Femtedit's fluid stability was defined by brief, recurring interventions, adjustments, and rearrangements or, in other words, ongoing or recurring – rather than finite – trials.

Absorbing Parts from the Outside

Another point at which Femtedit differed from the network metaphor has to do with the relation between the inside and the outside of the virtual environment. Apart from reestablishing the Femteditians' homes, the tasks in Femtedit involved making links from the homes in Femtedit to web pages on the Internet. The design encouraged children to look for URLs in their environments, not only in Femtedit but especially in other places. Also, the research forum contributed to a steady flow of alterations and revisions of the already-established links in Femtedit and to ongoing additions of new parts. This was a repeated pattern of Femtedit: new parts entered the virtual environment and altered the character of the technology. Some links came to stay, and others were exchanged or deleted, but either way the links involved contributed to the continuity (and mutation) of Femtedit.

In this way, external parts were absorbed by the Femtedit design. They were not opponents that contributed to the technology by challenging it, as described by the network metaphor. On the contrary, they were friends who joined the game, so to speak, who entered, influenced, and formed Femtedit. Not negatively as opponents but positively by becoming parts of the assemblage equal to other components. Let me again remind us of Law's (1989) description of the network: "They seek to dissociate hostile forces and to associate them with their enterprise by transforming them" (p. 121). In our case, however, external forces were not hostile, and they were not necessarily associated with Femtedit through mutation.

The flow of parts from the outside was decisive for Femtedit's continuity. The parts provided researchers with material for the feedback from the Femteditians, and thus for their reanimation. The aspect of ongoing absorption of external parts resonates with the network pattern of obligatory components that have to stay in place if the network is to remain whole.

However, the parts absorbed into this pattern of relations did not have to stay in place in order for the pattern to stay intact. On the contrary, they had to keep mutating. The researchers encouraged this, and it was inscribed in the frame story. The result was not a pattern of relations that, once constructed in opposition to external elements, stayed the same, as the network did. Instead, this pattern of relations continued changing through the absorption of external parts.

Critiques of the Network Metaphor

Femtedit performed patterns of relations that did not fit the network metaphor. Or, put the other way around, the network metaphor is not appropriate for characterizing the pattern of relations performed by and through Femtedit. Before discussing further what was performed, I look at the critiques of the network metaphor that have been posed by many authors. I focus especially on three points of critique concerning the managerial tendency of network stories as well as the stability and singularity produced by the network metaphor. The criticisms are posed by authors sympathetic to ANT. Hence, I take the critiques as attempts to further develop the line of thinking initiated by classic-ANT.

Managerial Perspective

Feminist and social interactionist Susan Leigh Star (1991) has observed that Michel Callon and Bruno Latour's writings start with heroes or near-heroes; people and things of great importance and great power: Louis Pasteur, Rudolf Diesel, the double Helix, and the Eagle computer, for example. "Some of us," Star modestly writes, "begin not with Pasteur, but with the monster, the outcast" (ibid., p. 29). Many of these "some" are feminists who wish to create descriptions that notice the peripheral, the ephemeral, the invisible, and the overseen, that is, what fails, what does not fit the standards. The powerless, if you wish. To these authors, the network descriptions of classic-ANT are too managerial, too centered, and too integral. Sociologist of childhood Nick Lee and social psychologist Steven D. Brown (Lee & Brown 1994) point to the colonial character of the network metaphor. It leaves no room for "Others" and "Otherness" and allows nothing to stand outside the network. Everything is integrated.

Metaphors, Star notes, create worlds and emphasize and give voice to some people, while silencing and ignoring others. Along with Haraway (1997), Star remarks that the network imaginary creates a "God's-eye view," which, looking at the world from above, sees everything as fitting together in one system. It is a managerial perspective, a perspective of one who creates worlds and aims for coherence and order. Philosopher and sociologist of science and technology Sergio Sismondo (2004) observes that the subtitle of Latour's *Science in Action*, "How to Follow Scientists and Engineers through Society," emphasizes the people at the center of inventions and technologies – the creators, the heroes.

But there is indeed more to the world than coherence, order, and central perspectives.[3] And there was indeed more to Femtedit than coherence and order. There were parts that did not stay in place and do their work as the network metaphor suggested. There were parts that did not fit in as permanent components of the assemblage but only briefly passed by and left again. These parts, however, did matter, as I have shown. We need a vocabulary that allows us to describe these different patterns. Following Star, Haraway, and other feminist writers, I therefore argue the need for metaphors that are capable of taking into account the failing, the changing, the ephemeral, and the overseen.

Focus on Stability

The network metaphor has furthermore been criticized for its focus on stability. This critique is closely related to the critique of the managerial character of network descriptions, but its focus is on the temporal

---

[3] That the world, facts, and technologies do not perform one central coherent order is partly what classic-ANT aimed at showing, as discussed in Chapter 2. The metaphor of construction undermines the view of order as a given, but, as we realize through classic-ANT analyses, it does not prevent the image of construction concluding in one centered order. It does not prevent total descriptions. See also this chapter, note 6.

stability, while the latter's focus is on spatial coherence. The process of constructing a network is a process that draws things tightly together and that aims at settling all components into an all-encompassing network. As we saw in the preceding descriptions, Femtedit was not like that. Or, it was, at least, not *only* like that. Trials occurred, as did ongoing constructions of the Femteditians and of the identity of the Femtedit world. Without these ongoing trials, Femtedit did not make much sense. There are technologies whose aims are not to fix, to settle, or to standardize processes. For example, think of open source software. Or think of a water pump (de Laet & Mol 2000) that serves different aims, that continuously changes, and whose creators and maintainers are temporarily available. The network metaphor cannot appropriately describe the pattern of relations that these technologies perform. Through discussions of such a pump – the Zimbabwe Bush Pump – Marianne de Laet and Annemarie Mol (2000) criticize the network metaphor for making a world of big, stable, and robust systems and for being incapable of describing assemblages that vary and do not settle. I return to this discussion later.

Singularity

The network metaphor was launched to do war on the concept that technology and facts among other things have essential, isolated existences (e.g., Latour 1987; Law 2002b). I would like to question whether war is the right idea to guide scientific work. Wars unmake worlds and make worlds. They unmake understandings and make understandings. In that sense war is singular. It accepts only one order, only one pattern of relations. The network metaphor has moved into the castle of the dethroned understanding. Only on the ruins of the past can the new emerge. "I'm much more willing to live with indigestible intellectual and political heritages. I need to hold on to impossible heritages more than I suspect Bruno [Latour] wants to," Haraway (Gane & Haraway 2006, my insertion) states. I hope to have the same tolerance for tension in my work. Latour rejects the old order but keeps the part of the order that lets him inhabit the castle as the new king. He does not open a community house or enact cross-generational cohabitation. Why not celebrate multiple orders next to one another, intertwined and coordinated, instead of celebrating only one order, Mol and Law ask (e.g., Law 2002a; Mol 2002; Mol & Law 1994).

Relations and Spaces

From Classic-ANT to after-ANT

The critiques of the network metaphor should not lead to a disposal of the term. Such a move would contradict the critique of the singularity of the network metaphor. The problem of singularity is closely related to those of managerialism and stability. Aiming to suggest alternative solutions to these problems, Law and Mol (e.g., Law 2002a; Mol 2002; Mol & Law 1994) have located the question of multiplicity at the core of their theorizing. Their works are central to the move from what I call classic-ANT to *after-ANT*. The term "after-ANT" was invented when a number of key ANT scholars met at a workshop in the late 1990s to discuss progresses in ANT. The meeting resulted in the excellent volume *Actor-Network Theory and After*, by John Law and John Hassard (1999), which displays ANT (or after-ANT) as an anti-dogmatic empirical approach that focuses on inventing new metaphors and theoretical insights rather than on consolidating a set vocabulary. Furthermore, the volume gives the impression that after-ANT is made up of a diverse collection of scholars (including Latour) who are inspired by poststructuralism and ethnomethodology and are occupied with questions such as ontology, materiality, multiplicity, semiotics, and translation, with a preference for ongoing discussion over closure.[4]

Law and Mol have intervened in the network metaphor in three ways that are indicative of the move from classic-ANT to after-ANT: First, they have turned the network metaphor into a metaphor that may be used for empirical descriptions, which is contrary to the network imaginary of classic-ANT, in which the network is a fundamental all-embracing and all-inclusive theoretical metaphor. Second, they have emphasized that the network metaphor does not create sensitivity to describing all empirical formations. And third, they have presented three additional metaphors next to the network metaphor. The four metaphors make available the creation of empirical descriptions sensitive to the various ways in which socio-material practices may be formed; they coexist rather than replacing one another. These three moves are helpful for dealing with the two

---

[4] The preference for ongoing discussions became even clearer in later discussions of methods emphasizing the search for new questions rather than the attainment of certainty (see Despret 2004b; Gomart 2004; Latour 2004a).

different descriptions of Femtedit that I have presented in this and the previous chapter, which I will return to shortly.

From Relations to Patterns of Relations

Although not the case for all writers of after-ANT, Law and Mol's approach is spatial, and they apply their metaphors to discuss *spatial formations*. In the previous chapter I argued that in order to understand materiality we need to move away from thinking of elements and move toward theorizing in terms of relations. I described how relations can be conceptualized through descriptions of interactions among the components that come together to make up an entity. The notion of relations makes us think of how elements are connected. Their connections are dynamic; they are interactions. They can be characterized in terms of trials of strength, as I discussed in reference to Law's work (1989), or as chains of translations, as Latour (1987) and Callon (1986) have suggested. When using notions like trials of strength or chains of translations to study the network, we are equipped with a vocabulary that makes us focus on relations and interactions among components and not on the assemblages of parts. I have therefore come to be wary of relational approaches. The notion of relations – and the imaginary of connections among components and of interaction that this notion implies – does not help us come to grips with the two different descriptions of Femtedit discussed in this and the previous chapter. I am concerned that the notion of relation makes us focus on more or less well-delimited entities that in one way or the other are linked and that it makes us forget that these entities are results not only of interactions but of webs of interactions – that interactions are embedded in patterns of relations and that patterns of relation also constitute relations. Patterns of relations form spaces. The two descriptions of Femtedit differ in the pattern of how the relations among the parts were formed. Their differences lie in their spatial formations. In order to increase our sensitivity to materiality as a relational phenomenon, we need words that help us focus less on relations or interactions and that instead assist us in describing spaces. We need to move from a relational approach to a spatial approach that focuses on the patterns performed through relations among parts. From a quite different theoretical stance, Marxist philosopher Henri Lefebvre (1991) identified the same problem and called for a shift from inquiring about things in space to investigations of the production of space.

The metaphor of the network emphasizes neither components nor their interactions or relations but the assemblage that each component and relation is part of, and it characterizes the pattern of relations that this assemblage forms. It characterizes its spatial formation. As long as we operate with only one spatial metaphor – the network – such a metaphor is a "space of no space." Sharon Traweek (1988) has ironically characterized the extremely objectivist culture of high-energy physics as a "culture of no culture," emphasizing thereby that any practice is a culture among other cultures no matter how deeply it is enveloped in purifications that deny its cultural nature. Likewise, through its all-encompassing character, the network metaphor in its classic-ANT gestalt denies that it is a space among spaces. By "reducing" the network to an empirical metaphor, Mol and Law (1994) turn the network metaphor into a spatial metaphor that describes one spatial formation next to others. Preserving the network metaphor and adding a metaphor that can characterize the pattern of relations in Femtedit described in this chapter is helpful in dealing with the different descriptions of Femtedit.

Spatial Imaginaries

> Not so many years ago, the word "space" had a strictly geometrical meaning: the idea it evoked was simply that of an empty area. In scholarly use it was generally accompanied by some such epithet as "Euclidian," "isotropic," or "infinite," and the general feeling was that the concept of space was ultimately a mathematical one. To speak of "social space," therefore, would have sounded strange. (Lefebvre 1991 [1974], p. 1)

With these words Lefebvre initiates his work titled *The Production of Space*. Further on in the book he emphasizes that we are confronted meanwhile (in 1974) with an indefinite multitude of spaces: geographical, economic, demographic, sociological, ecological, political, commercial, global, and mental. Disproportionate to this proliferation of the term, the notion of space is clearly under-theorized, Lefebvre notes, and how such diverse spaces come into being, how they are separated and interrelated, and how they are reproduced materially and in language remains generally unclear. Lefebvre develops a theory of space as a product to answer these questions. Whereas Lefebvre's aim is to theorize the production of space – in singular – as an overall societal characteristic, in order to be able to investigate materiality I concentrate on the spaces – in plural – emerging through the particular patterns in which materialities interrelate.

This is the first point about my understanding of space: Space is expanded, and the spatial approach helps us turn away from a perspectival approach that creates an imaginary of an arrangement viewed from a singular position,[5] and it helps us turn toward a dispersed view of patterns of relations as relative to one another. Geographer Chris Philo (2000) argues that a pivotal aspect of Foucault's theory is that he approaches social life and history in spatial terms:

> I would argue that when Foucault gazes out on the social world of the past, he sees not the order of (say) a mode of production determining the lines of class struggle nor the order of (say) a worldview energising everything from how the economy functions to how the most beautiful mural is painted: rather, he sees the *spaces of dispersion* through which the things under study are scattered across a landscape and are related one to another simply through their geography, the only order that there is here is discernible, by being near to one another or far away, by being positioned in certain locations or associated with certain types of environment, by being arranged in a certain way or possessed of a certain appearance thanks to their plans and architecture. (pp. 220–221, emphasis added)

Foucault replaces the traditional account of history as a series of progressive developmental stages seen from the current highest stage with descriptions of *spatial relations* deeply implicated in historical processes: the distribution and arrangement of people, activities, and buildings. Philo notes that this implicit critique of coherence targets the tendency of historical accounts to produce an overall form of civilization, a singular principle of society, and a unitary significance common to all phenomena of a period. Analogous to this, descriptions of technology are often total in character, focusing on the functioning of a machine in definite and singular terms, often presented through the view of the designer.

According to Philo (2000), Foucault finds such total descriptions suspect because of the measure of order they introduce: "[A total description] smoothes over the specific confusions, contradictions, and conflicts which have been the very 'stuff' of the lives led by 'real' historical people, powerful and powerless alike" (p. 210). Total descriptions remain alien to the

---

[5] Lefebvre (1991) provides an insightful description of how perspectivism in the Renaissance came to be embodied in the organization of the social life of the town: "Façades were harmonized to create perspectives; entrances and exits, doors and windows, were subordinated to façades – and hence also to perspective; streets and squares were arranged in concord with the public buildings and palaces of political leaders and institutions (with municipal authorities still predominating). At all levels, from family dwellings to monumental edifices, from 'private' areas to the territory as a whole, the elements of this space were disposed and composed in a manner at once familiar and surprising which even in the late twentieth century has not lost its charm" (p. 47).

details and differences of practice at particular times and particular places. They create an order in which everything fits to everything else, in which all components have their right place.

In his assault on what Philo calls "the castle of coherence," Foucault (1972) proposes the method of *general description* as an alternative to total descriptions:[6] "A total description draws all phenomena around a single centre – a principle, a meaning, a spirit, a world-view, an overall shape; a general history, on the contrary, would deploy the space of a dispersion" (p. 10). Similarly, describing the materiality of learning in spatial terms provides us with an approach in the midst of things that does not search for problems according to a pre-given norm or apply either a child-perspective (Christensen & James 2000) or a teacher's view (e.g., Marland 1993). Like Philo, the spatial approach I apply here sees "spaces of dispersion through which the things under study are scattered . . . and are related one to another simply through their geography" and characterizes the formation of these different spaces. Describing spatial imaginaries instead of order, principles, or significance allows us to create descriptions at the level of socio-material interactions, rather than elevating the descriptions to a "transcendental" (St. Pierre 1997) level of meaning, ideas, or generalities (see Thrift [1996], chapter 1, for discussions of a variety of theories that share this nonrepresentational aspiration).

Spatial imaginaries do not imply that time cannot be part of the study (Sørensen 2007). Foucault was not interested in excluding time from social research; rather, he fought against the particular depiction of time as a singular, orderly progression. I have described how my research object and research field came to be as a chain of encounters among components. But note that this is not a description of a development from simple to more complex or from primitive to more advanced; it is a development from being entangled in one network to becoming entangled in another – a spatial movement rather than a temporal progression. Instead of ignoring time, a spatial imaginary is about finding ways of conceptualizing time

[6] Foucault applied spatial strategies in his attack on progressive time as well as in his critique of totality. Whereas the attack on progressive time is convincing in his own and his followers' writing, the same works have demonstrated that the totalizing of descriptions is not necessarily overcome by applying spatial techniques. It is possible to create singular spatial descriptions "from above" with a "God's-eye view." Indeed, in his studies of power Foucault did not look at one singular totalizing power as the source of history, but his accounts do add up to describe one – the disciplinary – power as an effect of contingencies, practicalities, and particular located practices. As I discuss shortly, this risk of producing total spatial descriptions can be solved by applying multiple spatial metaphors, which imply that spaces never perform only one singular, total pattern of relations.

other than as progression, just as it is about conceptualizing space in a new way, which I discuss in more detail later in this text. In Table 4, which characterizes the four spatial formations I discuss in this book, I have indicated the different formations of time in the four spatial formations.

The spatial approach applied here is not an attempt to localize elements in space (as territories), or measure their geographic distance. Researchers of childhood have written remarkable works on children's places and spaces that demonstrate how modern childhood is indeed constituted through the design of specific kinds of landscapes (de Coninck-Smith & Gutman 2004). Such studies describe, for instance, places in which children play and learn. Childhood researcher Kim Rasmussen (2004) compares "places for children" created by adults with "children's places" that are "created out of children's symbolic work and creativity" (p. 158). The places Rasmussen describes – by means of child informants equipped with disposal cameras – are characterized by the condition that they can be photographed: for example, fields, courtyards, schoolyards, gardens. In his accounts of "the garden" as a "children's place" Rasmussen describes swings, a rabbit, a sandbox, siblings, and a birthday party and provides us with a spatial imaginary of the garden as a container of these elements, as well as of the play and other activities of the informants. This description of already existing places that are inhabited by children and thus are "children's places" is supplemented by approaches describing interactional spaces – sub-spaces within classrooms (Leander 2002) and playgrounds (Karsten 2003) that are composed out of children's interaction in those places. In these studies, places are described as created by human creativity and interaction, and the materials play the role of resources for or resistances to these human endeavors. Furthermore, these places are territories, fields, areas, surfaces, or regions in which action takes place (even though it is sometimes described as a mutual shaping of place and action). I use the notion of place[7] to refer to this imaginary of space as a container for human action – either preexisting or created through human interaction. My intent is to describe space as an expanded web of relations

---

[7] A common distinction between space and place is the phenomenologically inspired idea of space as being more "abstract" than place – the latter being more delimited, with specific subjective meanings and attributes. In this understanding, space exists only as places, as centers of human meaning expressed in the everyday experiences and consciousness of people within particular lifeworlds (Merleau-Ponty 1962). This exceedingly humanist conceptualization of space is not very helpful in the understanding of the materiality of learning, and I consequently treat "place" as one spatial (and thus socio-material) formation among others.

that may have nothing to do with geographic terrains. That is, space consists of emerging relational formations in which human and nonhuman components may take part, and the components that do take part contribute to performing these spatial formations.

I follow Law and Mol in their inquiries into spatiality (e.g., de Laet & Mol 2000; Law 2002b; Law & Mol 2001; Law & Singleton 2005; Mol & Law 1994). They emphasize that what is next to, above, beyond, and apart from is not necessarily defined in terms of metric distances; instead it may be defined in terms of identity, functionality, familiarity, or a mix of these or other attributes. The expanded web of relations accounted for by spatial descriptions may thus include any kind of materiality: human as well as nonhuman, social as well as physical, active as well as passive. Law and Mol (1994) discuss different spatial types in terms of topology:

> Unlike anatomy, topology doesn't localize objects in terms of a given set of coordinates. Instead, it articulates different rules for localizing in a variety of coordinate systems. Thus it doesn't limit itself to the three standard axes X, Y and Z, but invents alternative systems of axes. In each of these, another set of mathematical operations is permitted, which generates its own "points" and "lines." (p. 643)

Explaining what their spatial topology is not, they add in a footnote: "One could say that anatomy is a topography, a map-making practice. Like geographical topographies, it localizes its objects within a set of coordinates, taking these coordinates as tools, rather than as an object of reflection" (1994, p. 665, n. 5).

Let me be clear about this: what I am attempting to do is not to locate pre-given entities in an Euclidean three-dimensional X-Y-Z space but to describe different alternative "coordinate systems" and how they are formed in particular practices. Mol and Law have developed four spatial metaphors[8] (region, network, fluid, and fire) to emphasize that more than one space exists. Thereby they create sensitivities to different formations of

---

[8] "Metaphor" is not to be understood as an expression of prelinguistic entities that structure our understanding, as Lakoff and Johnson (1980) do. Nor do I take "metaphor" as a collection of representations that map already-existing understandings, as Quinn (1991) suggests. Rather, Law and Mol's spatial metaphors are images that create sensitivities to thinking about certain patterns of relations. A network makes us think about elements that are connected, regions makes us think of fields containing homogeneous entities, and fluid makes us sensitive to relations that vary and mutate. Hence, "metaphor" is close to the notion of "imaginary." However, whereas "metaphor" refers specifically to the verbal expression of "network" or "region" that allows a certain sensitivity to emerge, "imaginary" refers to the arrangement, infrastructure, or syntax implied by the metaphor.

spaces, to describing technological practices as performing more than one pattern of relations. Mol and Law's – and my – interest is to explore the variations in spatial formations performed through different practices. A particular space is identified by the pattern of relations of which it is made up and the principles they perform for what counts as an object, as differences and similarities, or as continuities and breaks.

Spatial formations are always situated, but not necessarily located, within a situation at a delimited moment and place. As was the case in the description of Femtedit through the metaphor of trials of strength, we saw that the network was constituted of components that, according to this definition of situation, lie inside as well as outside the situation. Relations can form patterns that are large or small, reaching across time and space in a Euclidian sense. But more than that, the spatial approach allows us to describe the particular temporality involved in this space, just as it provides us with the task of characterizing the parts of the space; the relations among the parts; the stability of the space and its dissolution, displacement, mutation, and demarcation; how differences and similarities emerge; the norms of the space; which form the space takes; and how it circulates. Describing an online 3D virtual environment in spatial terms is a matter of following the involved parts as they relate and of describing the pattern these relations form and characterizing them according to the previously mentioned list. Spatial imaginaries are about describing objects as patterns of relations. When discussing a spatial imaginary – the network, for instance – I name each space to distinguish between the formations that characterize it.

Anthropologists of education Hervé Varenne and Ray McDermott (1998, p. 12) note that entities that together make a pattern gain their particularities through the ways in which they are arranged with other entities. Even though Varenne and McDermott are not writing in spatial terms, their description is useful for my purposes. Spatial imaginaries are about describing the patterns in which parts are arranged or relate, which is a way of characterizing the particularities of the object under study. It is not, as the notion of patterns is sometimes understood, an attempt to generalize. On the contrary, it is a sensitivity to describing particularities as effects of relations. We may understand patterns of relations as the "coordinate systems" Mol and Law talk about – not as one general or universal coordinate system but as the particular coordinate systems performed by and through particular practices.

Fluid Patterns of Relations

This chapter's initial discussion of Femtedit confronted us with a description of the technology that did not fit the network metaphor. A spatial approach allows us to describe the spatial formations of a technology that differ from the network. The spatial metaphor of fluidity is helpful (Law 2002b; Law & Mol 2001; Mol & Law 1994; see also Elgaard Jensen 2001; de Laet & Mol 2000; Law 2002a). The classic example of a fluid technology is the Zimbabwe Bush Pump (de Laet & Mol 2000). De Laet and Mol show how the pump continuously changes shape. Of the many pipes and bolts that make the pump work, any one part is not in itself necessary to keep the pump working. Each part can be replaced with other components. With many of its bolts removed, the pump still keeps its capability to pump. Furthermore, the social and village relations that are connected to the pump are not always the same. Just as the purpose of the pump sometimes is to provide clean water and keep people healthy, sometimes its purpose is to contribute to creating Zimbabwe as a nation. Material bits and pieces as well as social relations and purposes vary with the different arrangements in which the pump becomes entangled. The success of the Bush Pump, it is concluded, is its ability to change shape. Obviously, the pump does not perform a network pattern of relations. De Laet and Mol call it a fluid technology.

Fields of invariant and gradual mutation are fluid (Mol & Law 1994). Components of fluidity are optional and exchangeable, whereas objects in a network are durable and held in place. Fluid objects are not well defined, and their mutual relations are variable. Stability in fluidity is not generated by fixed relations – as in a network – but by continuous mutation. Fluidity is variable in the sense that it does not collapse if objects are substituted with others, changed, or disappear. On the contrary, fluid patterns depend on including new parts. They encounter their limits the moment they no longer absorb their surroundings. See Table 4 (pp. 55–56) for a comparison of fluids and networks.

Femtedit as Fluid

I described Femtedit as a pattern of relations in which components could fail without the pattern dissolving, as an ongoing trial that did not settle but continued mutating, and finally as an assemblage that absorbs parts from outside, contrary to treating them as opponents. These three aspects are closely related. Because there were no opponents performed, there could be no trials of strength. Instead, an ongoing trial was performed, not as a fight among opponents but as a continuous exchange among "friendly" parts, as an ongoing trial that gradually altered Femtedit. All parts – "external" and "internal" – engaged in this exchange, and this made up the technology. This also implies that "failing" is not the right term for the components that did not stay in place. That was how they acted in network terms. In fluid terms these components contributed to the ongoing mutation of the fluid formation. "Failing" in fluid terms happened the moment mutation stopped.

The nonhuman components like graphic ruins, hyperlinks, interrelations between schools, and bandwidth were not the only parts that changed. Researchers changed as well. The plan for giving sequential feedback from the Femteditians turned out not to match the way in which the project was proceeding, but this did not lead to the falsification of the hypothesis inscribed[9] in the plan about how the project should proceed. Instead, it became a lesson for the future process and changed the relation between the plan and the Femteditians' feedback. Instead of using the plan as a guideline for how to proceed sequentially, the researches used the "steps" of the plan as inspiration for different ways of giving feedback.[10] In this way, Femtedit changed together with us, the researchers, as we learned a lesson. We changed our way of participating in the project, just as described by Emile Gomart (2004), who suggests that researchers participate as apprentices in the research process.

The identity of the Femteditians and the Femtedit virtual environment changed in the process, along with the researchers. Similarly, the children involved in the Femtedit project were continuously challenged through the feedback from the Femteditians. Rather than being given more or less isolated pieces of factual knowledge as final results that they could consider robust achievements, they were encouraged to keep revising, amplifying, and extending their work (see Chapter 4).

These patterns of ongoing mutation performed by and through the Femtedit technology implied and required continuous involvement of parts from outside, especially through hyperlinks, as well as the experiences

---

[9] The description of a "hypotheses inscribed" in technology or plans is taken from Akrich 1992.

[10] I keep in mind Suchman's (1987, 2007) insight that plans are involved as resources for action rather than prescriptions. However, I want to emphasize that there are variations in how decisive a role plans play in practice. Differentiating between "inspiration" and "guideline" is an attempt to formulate such variations.

and exchanges involved in bringing these hyperlinks into Femtedit. Together with the ongoing mutation, the involvement of new parts from "outside" is a key characteristic of fluidity. New parts – as well as the parts already entangled in the pattern of relations – may stay within a fluid assemblage for a long or short time. They are optional and gradually exchangeable.

To Be or Not to Be Fluid: A Few Examples

Before ending this section about the fluid characteristics of the Femtedit virtual environment design, I compare the fluid Femtedit design to a few classic educational computer programs. I need to make a provision about this section: It is crucial to my approach that technology be studied as an embedded practice. In the following, I discuss educational programs without basing my examination on empirical material about how they take part in practice. It may be the case that the technologies I describe do contribute to performing a greater variety of forms than I describe, including fluidity. However, I do not want to make an extended comparison at this point, but instead I let this asymmetric comparison simply clarify some characteristics of Femtedit and concretize some characteristics of fluidity. Inevitably, a comparison of the technological practices of Femtedit and the programs discussed in the following would show greater variety.

Mathematician and learning theorist Seymour Papert's computer program, entitled Logo (1980, 1993; see also Agalianos et al. 2006), allows children to program "turtles" on the screen to act according to the geometric rules children set. A rule could be that the turtle must keep moving one step forward until it bumps into a barrier or another turtle, at which point it must turn 135 degrees to the left. The turtle can also be programmed to draw a line on the screen while moving, which will create a graphic expression of the rule – as well as creating nice pictures of flowers, houses, or other objects. Logo is explorative and open-ended, with no predefined result. These aspects are fluid. However, the geometric operations that Logo is programmed to execute on specific commands are entirely fixed. They define the limits of the fluid pattern of relations. In comparison, most components involved in Femtedit were malleable. Femtedit defined the activities to involve building blocks and hyperlinks, which provided a large source of components from "outside" that could become part of Femtedit. The user of Logo has to stay within the discipline of geometry. Without that, the program dissolves.

Involving themes from children's everyday life has been an element of other educational software before Femtedit. Robert B. Davis's Plato computer system teaches children mathematics, as Logo does. Central to Plato is the fact that it builds on what children already know (Druin & Solomon 1996). For example, it introduces fractions by asking the child to share jumping beans with two friends. This is supposed to make the child draw on familiar experiences of sharing jumping beans and to reassemble these experiences into a new frame as he acquires new knowledge. Parts from outside are involved, as they are in a fluid pattern of relations. But they are not absorbed by the program in a way that changes its formation, as is characteristic for fluidity. Whereas Plato defines a very specific practice from the child's life – sharing jumping beans – as relevant and provides a quite limited way of using this experience in the computer program, the Femtedit fluid pattern of relations invites the children to define which practices are relevant for inclusion in the virtual environment and how.

Finally, by keeping the frame story relatively undefined, that is, relatively blank, Femtedit contributed to performing children as individuals who define which parts to include and how to do so. Lee and sociologist John Hetherington (Hetherington & Lee 2000) have proposed the notion of "blankness" in order to draw attention to how empty spaces, like the hole in the board of a peg solitaire game (which involves moving pegs around on a board that has holes cut into it), can be a pivotal contributor to action. It is not the pegs that drive the game ahead; it is the hole. Do not look only for the pegs, they note. Do not go after objects that are "full" and in motion. Social scientists, they continue, usually search among full objects and filled spaces in order to find sources for action. But sometimes it is not an interaction itself or a known interactor but a break in the interaction or an undefined identity that evokes further occurrences. Hetherington and Lee call such holes, breaks, and unidentified identities *blank objects*. The undefined character of the Femtedit frame story made it a blank object. This blankness, this empty space, was a crucial contributor to fluidity, creating a constant need for filling the blankness of the frame story. The children were in charge of filling this blankness, which put them in an active position, as I discuss further in Chapter 5. This blankness can be compared to a textbook, which does not involve blankness but conveys a full body of information for the reader to store, engrave, or copy. Indeed, a textbook is a full object that performs the reader as blank. It is up to the textbook to fill the reader with information. The textbook has no purpose if the reader is already familiar with the information it contains. In Femtedit it was the other way around: Femtedit was blank, which required the user to be "full," to be active. The blankness made it possible for the children to be active and hence, through the building process, to perform a fluid pattern.

Many educational interactive digital designs involve blank lines, for instance, *drill-and-practice* programs (also known as *interactive textbooks*). Based on Patrick Suppes's special version of behaviorism for computer curriculum (see Druin & Solomon 1996), many programs present an arithmetic exercise followed by a blank line. For example, $3 \times 9 = \underline{\hspace{1cm}}$. This "blankness" does not contribute to performing fluidity. It is not blank in terms of its answer being blank. Twenty-seven is the product. That is set. There is no discussion. If the user types in another number – 83 – the computer reacts with the message "TRY AGAIN." The right result – 27 – may not be presented for the user, but the way the exercise is presented and the repeated assessment of the answer provided makes it clear that a single right answer to the task exists. It is as if the unanswered math problem is unbalanced, and the program is just waiting for the 27 to be filled in and the balance to be reestablished.

As a result of these kinds of so-called *pseudo-questions* – a term that indicates that they are not questions that look for an answer, but questions to which the answers are already known (Lindblad & Sahlström 1998) – children are performed as *trivial machines*, to use a term from systems theorist Niklas Luhmann (2002, p. 77). These are pupils that, given a specific input, execute a certain function, which results in a specific output. The Femtedit frame story did not have such a predefined result. The blank space established by the frame story contributed to performing the characteristics of gradual mutation through the involvement of external exchange and optional parts.

Multiplicity

One question is still to be settled: did Femtedit perform a fluid space or a network space? Neither option is correct. It (they) performed both a fluid and a network pattern of relations. In order for the Femtedit technology to be able to move through the seven sessions without dissolving into its component parts, it had to be designed as a network that was immutable and mobile. At the same time, the virtual environment was quite flexible. While establishing a rigid network structure, Femtedit also – across other connection points – incorporated relations with considerable slack. This slack made it possible for the virtual environment to continue to relate to the involved parts while they varied over time – and while Femtedit also varied.

A technology can very well perform a network pattern of relations and a fluid pattern of relations at the same time; that is, a technology can very well be multiple. Postmodernist approaches suggest the idea of pluralism to emphasize that there is not only one right description of the world. Giving one description higher status than another is a political move, not an objective move. Using Wittgenstein's notion of language games, Lyotard (1984) emphasizes this concept is discussed in the plural. Language games are the patterns of activities and practices associated with particular families of linguistic expressions. The way an object like a 3D virtual environment is described depends on the language game used to describe it. A scientific language game, a pedagogic language game, and a peer language game all provide different descriptions and hence different ideas or representations of what the virtual environment is. In other words, what a virtual environment is depends on the perspective of the description. The network pattern of relations and the fluid pattern of relations can be seen as two such perspectives (see also Dreier [1999] for a more practice-oriented notion of perspective).

While sharing the postmodernists' desire to theorize beyond singularity, Law and Mol (e.g., Law 2002a; Mol 1999, 2002) suggest the notion of multiplicity, which differs from that of pluralism on two points. First, Law (2002b) notes that plurality may lead to a fragmented collection of descriptions. Nothing is gained by just having many instead of one, by simply listing a number of descriptions of Femtedit. Different patterns of relations intertwine and interrelate. Multiplicity and coordination go together, Law underlines. Mol suggests the notion of multiple versions of an object. "They are different and yet related objects. They are multiple forms of reality itself," she adds, almost poetically (Mol 1999, p. 77). Psychologist and philosopher Vinciane Despret (2004a) observes that in medieval Latin "version" (*versio*) meant change. A version overturns and changes what it prolongs, and it is able to integrate other versions or be joined with them because it keeps its connections to what it changes. Following this understanding of version, I however apply here the notion of form instead of version. In the previous quote Mol applies the two terms synonymously, and because "form" is already part of my vocabulary in terms of formations, I apply this term in the following in the understanding that technology may take multiple forms. With Law, Mol, and

Despret, we do not understand the network and the fluid pattern of relations as two independent perspectives that have nothing to do with each other and that would each happily exist without the other. Instead, the two patterns of relations coexist and depend on each other. The fluid pattern of relations could not have existed if the network had not ensured the movement through the seven sessions and the enrollment of the children, the virtual environment, and the other components. On the other hand, the network pattern of relations could not have been capable of keeping the components together if the researchers had not provided their flexible and changing repair work, if the children had not continuously brought in new parts from outside, and if the components had not been optional, allowing the graphic ruins to change the participation of the components.

In her study of atherosclerosis, Mol (2002) visited two hospitals and went to different departments within the hospitals: the outpatient clinic, the operating room, and the department of pathology. In each place she found a distinct form of atherosclerosis, enacted through different human actors, different technologies, and different practices. Many atheroscleroses were enacted. They were multiple but not plural, because several strategies existed for coordinating the forms: layering, smooth narratives, translations, and hierarchies (see also Law 2004). Whereas such coordination strategies also keep each atherosclerosis more or less well delimited, allowing connections to be established among them, we may observe that the patterns of relations are different, yet inseparably entangled with one another. The latter fashion was one of the ways in which the construction of Femtedit as a network and its life as fluid were amalgamated.

When I first started writing, my intention was to focus on Femtedit without discussing the FEMTEDIM pilot project. It however appeared impossible. So many solutions, experiences, and consequences of FEMTEDIM were continued into Femtedit that I finally had to give up the attempt to exclude FEMTEDIM from this book. This led me to write a draft version describing FEMTEDIM in one chapter and Femtedit in the following, creating a narrative of the construction of the technology in the form of a linear timeline. This linear presentation, however, was dull, and reading through a long description of a technology only because of its promised eventual relevance seemed unnecessary. If the description of FEMTEDIM were imperative for showing how Femtedit was constructed, it should be possible to include it into the description of Femtedit. Law's heterogeneous engineering approach made this possible. It enabled me to describe the presence of opponents to FEMTEDIM in Femtedit's trials of strength. The description captured the way in which FEMTEDIM was entangled with Femtedit.[11]

Similarly, the network construction of Femtedit was entangled with its fluid existence. It would be impossible to understand Femtedit if only the fluid pattern of relations was described. This becomes especially clear because we are working with technologies with which most people are not familiar. Without the story of how these technologies were connected and worked as a coherent machine, it would be difficult to understand the ongoing process of trials of optional and exchanging components, of absorption of parts from outside, and of stability without sameness. But more important, the humans and things involved in this fluid process also acknowledged the existence of a Femtedit network through the very way in which they each respected and enacted the network while also being fluid. The network Femtedit was entangled with the fluid Femtedit, and vice versa. The following chapters reveal more such entanglements of different spaces.

It is important to see the concept of entangling as a supplement to that of coordination, as suggested by Mol. Mol describes the different forms of atherosclerosis on the basis of empirical observations in different departments of a hospital. This may mislead us into thinking that objects appear differently in different places, whereas coordination is established between these places and their objects. It may mislead us into a Euclidian way of thinking of space. My discussions of Femtedit all have the same source, but I still have found different forms. This is important. A technology is multiple because it is crisscrossed by a variety of relations that belong to different spatial formations, all of which are entangled with one another.

In addition, the notion of multiplicity implies criticism of postmodern *perspectivalism*. Mol notes that perspectivalism ends up dealing with perspectives, language games, and interpretations, leaving the subject matter behind. In her book on atherosclerosis Mol (2002) writes with reference to perspectivalism:

> In a world of meaning, nobody is in touch with the reality of diseases, everybody "merely" interprets them. There are different interpretations

---

[11] Note that this understanding also implies a conceptualization – or performance – of time that is quite different from the developmentalist notion of time that would be implied in a description of FEMTEDIM as the history of Femtedit. In heterogeneous engineering, the description of history is entangled with the present. History does not belong to the past; it is not gone and does not only exist in memory or congealed into physical entities. On the contrary, history is materially entangled with the present.

around, and "the disease" – forever unknown – is nowhere to be found. The disease recedes behind the interpretations. In a world of meaning alone, words are related to the places from where they are spoken. Whatever it is they are spoken about fades away. (pp. 11–12)

Postmodern approaches find plurality in perspectives, in interpretations, and in language games, not in materialities. Plurality applies not to the objects interpreted but to the interpretations of them. Despret (2004a) notes that when understanding visions (perspectives) as determining the relation to the object of study, sciences have no function other than to "discover that which predated their questions, to continue and explain the vision they gave of their object . . . When we speak of vision . . . we affirm at the same time that this vision is what prevents authentic access to what should be known" (p. 29). Latour (1993, p. 61) concludes that postmodern perspectivalism creates a hyper-incommensurability between subject and object. Instead of the plurality of interpretations, Mol suggests we describe the multiple versions (forms) of objects, just as Despret notes that versions (forms) of objects are versions (forms) of the world. Following Despret, Law, and Mol, the network pattern of relations and the fluid pattern of relations are two forms of the Femtedit virtual environment, two coexisting forms that partly involve different components and whose relations among components form different patterns. They are different ways of making the virtual environment technology – to which my vocabulary and metaphors contribute.

Conclusion: Spatial Formations and Flexible, Multiple Technology

The metaphor of fluidity allows us to think about technology as changing and varying. It teaches us that changing and varying processes can also be stable, and that stability may lie elsewhere than in immutability and control – that it may lie in the process of change. Hence, we do not have to think about technologies and other assemblages that change as failing or dissolving, even when their boundaries are vague due to dependency on components from outside. On the contrary, these aspects can even be what maintains the stability, and what keeps the assemblage in place. The network metaphor limits our understanding of stability and change and of success and failure. The fluid metaphor offers itself as an alternative, in which variability and failing are not residual categories, but rather a pattern of relations with its own logic as to what counts as parts, relations, stability, and dissolution. Returning to Law's (1989) definition of technology that was quoted previously, we need to abandon his classification of technology as a "relatively stable system." Indeed, technology may be a "relatively flexible system."

Law, Mol, and others discuss fluidity in the frame of after-ANT with the purpose of developing some of the theoretical investments of classic-ANT to embrace the temporary and varying. I feel that it is important to emphasize that this is not just a matter of a new aim. It is also a matter of different kinds of empirical material. The strong currents from the Canaries and the northeast trade winds that Law discusses in relation to the Portuguese vessels have different materialities from children, research practices, and online conversations. These materialities are a matter of life or death. If the heterogeneous components of the Portuguese galleys were not tied together properly, the wind and the currents would have indeed caused the ships to sink. The distance between integrity and dissolution was short. One moment they could have been floating proudly along the west coast of Africa, and the next they could have been hit by a storm, split into thousand pieces, and sunk into the ocean. The conditions of the Portuguese vessels were quite different from the conditions of Femtedit. They were dramatic. The components of Femtedit were weaker, and many of them could disagree without anyone suffering major pain. Fluid patterns of relations were more pronounced in Femtedit, whereas network patterns of relations dominated the Portuguese vessels. Fluidity is an empirical discovery. It is not simply a result of researchers' wish to describe the ephemeral, the varying, the invisible, and the overseen. It emerged when after-ANT turned to new empirical fields: clinical practice (Law & Singleton 2005; Mol 2002; Winthereik & Vikkelsø 2005), corporate identity (Elgaard Jensen 2007), water management (Medd & Marvin 2007), a local community pump (de Laet & Mol 2000), and school practice. These fields are different from classic-ANT's preference for scientific facts and large technological systems. The latter may involve fluid patterns of relations, but they perform another level of network stability than, for instance, the Femtedit online 3D virtual environment. Indeed, the ways in which patterns of relations are combined, intertwined, and entangled with one another are what characterize different technological practices.

This leads to a further point about Femtedit as a multiple object. Technology use is often described in plural terms, whereas technology is discussed in the singular. My descriptions of the fluid Femtedit do not discuss the use of technology more than those of the Femtedit network. Both discuss components and the ways in which they were related in making up the technology. But they account for Femtedit as two different patterns of relations, that is, patterns of relations that share components and that are intertwined and dependent on one another. This is how Femtedit was a multiple object.

The notion of fluidity undermines the common understanding of technology as a system whose singular function is to solve problems or fulfill goals (Hughes 1989) and allows us to take seriously forms of technology that are otherwise considered residual. By taking the alternative – fluid – form of Femtedit seriously, the focus of this chapter has turned away from how to design a technology that can work stably and predictably to a focus on the varying and on what in other (network) terms would be "failing."

Introducing the fluid imaginary alongside the network turned the focus from relations and interaction to sensitivity to spatiality. Chapter 2 discussed the construction of a research object and a research field. I described the research object as the virtual environment and the educational context as the research field. This account resonates with the way in which we usually conceptualize "space": as a field or container in which an object is located. In accordance with the empirical report on how field and object emerged as one inseparable process, I modified this formulation by the end of Chapter 2 and described the totality of object and field as a network. The network imaginary describes a spatial formation. Space is not a container in which objects are located. Space is an association of parts that make up an expanded web of relations. The virtual environment was described as an intimate part of this expanded web of relations, and, using the spatial imaginaries of network and fluidity, I characterized the pattern of relations emerging by and through the involvement of the technology. By characterizing the spatial formations of which technology is a part, a spatial approach takes us beyond interactionist accounts of the relations of technology and humans. And we learn to talk about forms of technology instead of a singular technology.

The Methodology of the Materiality of Learning
Lesson 3: Spatiality
As given by the definition of materiality, the ability of a hybrid to relate to others is achieved. The Femtedit technology was neither robust nor variable in and of "itself" but due to its relations to other parts. But materiality is not simply relational. My accounts of Femtedit display complex entanglements of a

number of relations. Relations are never singular. In order to describe the materiality of learning, attending to connection points, to interactions, and to relations among parts is not sufficient. We need to account for the formation of the multiple relations that make up technology, not only for the relations, but for the formation of relations. Multiple relations form spaces. By attending to space, we can describe the patterns relations form. We may characterize one such pattern as a network, another as fluid, and yet others as something different.

In his definition of technology Law (1989) emphasized that "technology does not act as a kind of traffic policeman that is distinct in nature from the traffic it directs" (p. 116). Accounting for a technology – or a traffic policeman – in spatial terms thus means describing the space formed through the channeled forces or associated parts, which at the same time are methods for associating and channeling these parts and forces. The traffic is not simply directed by the policeman; the policeman's directing is directed by the traffic, of which the policeman thus becomes a part. Describing a technology in spatial terms implies an account of the character of the expanded web of relations that these parts form. It is about characterizing the pattern of relations that is formed through the participation of the technology.

We observed, furthermore, that following the relations formed by and through the virtual environment leads us to an account of two different and mutually logically incongruent spatial formations. The network space and the fluid space, however, coexisted and were entangled with each other's existence.

To describe the materiality of learning in spatial terms we will have to account for technology as an intimate participant in the performance of learning, and we must characterize the spatial formations emerging through this performance, including the spatial forms technology takes.

4   Forms of Knowledge

Over the past few decades, a growing number of scholars have contributed
to developing a way of thinking about knowledge as situated in practice.
More than anything, this movement is a reaction to a long tradition of
understanding knowledge as located in the mind (Taylor 1985). Rooted in
Plato's dialogues, rationalism was founded on a conception of knowledge
as elicited from the mind by making the mind itself draw attention to that
which it already processes. In Locke's empiricism, the mind is a *tabula rasa*
(a blank slate) at birth, and knowledge is inscribed in the mind through
observations of the world. Like the rationalists, empiricists understand
knowledge as located in the mind, but the source is beyond the mind, in the
world (Scheffler 1999). Some of the central points of critique targeted at
these and their more or less direct descendants' approaches to knowledge
as located in the mind (e.g., von Glasersfeld 1985; Piaget 1972) concern the
private nature of knowledge that these theories convey, their individualism, and the essential character of knowledge that they imply (e.g., Dreier
2003; Roth 1999).

Alternatively, approaches to situated knowledge view knowledge not as
essential but as constructed in action; not as individual but as placed in the
"lived-in world"; not as private but as belonging to communities of
practice. Lave (1988) has studied the situated mathematic cognition in
everyday practices in supermarkets. (See also my similar study concerning
how children in supermarket situations apply knowledge achieved from
playing health education computer games [Sørensen 1998].) Lave and
Wenger (1991) have followed learning as embedded in communities of
practice by studying Yuctec midwives, Vai and Gola tailors, meat cutters,
and non-drinking alcoholics. Cultural anthropologist and cognitive scientist Edwin Hutchins (1995) has observed how knowledge is distributed
in character in the daily practice of naval quartermasters on the U.S.
marine transporter UUS *Palau*. And linguist Charles Goodwin (1994) has
explored the construction of "professional vision" in archaeologists'
practice and in courtroom practice. These scholars move knowledge from

the mind to the social sphere, which implies that knowledge is more than the content of the mind, and more than a set of technical knowledgeable skills. Knowledge becomes located within "a set of relations among persons, activity, and world, over time and in relation with other tangential and overlapping communities of practice" (Lave & Wenger 1991, p. 98).

What, then, is the role of materials in situated knowledge? Lave and Wenger (1991) note: "In general, social scientists who concern themselves with learning treat technology as a given and are not analytic about its interrelations with other aspects of a community of practice" (p. 101). According to the situated learning theory, artifacts provide a good arena in which to discuss the problem of access to knowledge. Technology, Lave and Wenger continue, carries a substantial portion of a practice's heritage, and understanding technology is a way of connecting with the history of the practice and of participating more directly in its cultural life. Following science studies scholars Karin Knorr Cetina (1999), Latour and Woolgar (1986), Andrew Pickering (1995), and Traweek's (1988) ethnographic studies of how scientific knowledge and facts are constructed in laboratories as a result of social and material arrangements, and after having discussed materials in the previous two chapters, the concept of technology and artifacts as simply providing an understanding of the history of a practice seems weak. We have seen how technology becomes involved in all aspects of establishing and performing practices, and we should therefore wish for a more varied understanding of how materials contribute to knowledge than the idea that materials simply give access to its history. Indeed, considering the lessons taught by the fluid Femtedit, we might expect technology to create mutation and change in knowledge rather than being a source for the archaeology of practice.

I accept the general picture of knowledge as part of "a set of relations among persons, activity, and world," even though I prefer to talk about knowledge as part of a set of relations without predefining the components related and thereby simultaneously dividing practice into pre-given elements. If we are to hint at the components involved, then we should at least add materials to the list. Let me treat these as preliminary parts that come together in particular patterns, which are the focus of study. Consequently, in this chapter I talk about knowledge as spatial formations.

Lave and Wenger emphasize that "abstract" and "concrete" knowledge do not reside in the world as distinct forms of knowledge. They insist that only one form of knowledge and one form of learning exist: situated knowledge and situated learning. I agree that knowledge is a practical achievement, but as we shall see this does not necessarily contradict the idea that different forms of knowledge – for example, concrete and abstract – emerge in practice. If we insist on knowledge being part of, and an effect of, practice or space, then knowledge necessarily varies with practice. Some forms of knowledge may be performed as abstract and others as concrete. This is a question of the ontology of knowledge, of what knowledge is – a question that must be settled empirically. In order to do so we must methodologically approach knowledge as situated, practical, and distributed. This is however only the point of departure of our study, not the result. The result tells us about the ontology of knowledge as empirically achieved, and here a variety of forms of knowledge may emerge.

One of the points of the spatial approach resonates with a central point of approaches to situated knowledge: both are especially concerned with the relations involved in constituting knowledge that lie beyond the mind. Consequently, such approaches to knowledge and cognition are known as *distributed cognition* or *distributed knowledge* (e.g., Hutchins 1995; Lave 1988; Salomon 1993). In his discussion of theories of distributed cognition, P. D. Magnus (2007) concludes that the distribution of distributed cognition occurs only at the level of the process or implementation of a task. The task itself, Magnus states, could in principle just as well have been carried out in the mind. Illustrating this claim, Magnus notes that he applies a pencil and paper to calculate three-figure multiplication problems – which turns the process into cognition distributed among Magnus, the paper, and the pencil – but that he in principle just as well could have calculated this multiplication without material aid.

This conclusion makes the crucial mistake of dividing the task from the process of cognition, and by this move the pencil and paper become transparent tools that have influence only on the process, but not on the task. Consequently, materials have no effect on the knowledge aimed for nor on the knowledge produced. The knowledge is in principle the same regardless of whether it is distributed or mental. It is irrelevant whether it is Magnus's "mind" or the Magnus-pen-paper assemblage that performs the calculation. The materials become arbitrary to the ontology of knowledge. Magnus misses an important point in distributed cognition theory, namely that cognition is not computational but situated in practice, hence the division of cognition into task and process is inconsistent with this approach. He misunderstands the attempt to grasp materials as part of practice and hence part of cognition and knowledge. At the same time, however, I believe Magnus does reveal an Achilles' heel of these theories, namely their avoidance of taking a position on what knowledge's practical, distributed, and, especially, material character means for the ontology of knowledge. The focus on the location of knowledge – in the world and not in the mind – seems to drive out the question of the ontology of knowledge.

Enthralled by the account of knowledge as located in the world, Lave and Wenger neglect the possibility that "in-the-world-knowledge" may differ when different materials are involved in producing it. Only by ultimately rendering materials irrelevant is it possible to insist that knowledge as part of a "set of relations among persons, activity, and world" takes only one form. When we turn to spatial formations, however, it becomes clear that the ontology of knowledge constructed with a pencil and paper is quite different from the one constructed in the mind. This is the focus of this chapter: how different materials contribute to constituting different forms of knowledge. As argued in the previous chapter, we need to apply the principle of multiplicity.

On the basis of these two points of discontent with the theory of situated learning (the limited role of technology and the singular approach to knowledge), I apply in this chapter a spatial approach to the study of the materiality of knowledge, which allows me to examine empirically which forms of knowledge were performed practically in the classroom and with the online 3D virtual environment. We will see different forms of knowledge performed with different materials, which toward the end of the chapter allows us to start discussing learning.

The Quest for Resemblance

"It doesn't resemble reality," Grethe said. The teacher was commenting on the activities in the virtual environment and especially on what she saw on the computer screens as the children were engaged in saving the Femtedians in the virtual world. My colleague Nina Armand's field note describes the situation like this:

> I went up to Grethe and said that I appreciated her helping Ronny to find codes for the objects he wanted to build. She answered by saying that she couldn't see the children were learning anything, that it was frustrating for them not to all learn the same thing and that many of them did not know what it was all about. She and the children had expected to link to web pages and discuss with the Swedes about what to build. She couldn't see any collaboration, and they built all kinds of mixed-up jumble. It didn't resemble reality. She would have preferred, she said, if they had sketched out a Viking village and learned to plan what such a village could look like. She didn't understand, she said, why we didn't initiate each lesson by telling the children collectively what they had to do. (Nina's field note 1511_1)

Nina was shocked by the sudden dressing-down that her compliment had given rise to. She promised to discuss the issue with the group of researchers and closed the conversation. After discussing the incidence we made a few changes to Femtedit, as I discuss in the following. Grethe said a lot in these few sentences, enough to form the basis of this chapter's discussion of knowledge and of which forms of knowledge were – and were not – performed with the virtual world. Her emphasis on the lack of resemblance to reality particularly catches my attention, along with her categorization of the children's building as a "mixed-up jumble." I take her dissatisfaction to be a result of being confronted in the computer lab with a different and probably even conflicting form of knowledge, compared to the one she was part of and daily took part in performing in the classroom. Scrutinizing further, the difference between the "proper knowledge" and the "mixed-up jumble" is the focus of this chapter: How was the knowledge with which the teacher was dissatisfied formed, and what shape did the knowledge take that she would have preferred?

Taking this point of departure for the discussion of knowledge in schools, I grant Grethe the role of the spokesperson for the standard form of knowledge performed in school. Grethe had been a teacher at St. Marc Street School for more than two decades. She was a very engaged and respected teacher among colleagues, the headmaster, parents, and pupils. The Danish elementary school is unitary in the sense that all children attend the same school type from first to ninth grade.[1] Thereafter pupils can chose to attend grammar school, vocational school, and technical school, among others. A central principle in Danish elementary schools is the "class teacher," which is the main teacher of a class and the person who takes cares of the children's well-being. The class teacher follows one class for all nine years – from when the pupils enter elementary school until they leave. Grethe was class teacher for the third time, now for a group of twenty-four pupils halfway through their elementary schooling. Her long experience had helped her become a confident figure in the eyes of the children, colleagues, and parents. She had been head of the teacher's council and was reflective about her teaching principles and critical of the current political trends toward stronger control of schools, teaching, and pupils through audit mechanisms. She frequently attended further education programs, learning about new educational methods and principles.

---

[1] There are public schools, private schools, free schools (*friskoler*), and progressive free schools (*lilleskoler*) in Denmark that follow different pedagogic principles. But in all these schools classes stay together the first nine years of primary education.

During my classroom observation I recognized many of the teaching principles I knew from my own schooling decades back, but Grethe also emphasized that even though standard teaching methods were good and necessary, it was important for her to interrupt this with "alternative" projects such as theater, competitions, sports, cooking, visits to cultural sites, and collaboration with other schools or classes. This preference for educational experiments was probably also what made her and her colleague from the same class, Hans, approach my research team and suggest that we set up the Femtedit project in their class. Grethe is probably neither as a person nor as a professional typical among Danish elementary school teachers. But based on the debates among elementary school teachers and in their trade union, the image of what passes as a "good teacher" matches quite well with how I experienced Grethe: liked and respected, sovereign in the classroom, and following traditional principles while interspersing them with more experimental and alternative projects that generally gained great approval among other teachers and parents. I take Grethe's critique of Femtedit as a continuance of her professional expertise, which, more than a personal critique, makes it an evaluation based on the longer tradition and culture of Danish primary education, and on the standard form of knowledge performed in this tradition.

Grethe's critique forms a puzzle to be solved. I focus especially on her complaint about the lack of resemblance. I describe the space performed with the virtual environment and look at how it was possible that a mixed-up jumble that had no resemblance to reality and displayed no collaboration was performed. This does not mean that I examine knowledge from Grethe's perspective. Rather, I enquire about the space through which the knowledge is performed as a mixed-up jumble, in contrast to the space of which Grethe – and thus Grethe's judgments – was a habitual part. The contrast is described by first discussing knowledge performed in the classroom that was less mixed up, that resembled reality, and that was shared by the whole class, and subsequently by examining the form of knowledge established by the virtual environment.

Classroom Jumping Demonstration: The Standard Measurement and Resemblance

I start my discussion of forms of knowledge in the classroom. Let me report from my field notes, taken during a math lesson:

> *The teacher is standing next to her desk with the textbook in her hand, reading out loud.*

T: "Fourth B is doing physical education. Today they are on the athletics pitch. They do long jumping. First, it is Jens's turn. He runs as fast as he can and jumps. Mette is the linesman. She takes out the tape measure and measures his jump: Two meters."

The teacher looks up from the book.

T: Two meters – is that a long or a short jump?

Three children raise their hands. Ben doesn't.

T: Ben – two meters, is that a long or a short jump?

Ben looks bewildered at the pupils around him, but no one comes to his rescue.

B: Short . . . [low voice]

The teacher walks toward the blackboard.

T: Well, Ben . . . let's see . . .

She takes a piece of chalk and a big one-meter ruler down from a hook on the wall. She turns around and walks toward the middle of the classroom.

T: Come here, Ben.

Ben gets up and walks over to her.

T: Ok, stand here . . .

The teacher draws a chalk line on the floor. Ben looks at it and shuffles his feet. The teacher walks backwards toward the blackboard.

T: So . . . just stay there . . . Ben, now jump from that line ahead as far as you can.

Ben looks at her, looks back at the chalk line, takes a step back, and jumps ahead with great effort.

T: Stay there, stay there . . .

The teacher grabs Ben's shoulder. She bends down and draws a chalk line on the floor where he stands.

T: Ok, Ben. Let's see how long you jumped. This ruler is one meter long.

The teacher puts the ruler on the floor and measures the length between the two chalk lines.

T: Ninety . . . three centimeters . . . Almost one meter . . . You jumped ninety-three centimeters. Not too bad. So . . . what do you think? Jens jumped two meters. Was that a long or a short jump?

B: Long.

T: That's right, Ben. Two meters is quite a long jump . . . Now, please sit down. (Field note 2609_82)

Knowledge is performed in this sequence – knowledge about the length of Jens's jump. This was done through the use of a standard measurement instrument, the one-meter ruler. This standard allowed the teacher to compare two entirely different activities. If he had been able to refer to the standard, Ben could have known in advance whether Jens's jump was long or short, without jumping and measuring. But Ben was not familiar with the metric standard, and so he could not make much sense of the length of Jens's jump from the teacher's reading of the math textbook. Through the teacher's nice little demonstration Ben gained bodily experience about the length of a jump. But this still would not allow him to compare his own jump with Jens's from the math book because Jens's jump was only presented as a measurement. If Jens had been jumping next to Ben in the classroom, they could have gained knowledge about their jumps through direct comparison, without needing to involve any measurement. But because Jens was absent from the classroom and present only in the text-book, knowledge about Jens's jump could only be gained by involving the standard measurement.

This is the amazing ability of the standard. It can link two distant and entirely different situations. And it can do this only because it is isolated from each of the two. Because each of the jumps was known through their reference to the standard measurement, they could be compared to each other. But remember, the standard did not do this on its own. Ben jumped. The ruler was placed and read. And the teacher drew chalk lines on the floor. These things and these efforts were not unimportant. Without them, the knowledge about the length of the jumps could not have been performed.

However, the result of the demonstration did not involve all these heterogeneous components. The result was that Jens's jump was long. This result was the knowledge Ben in principle could have held prior to the demonstration, which would have rendered the demonstration redundant. In the knowledge resulting from the demonstration, the efforts of the ruler, the chalk lines, Ben's bodily efforts, and the teacher's hand on his shoulder were all discounted. The resulting knowledge was pure and simple: Ben's jump was 93 cm, which meant that Jens's jump was long. The knowledge about the length of the jump was not performed as residing in the material activities of the classroom but as residing in Ben. Before, he did not possess the knowledge; now he did.

The standard was beyond the jumping demonstration in the classroom. It was somewhere else. The knowledge performed referred to something located elsewhere. But there was resemblance among the elements: the measurement of the length in the classroom, the measurement of the length in the book, and the standard metric measurement. They resembled one another. They were all metric measurements. Ben's jump resembled reality – as long as we can consider the standard measurement reality. This resemblance involved a boundary between the activities in the classroom and the standard measurement. The activities in the classroom simply contributed to revealing knowledge about the length, whereas the standard was beyond the classroom and was referred to from the classroom. There is a spatial metaphor that characterizes well this form of knowledge performed in the classroom: the region.

Regional Space

The Regional Imaginary

I will briefly leave the classroom and introduce the regional imaginary. The region is a third spatial metaphor presented by Mol and Law (1994). Something performed as a region takes the shape of a container or field in which objects are located, where people act, or where entities belong. Think of a map. One can point at a map and say "look, there are the mountains, there is a forest, there is the city." Maps perform regions that are each defined by their content: rocks, trees, houses. It is a forest because it consists of trees. The region is defined by what is in it: a school is a region for teaching, a club is a region of members (Elgaard Jensen 2001), and Dutch anemia diagnostics is a region for measuring hemoglobin levels (Mol 1999). The regional space is performed in a way that makes what is inside it homogeneous in the sense that all inhabitants of the region have the same regional identity or are all of the same kind.

The relationship between content and field is not simple in the regional imaginary. It is not necessarily the case that the content defines the region, that is, that one sees a clump of trees and knows it is a forest. It may also be the case that one defines a region to be "Denmark," in which case it follows that the inhabitants, traditions, and things within this region are Danish. It goes both ways. Content and field mutually define each other in the way regions are performed: trees define the field as a forest, while the forest defines its content as trees. Denmark defines its content as Danish, just like the Danish content defines its field as Denmark. Or, one identifies a group of people as women and, consequently, what they do is identified as female.

Furthermore, regions have boundaries. The forest, mountains, and cities are performed with certain, limited extensions, just as regional genders are. It may be difficult to define the boundary of the city, but in principle a specific point can only be either inside the city or outside of it. A road sign tells travelers when they are leaving the city, and documents at the city planning division display its boundaries. Because of difficulties in defining boundaries, one may define sub-regions of suburbs and settlements, but that does not change the fact that the region is always performed with a clear inside and outside – of regions or of sub-regions. In the regional imaginary, a person is either in the school and involved in the teaching or learning practices, or does not belong to the school. One is either a member of a club, or one is not. Either a person measures the hemoglobin level, or they do not belong to the Dutch anemia diagnostics region. Regions have boundaries; they have an inside and an outside.

The reader may object, noting that there are cleaning staff in a school; that there is a hierarchy of members in a club; that it does happen that a nurse in the Dutch anemia diagnostics system looks into her patient's pale eyes and, without measuring the hemoglobin level, concludes that he suffers from anemia; and that there are "queer" genders (Butler 1993). One may claim therefore that the content of a school, a club, or a diagnostic system is not that homogeneous. Indeed, one may be right if one is arguing in terms of network or fluid imaginaries, but not in the regional imaginary. The "different" is not what defines the inside of a region. In the regional imaginary differences inside the region are suppressed. If one is inside a region and does not fit the definition of the regional identity, then one is performed as an exception, or as belonging to the sub-region of deviance.

Whereas similarity is to be found inside regions, differences in a regional pattern of relations are performed among regions, across boundaries. There are different ways of diagnosing anemia in the Netherlands and in Africa, city and countryside are different in population density, Sweden and Denmark are different nations, and men are different from women. If one compares one region with another, one will find differences in content.

Finally, regions are stable and immutable. The description of a region as a field with boundaries that is homogeneous within but different from other fields is not a very dynamic description. The region is a rather firm structure. It is a pattern of relations that stays as it is and where it is (see Table 4, pp. 55–56).

Regional Knowledge in the Classroom

In the previous discussion of the field note excerpt, I showed how, by using a standard measurement, knowledge was performed as referring to something somewhere else. Two regions were performed. Before the jumping demonstration, knowledge was performed as residing in a region of thoughts, ideas, and knowledge inside Ben (probably in his head) from which knowledge could be derived and expressed out loud – if Ben had possessed the knowledge. This mental knowledge was performed as referring to another region, the one-meter standard measurement that was delimited and separate from the first. The one-meter measurement belonged to a region of exact measurements and facts about distances – a region made up of different kinds of entities than the knowledge inside Ben. The knowledge in this second region would not necessarily be inside Ben. It could be in a textbook as a written representation, in images, and on the blackboard. No matter where this form of knowledge is located, it is performed as separate from and referring to another region, to that which it is about. And it is performed as different from what it is about – it is a representation, whereas what it refers to is reality.

Because Ben could not deliver the knowledge about Jens's jump, the knowledge had to be constructed in the classroom. If Ben and Jens had both been present in the classroom, jumping next to each other and comparing the lengths of their jumps, no regions would have been performed. The form of knowledge hence performed would be in the activity – in the bodies, the jumps. Or, more precisely, it would not be *in* the activity; it would *be* the activity. It would be the bodies, the jumps. There would be no reference to anything anywhere else. This form of knowledge would be performed as local, as embedded in the assemblage of which it is made up.

The meter measurement enrolled made Jens present while absent by bridging Jens's region – the textbook – with the region in which Ben's jump was present. By making both of them refer to the same third region, the standard, which was separate from both of them, their jumps could be compared. Through this regional triangle, the length of Ben's and Jens's jumps was performed as mirroring the length given by the standard measurement.

In order for this regional pattern to be performed, the regions had to be stable. If the standard changed and if its length varied from time to time, it would not work to bridge the jumps. The jumps could only be compared because the system of measurement Jens had used to measure his jump was exactly the same as the system the teacher used to measure Ben's jump and because this system had not changed in the meantime. The stability of the standard measurement was crucial.

The other region, the one performed with the jumping demonstration in the classroom, also had to be made constant. If it varied, the comparison would not be possible. The length of Jens's jump was noted in the textbook, and, due to the materiality of the printing ink, it could not change. It was immutably two meters long. The length of Ben's jump was fixed by the chalk lines drawn by the teacher on the classroom floor. These lines performed a fixed distance, without which the length could not be measured. Even though the teacher kept Ben in place by putting her hand on his shoulder, Ben's shuffling feet might have been too inconstant to make the measurement. Finally, the other pupils contributed to the constancy of the knowledge. By witnessing the measurement of 93 cm, they as a collective contributed to performing it as a stable and immutable figure. If one pupil would later say that Ben's jump was only 78 cm or that it was 124 cm, she would have to convince all other pupils. This would probably be hard, considering she was one against more than twenty. By their bare perception of the jump as a group, the pupils contributed to making the knowledge constant.

What happened next was important. The result of the demonstration was that Jens's jump was simply "long." It was purified of all the heterogeneity of bodily efforts, chalk lines, and witnessing. Those were not the entities the teacher would want to hear about if she were to review measurements with the class the following day. She would want the facts: the measurements and nothing else. Thereby the knowledge resulting from the demonstration was performed as identical to the knowledge Ben was supposed to have held prior to the demonstration. By being performed as residing inside Ben, the socio-material processes involved in the demonstration were black boxed.[2]

This way, two immutable regions were performed. The form of knowledge performed in the occurrence discussed in the classroom was regional. It performed two stable regions, one referring to the other. I return to this shortly. First, I turn to a classic concept in science studies that can teach us more about this form of knowledge.

Boyle's Experiment: The Material Technology

Let us look back to the debates over what counts as knowledge that took place in the mid-seventeenth century. Robert Boyle (1627–1691) argued for

---

[2] In my description of the demonstration in the classroom I make use of the network imaginary to describe the performance of the region. I show how heterogeneous elements are connected. A central endeavor in classic-ANT has been to demonstrate that regions are performed through networks, that is, that regions depend on networks. Network patterns of relations are thus involved in performing the representational knowledge discussed.

an experimental basis of the specific form of knowledge called "matters of facts." He did this through pneumatic experiments. These experiments and Boyle's discussions with his rival, Thomas Hobbes, are thoroughly described and discussed by historians of science Steven Shapin and Steven Schaffer (1985). Operated by his assistants, Boyle's air pump could evacuate the air from a transparent glass container. Or so, at least, was what he with great effort sought to demonstrate. Shapin and Schaffer describe how three technologies were involved in the production and validation of matters of fact: a material, a literary, and a social technology. These three technologies were not distinct, and their workings depended on one another. However, I deal with them separately, as Shapin and Schaffer do. Indeed, I will separate them more than Shapin and Schaffer do. In this section, I present the material technology and return to the literary and social technologies in relation to a second field note excerpt I discuss later. Juxtaposing the descriptions of Boyle's experimental knowledge provokes new questions about the analysis of the forms of knowledge in the classroom and in the virtual environment and thus provides clarifications of the forms of knowledge.

We set out by taking a look at Boyle's air pump apparatus. As a committed contributor to the mid-seventeenth-century discussions on the vacuum, Boyle made dozens of experiments in pneumatics. His air pump consisted of two main parts: a glass globe (or "receiver") and a pumping apparatus. The air was to be removed from the glass globe. The narrow base of the glass globe was connected to a hollow brass cylinder. To fit into the brass cylinder, the glass globe was equipped with a brass device containing a stopcock. By way of the stopcock, the glass globe was attached to a small hole at the top of the brass cylinder into which a brass valve was inserted. Within the brass valve was a wooden piston topped with "a good thick piece of tanned show leather" (ibid., p. 28). The piston was worked up and down by means of an iron rack-and-pinion device, and the whole thing rested on a wooden frame. Boyle argued that, when activated, this assemblage pumped the air out of the glass globe.

I will not dwell too much on this device. I am not particularly interested in the pumping of air. What is relevant here is that this material technology was carefully set up in a way that allowed Boyle to detach his findings – the matters of fact – from himself as a person. "The matters of fact in Boyle's new pneumatics were machine-made" (ibid., p. 26), Shapin and Schaffer note. This is crucial. The product of the experiment, the knowledge, was observed and recorded by Boyle, but it was not he who invented it. The power of the air pump, like that of other new scientific instruments at the time – the microscope and telescope – resided in its capacity to enhance perception and to constitute new perceptual objects. Information obtained through the senses assisted by instruments was preferable to information from the senses alone, Boyle stated. This implied a new understanding of the senses, namely that senses alone were inadequate for constituting knowledge. Only senses assisted by instruments and disciplined to follow the workings of the instruments could produce "proper knowledge."

The machine not only degraded the senses; it also factored out human agency in the knowledge it produced. Shapin and Schaffer depict how Boyle struggled with this material technology to produce "proper knowledge." They present several designs of the air pump and describe Boyle's efforts to prevent the glass globe from imploding when the air was evacuated and to avoid leakages. The machine had to be carefully calibrated in order to produce factual knowledge. Its capacity to produce matters of fact crucially depended on the physical integrity of the air pump. The machine had to perform in a way that convinced the human witnesses that it was airtight, for all practical purposes. When this was the case, Boyle could lean back and state, "It is not I who says this; it is the machine" (ibid., p. 77). The knowledge produced by the machine was superior to that produced by the human senses alone, and it was detached from human agency. The knowledge was "over there" by the machine, and Boyle was standing here, modestly watching, recording.

We need some context. Boyle's experiments took place in the 1660s, in post–civil war Restoration England. During this time, fights over beliefs were lethal. Boyle's construction of knowledge as separate from the domain of humans was a remarkable contribution in the battle. This form of knowledge was set apart from beliefs and opinions. It required the humans only to discover, pick up, and register what nature showed. Thus, it would make no sense to fight over believes or opinions anymore. The construction of knowledge was out of the hands of humans. Knowledge simply mirrored nature. This form of knowledge created a firm boundary between the human and the natural. Furthermore, it performed a direct correspondence between knowledge produced in the laboratory and what is "out there" to be known. Knowledge was a representation of what is "out there." Today, we still use this empirical style, Latour (1993, p. 18) notes. And today, we still find this form of knowledge in schools.

Representational Knowledge

The material technology making up the knowledge in Boyle's laboratory created two regions: nature acting through the air pump and the experimenter, who perceived and registered the knowledge, which the pump brought about. This is analogous to the two-meter jump example – the length of Ben's jump was given by the standard in the classroom, and the pupils only perceived and registered the knowledge, which the one-meter ruler brought about. The carefully calibrated setup of Boyle's experiment performed a boundary between the knowledge it produced and the human being. The knowledge was simply an expression of the "nature" it represented. Let me call this form of knowledge performed in the experiment and in the classroom *representational knowledge*. In English, knowledge is a very broad term. In French, German, and the Scandinavian languages, several terms are used to describe different aspects of knowledge. Representational knowledge resonates with what is usually referred to as *"Wissen"* in German, as *"savoir"*[3] in French, and as *"viden"* in Danish.

Neither Ben's jump nor Boyle's experiment were more than demonstrations – one of the length of a jump, the other of the facts of nature. Of course, the experiment was supposed to reveal "new" knowledge. But the "news" of the experimental knowledge did not refer to the object of study. It referred to the knowledge – apart from the object – that was new to us (humans). The object was not new; it already existed – apart from us (humans). The knowledge in the classroom was performed as new to the pupils, but the reality – or the standard the knowledge referred to – was performed as existing prior to and independent of the classroom activities. The experiment and the classroom shared the characteristic of performing a representational form of knowledge.

By looking at Boyle's experimental practices, Shapin and Schaffer describe that it was never entirely possible to set up a machine that unambiguously performed the boundary between man and nature. After all, human investments were involved in setting up the machine that factored out human agency, and humans were disciplined by these machines to perceive matters of fact in certain ways. In addition, the calibration of the machine never resulted in unequivocal facts. This however does not change the fact that the efforts involved in this assemblage contributed to performing a regional pattern of relations, and thus representational

---

[3] Foucault (1972) and Lefebvre (1991) apply the distinction between *savoir* and *connaissance* in their discussions of knowledge. My use of these notions is less fundamental than those two philosophers', who describe them as different layers of discourse or social space – respectively – that in different ways function to establish, maintain, and change those formations. I apply the terms to characterize different forms of knowledge out of many; each of which however does not have a theoretical or principle function in the formation of an overall discourse or space.

knowledge. The form of knowledge performed in the classroom was purified from the ruler, the chalk lines, and the jumping body, as I described.[4] Similarly, the experimental setup in Boyle's laboratory was discounted after the experiment, and only the black boxed findings or facts of the experiment were taken into account as knowledge. The representational form of knowledge performed two stable regions with a boundary between them. The pattern of relations this representational form of knowledge contributed to performing was regional.

The Bed-Loft Inaugural Ceremony: Resonance Space

The story of representational knowledge is not the whole story – or the only story – about forms of knowledge in the classroom. There were occurrences in the classroom in which representational knowledge was either not performed or was less prominent. An inventory of the classroom revealed stories of former projects:

- On the wall were two posters. They displayed paintings showing how to sort garbage and keep the environment clean. The class had made them the previous year for a school contest about environmental issues. They had won the first prize and a considerable sum of money.
- Next to the posters hung some pictures of Hans Christian Andersen's fairy tale the Snow Queen. They were placed there to inspire a current project. The class was preparing a play based on the Snow Queen to be shown to the parents at Christmastime.
- There was a miniature cardboard model of a school in the corner. It was three storeys tall and stood about a meter high. On each storey were two or three rooms, in which items such as miniature furniture, animals, wooden bricks, cooking utensils, and a water basin were organized. The class had made the model in an earlier project about the ideal future school.
- I spent most of my classroom observation time seated under a big bed-loft. St. Marc Street School was built in 1882 and lives up to the ideal of the day that schools should be stout and tall, looking down on the surrounding tenement houses. Consequently, the classrooms

---

[4] There were other occurrences with other materials in the classroom during which representational knowledge was performed. Textbooks are good examples. They are representational in character. They talk about something that exists somewhere else. Law (2002a) describes a textbook on lower-limb arteriosclerosis: "It [the textbook] assumes that there is an object – lower-limb arteriosclerosis – out there that manifests itself in various ways" (p. 17, my insertion). This is what textbooks do.

Figure 5. Children and adults exploring the bed-loft, photographed during the inaugural ceremony.

are high-ceilinged. In collaboration with a school of carpentry, the fourth-grade class had built a large wooden bed-loft, about six meters square and two meters tall, in the corner of the classroom as a refuge for pupils during breaks and for group work.

At least two of these projects involve some aspects of representational knowledge. But it is far from obvious from the descriptions that regional spaces were performed with these materials. Therefore, in this section I turn to one of these materials, the bed-loft, and discuss the form of knowledge performed with it. The bed-loft was central on the class agenda during my visit. Consider this field note excerpt:

Wednesday morning. For an hour the class is busy preparing the bed-loft inaugural ceremony [see Figure 5]. They bring up soft drinks and sandwiches made by Suzan's mum. They arrange the food and drinks nicely like a buffet on a few desks put together. Some pupils sweep the floor and decorate the windows, windowsills, and the blackboard. They put all school bags against the wall. A song for the occasion, written by the teacher, is distributed on printed sheets. The classroom door is open. Children pass in and out and into the neighboring class, who is preparing as well. The other class was also part of the carpentry project and is also celebrating their new bed-loft. Around eleven o'clock parents start turning up. They chat with the teachers and with children. Some sit down at the pupils' desks, some stand. The principal arrives. At 11:15 the bell rings. One of the teachers comes into the classroom and says, "It's time, come over"! We all pass to the neighboring class, where we are told to gather by the walls. There are almost seventy people packed by the four walls of the classroom. One of the teachers initiates the song, and we all read from the printed sheet in our hands, singing about the fabrication and erection of the bed-lofts. After the song, the principal makes a speech celebrating the project and the pupils' hard work. Then follows three speeches made by pupils, who are all a bit tense and clearly excited by their performances. The speeches are each followed by long applauses. One of the teachers invites everyone for drinks and sandwiches, and the crowd moves to the other classroom. (Field note 2609_56)

Being new, unusual, and spectacular, the bed-loft was a remarkable object, an object to be noticed and experienced. Because of its immensity and the fact that it was nailed to the walls of the classroom, anyone who wanted to set eyes on it would have to be bodily present in the classroom. The bed-loft thereby constituted a magnet, drawing people who were interested in the class's work to the classroom. Along with this materiality, the bed-loft was also an occasion for celebration. The inaugural ceremony on the one hand reinforced the magnetism of the bed-loft and its ability to draw people toward the classroom. Moreover, the celebration made people come together in the classroom at the same time, and it thereby established a collective witnessing of the bed-loft. Like the three other projects mentioned previously, the bed-loft made available a gathering of groups of people who were otherwise external to the class. Because of the erection of the bed-loft, external people were invited to visit the classroom, and, due to this, a song and several speeches were written and performed for the occasion. Like a festival, this gathering gave the participants a communal experience of the bed-loft that contributed to maintaining and extending a community centered around the class. The inaugural ceremony worked as a temporary hub or a passage point (Latour 1987, 1990) for the community's participants. After sharing the experience of the bed-loft, they left the school enriched by an impression that was communal and that therefore allowed each of them a sense of communality or shared culture even when separate and distant from the class.

I call the space performed by and through the bed-loft *resonance space*. It has much in common with network space, but it differs on crucial points: Resonance space has and maintains a center, here the bed-loft. It spreads out from the center, and it is crucial that closure is obtained concerning the center. This does not mean that all parts and relations of the space must be alike. Diversity is tolerated as long as each part and relation is in sufficient harmony with the surrounding ones such that they keep up a relative consensus regarding the center. The space starts to dissolve only when the diversity takes the form of dissonance that compromises the identity of the center.

Boyle's Experiment: Literary and Social Technologies

I wrote in a previous section that Shapin and Schaffer (1985) present Boyle's experiment as performed through three technologies. I discussed the material technology and how it contributed to performing a representational form of knowledge that was detached from man.[5] In this section, I discuss his social and literary technologies. Crucial for these is their contribution to performing knowledge as communal.

In order to produce "proper knowledge" – matters of fact – it was not enough for an experiment to apply material technology. No matter how perfectly calibrated the experimental setup, it could not claim to have produced any knowledge if it was accomplished by a lonely individual in a remote laboratory. One of the crucial elements of the material technology – the glass globe – was also one of the pivotal components for the social and literary technologies. Made out of transparent glass, it allowed people to witness how small animals were suffocated and candles put out as a consequence of emptying the container of air. Witnessing was the crucial point in the experiment. The experimenter had the modest task of perceiving and registering the facts "spoken" by nature through the machine.[6] But the experimenter should not be the only witness. The capacity of the experiment to yield matters of fact depended essentially on the assurance of the relevant community. Witnessing had to be a collective act, and the laboratory had to be a public space. One witness could be mistaken in his observations, but two or even ten or a hundred who confirmed the perception were likely to be right. So, Boyle engaged witnesses in his experiments.[7]

---

[5] We can legitimately equate "man" with "human," because there were hardly any women in Boyle's experimental world (see Haraway 1997, p. 26ff.).

[6] "Modesty" is a central term in Shapin and Schaffer's description of the experimental way of life, which is however beyond this book to discuss; see also Haraway (1997).

[7] The way in which witnesses were selectively picked for the experiment is a central part of Shapin and Schaffer's argument. I return to this point later in this chapter, where the comparison between the classroom and the online 3D virtual environment makes it apparent that it did indeed matter who the witnesses of the knowledge were, especially in a school context.

The laboratory, however, had a limited capacity and limited access. Written reports could guarantee the multiplication of witnesses of an experiment. This *literary technology*, completed in an unadorned, factual, compelling style, could make the experiments known to those who were not direct witnesses of the experiment, to *virtual witnesses* as Shapin and Schaffer call them. Knowledge would not count as such just by being conducted in a laboratory and witnessed by gentlemen. It had to spread beyond the walls of the laboratory to be acknowledged and accepted. It had to be made communal:

> Radical individualism – the state in which each individual set himself up as an ultimate judge of knowledge – would destruct the conventional basis of proper knowledge, while the disciplined collective social structure of the experimental form of life would create and sustain that factual basis . . . No one man was to have the right to lay down what was to count as knowledge. (Shapin & Schaffer 1985, p. 78)

To the literary technology the *social technology* was added. Shapin and Schaffer describe in detail the conventions Boyle set up for experimenters to use in dealing with one another and in considering knowledge claims. Disputes should for instance be strictly about knowledge – about matters of fact – and not about persons. By separating knowledge from humans, the social technology also contributed to the regional pattern of relations (to "objectifying," as Shapin and Schaffer call it).

Communal Knowledge

Each of the participants – the parents, the headmaster, the teachers, the pupils, the bed-loft, the speeches, and the song – contributed to performing the shared experience that I call *communal knowledge*. The communal knowledge performed a resonance space. It did not create a formation of knowledge located inside the human knower while referring to an object distant from the human, but it was rather a feeling of interconnectedness that cannot be clearly separated from the web of participants of which it is made up. If one human or nonhuman participant let go of its relations to the others, then the community feeling would no longer include that participant. I apply the notion of "feeling" loosely, not to imply that we are dealing with emotion rather than cognition (if that is at all a valid division), but to point to the aspect of knowledge that has to do with acquaintance or familiarity, regardless of whether it is granted, emotional, cognitive, or practical. This is frequently referred to as "*Kenntnis*" in

German, as "*connaissance*" in French (see footnote 3, this chapter), and as "*kendskab*" in Danish. This aspect of knowledge has to do with interplay among participants. For example: "Do you know the foxtrot?" "Oh, yes, I do ... eh ... well, I can't dance it myself, but I know how it goes." The "yes I do ... I know how it goes" refers to a representational knowledge, to *savoir*: I possess knowledge of this dance; my knowledge represents the dance out there, in the world, in a different place. The "well, I can't dance it myself" refers to communal knowledge, to *connaissance*, to whether the two figures have mutual relations in terms of proximity of identity. It is not necessarily know-how, as *connaissance* can also refer to familiarity with a friend or relative.

Communal knowledge is not located within any one participant. Accordingly, knowledge does not necessarily imply that someone or something is carrying out the act of knowing. Representational knowledge performs a knowing person through the formation of the regional space, but the resonance space that forms communal knowledge does not. Communal knowledge spreads as and through the resonance space. The regional space performed knowledge as knowledge *about* something – length, for instance. In resonance space the communal knowledge was not performed as knowledge *about* the bed-loft, because a clear boundary was not established between the known and the knowing. Nevertheless, the bed-loft had a central position in the communal knowledge, which did indeed concern that object. To distinguish it from regional knowledge *about*, I refer to it as knowledge *of* the bed-loft. The communal knowledge was the bed-loft's knowledge. It had to do with the bed-loft; it was the knowledge of the bed-loft, not separate from, but a result of, the bed-loft.

As is typical for resonance space, the communal knowledge spread. It did not evaporate as the parents and the headmaster left the inaugural ceremony. On the contrary, the circulation of the participants allowed the communal knowledge to spread, by children and parents presenting the song to their family members at the dinner table and through talk and stories about the bed-loft and the inaugural ceremony. Communal knowledge was part of such extended practices – it drew the participants together, it went through the obligatory passage point of the inaugural ceremony, it centered around the bed-loft, and it was the knowledge of the bed-loft.

Similarly, the witnesses of Boyle's experiment contributed to performing communal knowledge of the vacuum machine by sharing the experience of the experiment and by spreading this experience through further interactions beyond the laboratory. An important difference between Shapin and Schaffer's account of knowledge in Boyle's experiment and my account of knowledge in the classroom is that what I call representational and communal knowledge emerge through one and the same event in Boyle's experiment, whereas I describe two distinct events in the classroom to account for the two forms of knowledge. We need to move beyond the classroom and beyond the laboratory in order to understand this difference: In the mid-seventeenth century, no references to "vacuum" were to be found on coffee packages on the grocery shelves, nor did people have vacuum cleaners or vacuum flasks that, as a matter of course, would make them associate the term "vacuum" with the suction of air and airtight containers. The knowledge Boyle's experiments produced did not have extended allies beyond the laboratory that could grant it validity, and Boyle's experimental knowledge was thus local and vacuous. It was "radical individual."

Literary and social technologies extended Boyle's knowledge of vacuum and enrolled a vast number of virtual witnesses through whom it could gain degrees of recognition and authority that by far exceeded what a knowledge claim given by any individual could ever obtain. However, representational knowledge produced the problem of radical individualism by establishing a distance between the knower and the known and thus producing knowledge as situated in the individual mind. This problem could be remedied by communal knowledge, which specifically turned individual knowledge into communal knowledge. Furthermore, this was crucial for the political importance of this form of knowledge, as discussed previously. In this way, communal knowledge was decisive for the establishment and extension of representational knowledge. Representational and communal aspects were inseparable and interdependent in Boyle's experimental knowledge. His matters of fact could be representational only if they were also communal.

The representational knowledge established in the classroom did not have the same need for support from communal knowledge. The metric standard worked, I explained, because Jens's jump in the math textbook referred to the same immutable measurement as did the ruler in the classroom. Jens's and Ben's jumps were local and separate from one another, but the standard bound them together across the boundaries of the school, across the distant places in which the jumps took place. The assemblages that made it possible to perform the metric standard in the textbook and in the situation the textbook referred to, as well as in the classroom, were in place. There was already an infrastructure of math textbooks with references to metric measurements and one-meter rulers distributed to all classrooms. But more than that, references to the metric standard that lay beyond the classroom and the materials immediately present in the classroom were crucial for the performance of the representational knowledge. Maybe Ben's family went to IKEA last week and bought a new dining table. The product description tag attached to the table informed buyers of the dimensions of the table in metric values. This was fortunate, because we may imagine that Ben's mother had written down the size of their dining room on a note, which, by using the disposable paper tape measures that hung at numerous locations on the walls of the furniture warehouse, allowed her to compare the size of her distant dining room to the product description. Thereby she was able to conclude whether the table would fit into the room. In addition to the dimensions of their dining table, Ben's parents could probably refer in metric terms to their own jumping abilities, to measurements from sports events, and to Ben's and his siblings' heights, which were measured during their yearly checkups. The ubiquitous presence – the infrastructure – of the metric standard made it possible for the pupils to discuss what they learned in class with their parents and anyone else who shared references[8] to the metric standard. Furthermore, the infrastructure of references already in place beyond the boundaries of the school granted representational knowledge in the classroom universality and validity. Indeed, this knowledge was not radical individual knowledge. Rather, it was widely present. For the same reason, the representational knowledge established through the classroom jumping demonstration was not dependent on communal knowledge – as was the case in Boyle's experiment – and it did not perform this form of knowledge. In order to find communal knowledge I had to turn to a different event.

Whereas the representational knowledge in the classroom demonstration was associated with an already-established infrastructure, the knowledge performed with the bed-loft was not. It was local and without much reference beyond parents', pupils', and teachers' particular, local efforts. Like the knowledge in Boyle's experiments, it lacked an infrastructure to grant it universality and validity. However, similar to the transparent materiality of the glass globe in Boyle's experiment, the visual

---

[8] We should be careful not to imply by the formulation of "references" to the metric standard that the metric standard exists somewhere beyond these references. According to the regional imaginary, each emergence of the metric standard does refer to a "real" meter, which is why it is adequate to talk about "references." Considering the metric standard from, for instance, a network imaginary, it is clear that there is nothing but references, that each reference enacts itself as a reference to the standard as well as enacting the standard with the characteristic of being distant from itself.

forms of the bed-loft, the environment posters, the pictures relating to the Snow Queen play, and the school model were visible objects of a noticeable character, which made them available for witnessing and thus for the formation of communal knowledge.

The formation of communal knowledge was just as vital for the school as it was for the scientific validity of Boyle's experiment. The value of the learning taking place in school is constantly questioned by parents and employers and in the press. That is one of the reasons for introducing increased audit of schools and teaching. Due to the form of the regional space performed with the metric standard and with other objects that had a materiality that made references available, such knowledge is easily validated. This was not the case with materials like the environment posters, the pictures relating to the Snow Queen play, the school model, and the bed-loft. The production of communal knowledge that moves beyond the classroom was crucial to establish if not validity then at least acceptance of this kind of school activity. Without this, the knowledge produced by the bed-loft was likely to be identified as radical individual. Through the formation of communal knowledge, it reached out beyond the walls of the classroom, just as representational knowledge does, only in a different way.

Tvia's Twin Towers: Fluid Space in Femtedit

The Creation of the "Twin Towers"

I now turn away from the classroom and toward the virtual environment. The analyses of the classroom and the virtual environment were created not sequentially but as a result of continuous adjustments of an oscillating movement between analyses of the two places. I moved back and forth between the data from the classroom and the data from the virtual environment, continuously analyzing, reading, re-reading, comparing, questioning, writing, and re-writing each set of materials in relation to changes to the other set. Even though the rest of this chapter focuses on forms of knowledge as they were constituted by and through the virtual environment, I repeatedly return to the analyses of forms of knowledge in the classroom, comparing, clarifying, and developing those analyses further.

The children's task in the Femtedit project was to build up homes for the Femteditians, as well as creating their identities by making hyperlinks to Internet web pages. The following field report is created out of a combination of field notes, of what children and researchers wrote in the blog, and of the visual appearance of the online 3D virtual environment. The compression of materials from almost the whole project period makes the report appear as one unbroken sequence. It however covers a period of several weeks, over which many other things happened:

> Five boys were busy building a house for the Femteditian Tvia. Michael, Tim, and Pete from the Danish group had chosen dun brown granite wall plates and were arranging them in two big squares, slightly staggered. They wanted to build something "big and pretty." It was not easy to get the wall plates to fit. While struggling with the plates the following week, they explained that the wall had to be as tall as possible. But they had not even managed to complete the first floor yet. More granite wall plates were attached. Ola and David, their Swedish teammates, put a TV in front of the "empty" Tvia, to make sure she wasn't bored while waiting for them to reanimate her. And they put in floors and walls of water inside the house and added the sound of water to these components.
>
> Tvia responded in the blog: "Great building!!! Please, link to some good pages . . . weak . . . help . . . oh . . . need more memory . . ." Tvia required more hyperlinks for her reanimation.
>
> Michael, Tim, and Pete started surfing. Tim found an animation on the Internet and linked it to the TV their Swedish partners had built in the house. "I have made a film," he wrote in the blog. Michael linked to satiric anti-terrorist web pages. There was an animation about Osama Bin Laden. "Look at this, look at this," Pete said excitedly, handing over the head-phones to Tine Jensen, my colleague. Tine watched and listened to the animation about how to "bash" Mr. Laden. She didn't know how to react. She found it repellent and felt the urge to forbid the link immediately. On the other hand, she wanted to be in accordance with the frame story, which implied that feedback was motivated by the relations and happenings inside the virtual environment and not by external criteria about what was good or bad. She told Pete that she personally found the joke distasteful because of its glorification of violence, its dumb U.S. centrism, and its ignorance of the complexities of the conflicts between the U.S. government and its Muslim enemies. Pete shrugged his shoulders and turned to the virtual environment. The teacher passed by and started reprimanding Pete for the worthlessness of what he was doing, for the lack of quality in the web pages he was visiting. Turning to Tine, she stated that "that's the problem with the Internet; you never know what sort of rubbish the children get in touch with."
>
> Tvia didn't comment on the satiric web pages but on the divergence in what the children built: "Thanks for all you have built. It is so nice. It gives me strength, but my mind is divided. I am CONFUSED. It is as if I were two persons. It is because you do not collaborate. The Swedish children

try to rebuild my old house. The Danish children try to build as big as possible – you need to start agreeing."

Pete changed the surface of the "water" walls and floor to granite and industrial metal, respectively. Ola put a skating image on the TV and two armchairs in front of it. Michael changed the skating image to a Digimon[9] figure, which David overwrote with an image of a speedboat. Tim found a web page with pictures of bombs, which he put right in front of their house and next to a few animations of fireworks, and he called this "explosions": "It's the Twin Towers," he said, smiling proudly at Tine.

How do we account for this mess of events? One way is to create a narrative beginning with the wish to build something big and pretty and concluding in naming the building the Twin Towers. This would be an account that grants the children the agency of building and naming and that implies a course of events directed by the children's intention. By giving privilege to the humans, such an account – that indeed follows the formula of most accounts in the literature of educational technology – overlooks the contributions of the material participants. Furthermore, such an account implies that the children's actions were prescribed by a pre-given plan.[10] This was not necessarily the case.

We can easily follow the association of the dark granite surface of the virtual building with the Twin Towers. The name given fits well with the look the building had come to possess, which it did not have initially, when it was given the "water" texture and the sound of flowing water. The field report gives us reason to think about other parts and patterns as crucial to the course of events: naming the building the Twin Towers could have been a continuation provoked by the confrontation between Pete, Tine, and the teacher concerning the anti-terrorist websites. Furthermore, it was late 2001, only a few months after two planes crashed into the Twin Towers in New York City's lower Manhattan. The children were asked to attach whatever links they wanted to the buildings in Femtedit, and, being the most exposed issue in the media that autumn, it was no surprise that 9/11 found its way to Femtedit. Two of the Danish boys involved in the building were twin brothers. All of these conditions as well as the phonetic likeness of "Tvia" and "twin" (especially with a Danish accent) may have

---

[9] "Digimon" is an abbreviation of Digital Monsters. Digimon is a Japanese franchise focused around an anime TV series and includes collectible card games, digital games, comics, and movies. At the time of the study, Digimon was one of the most popular global figures in child culture.

[10] For discussion of plans and situated action, see Suchman (1987, 2007).

contributed to the emergence of the naming of the "Twin Towers" in the course of the Femtedit building.

When refraining from basing analysis on assumed human intention, studies of social science often experience difficulties in accounting for occurrences in terms of causality or reasoned action that proceeds linearly from A to B. The field report describes a vast number of objects, utterances, considerations, interactions, and relations, and, taking these into account, we may instead describe the course of events as a number of single elements – more or less independent – coming together one after the other, neither following any set plan nor directed toward a goal. We need not understand the naming of the "Twin Towers" as the conclusion of the story, as summing up or embracing all other parts. I suggest that it was simply added on the same level as the parts already connected. Even though the naming of the "Twin Towers" must thus be seen as a weak actor, compared to a plan that cognitivists conceptualized as a strong actor, this naming most likely influenced the character of the flow of parts. Similarly, associating the anti-terrorist web pages with the tall granite building and putting together the granite wall plates might well have shaped the idea of building something big. The empirical material does not provide us with evidence that the idea was prior to the building activities. It may just as well have been a result of them. Instead of starting from a central participant, as did the resonance space, each part influenced the flow process. Step-by-step, parts came together, each contributing to the direction of the journey.

We see in the field report that the continual mutation emerged out of some links and building blocks being replaced and others changing or losing effect. First we saw a TV set erected. Then an animation was added to the TV, which was replaced by a still picture. Tvia's feedback was read, the blog was activated, and a researcher provided her reflections on the buildings. Statements were written; links added. First it was a sound; then it was a granite wall; then it was the Femteditian's feedback. Then it was something else. Due to its individual building blocks, the parts of the virtual environment were optional and exchangeable. Some parts were in focus at one moment, but at others they faded into the background. Sometimes they were exchanged and replaced, just as some reappeared and regained importance. The relations among parts in fluid space are varying. This varying involvement and omission of entities contributed to Femtedit as a process of continual mutation.

The fluid metaphor describes a pattern of parts coming together one after the other; not a pattern that adds up to form a more and more robust object, but a pattern in which the latest parts attached influence the direction of the process. What was on the top of the blog was always what was read and what counted. I never saw anybody scrolling down to be reminded of what had been written earlier. The past discussions were indeed over. Hence, the story of the "Twin Towers" is a product of talking about the process from a specific point in time. Had the project continued, then the story might have turned away from the "Twin Towers." This is important when we investigate the form of knowledge performed. Knowledge is usually understood as a product, and indeed – as I have discussed concerning representational knowledge – as a quite stable product. This characteristic does not apply to knowledge in fluid space. If we accept that we are dealing with a process of parts coming together one after the other, without any master plan, it makes no sense to conclude that the "Twin Towers" were the core of the knowledge produced in the occurrence in question, like the bed-loft was the center of the communal knowledge discussed previously. Any account of knowledge in this fluid space has to be a description of a process without closure.

The Lack of Representation in Fluidity

The fluid space performed with Femtedit differed significantly from regional space and the representational form of knowledge discussed in the previous chapter. In order to examine the knowledge produced by and through fluid space, it is helpful to look at how this differed from regional space and thus from representational knowledge. My approach to investigating this is to look for regional patterns performed with Femtedit, and, when they fail to appear, to describe the differences between the space in question and the formation of regional knowledge.

Femtedit consisted, among other things, of the Femtedit website, which included a web page for each Femteditian that contained a few pictures and a few sentences about the virtual creatures, as shown in Figure 3. But there was no total account or map that allowed the children to rebuild what they saw in the pictures and read in the presentation of the Femteditians. The Femtedit website presented a partial story of the life and concerns of Femtedit, rather than a model of it. The phrases on each Femteditian's web page were rather cryptic. Look for example at the ones on Tvia's web page:

"I was here first."
"I give good advice if you ask."
"My color is green."

The frame story provided more context for the phrases. The children first met Tvia as one of the protagonists in the frame story. She was the oldest and wisest Femteditian, the one who arrived first in Femtedit. This and other information about Femtedit and the Femteditians was written in Jaga's diary, which could also be read on the Femtedit website.

Tvia noted in the blog that her Swedish helpers were trying to rebuild her old house, while the Danish helpers were focused on building something big. The Swedish part of the team, David and Ola, indeed attempted to create a representation of what was on the pictures on Tvia's web page.[11] However, they received little support from the design of the virtual environment. The design provided only a few ambiguous sentences on a web page and a bit more information for those who read the frame story carefully. The children were "thrown" into the Femtedit world in an almost Heideggerian way,[12] without any definite model of what to do. There was neither a standard available that could show the children how the Femteditians' homes had to be built nor an unambiguous story telling how their identities had to be formed through hyperlinks. There was nothing like the one-meter ruler in the classroom, which made available a regional reference in the performance of knowledge.

What about the Twin Towers? They were not depicted on the Femtedit website, but they were (or at least had been) "out there," somewhere other than the virtual environment. Did those relations not shape representational knowledge? We need to look carefully at the relations between the "Twin Towers" in the virtual environment and the late World Trade Center in order to establish whether the relation is representational. Satiric anti-terrorist websites were linked to the "Twin Towers" in Femtedit as well as an image of a bomb and explosions. Together, these parts did not in any naturalistic sense mirror the "real" Twin Towers. They rather built on – or continued while mutating – the legendary New York buildings. They involved historic material in their activities but mixed it with fictional

---

[11] The Danish researchers urged the children to build the Femteditians' homes by involving hyperlinks and inspiration from external sources, while the Swedish researchers supported their children in recreating what was shown in the pictures. As we see in Chapter 5, the degree to which the researchers' and teachers' advice was included in the virtual environment varied. The design did not allow the teachers to control what children were doing in the environment. Their presence and advice were involved in the children's activities as component parts on par with web pages, images, chat messages, and other parts available for solving the tasks.

[12] Martin Heidegger describes a primordial feature of *Dasein* (being-there) as thrownness, which on the one hand means to be fundamentally lost and on the other allows *Dasein* to disseminate itself into the multiplicity of "being which it is not" (Casey 1998, p. 260).

and other materials that would probably be considered incorrect in regional space and representational knowledge. The pattern of relations performed with the Twin Towers in Femtedit did not regionally represent something "out there"; rather it fluidly connected parts – real and fictional on the same footing – in an ongoing transformative process. It did not constitute the spatial arrangement characterized by boundaries and separate regions necessary for performing the representational form of knowledge.

Not only the spatial but also the temporal arrangement of the virtual environment stood in the way of performing representational knowledge. The activities of the virtual environment changed gradually, as I noted previously. The buildings were not the "Twin Towers" from the beginning. I have described how both the metric standard and the knowledge about Ben's and Jens's jumps had to be constant in order to create a regional pattern of relations. Because it continuously transformed and because its relations varied, the virtual environment did not contribute to performing such constancy. A construction like Tvia's home in Femtedit could not be a mirror image of something "out there" that stayed the same – or that was changing (as the World Trade Center actually is). The fluid space performed by and through the virtual environment did not produce the temporal constancy required to form a regional space and a representational form of knowledge.

The teacher complained about this. She reprimanded Pete for the worthlessness of what he was doing. Indeed, in regional space, an arrangement that does not perform representation, like the buildings in the virtual environment, is worthless. Note that the teacher did not reprimand the assemblage; she told *Pete* off. As a participant of a regional space in which knowledge and agency is located in individuals who are consequently responsible for what is taking place, her performance clashed with the dispersed shape of the fluidity of Femtedit. Fluid space performs neither regions nor representation, and thus the virtual environment lacked resemblance to reality.

The Pakistani Song: What Form of Knowledge?

The Linking of the Pakistani Song

Before we turn to the form of knowledge performed with fluid space, this section examines to what extent communal knowledge was performed with Femtedit. I do this through a discussion of another field note report. The following account is put together from a few excerpts from my field notes, which were written over a period of two weeks:

> Hajjah told me she would like to have some Pakistani music in the house of her Femteditian. I said that was indeed possible; we could search for a song by typing in the title in Google. This, however, turned out to be difficult because she didn't know how to write the title in Latin letters. Her cousin in sixth grade would probably know, she said, so she could go and ask her. "Ok," I answered, and off she went. Only a few minutes later she returned but unfortunately without any song title.
>
> During the next week I spent an evening digging out a Pakistani song from the Internet. Not knowing anything about Pakistani music, I was searching in the dark, but, with the help of hit lists, I finally had one downloaded. I was excited to have my efforts evaluated, but before I could play the song for Hajjah she came running up to me at the next Femtedit session, telling me that she had found a music website. She pushed up her sleeve and revealed a URL written with India ink on her forearm: xxx.com. Some of the older boys had written it, she said. I don't know why, but I naïvely sat down with her at the computer and typed in the URL. A pornography site, of course, appeared on the screen – a responsible one, though, with a non-explicit first page and warnings about the explicit material that could be displayed by clicking on any of the links on the page. We concluded that the boys had played a trick on her, and indeed on me as well.
>
> Therefore, we were both quite satisfied when it turned out that the Pakistani song I had brought was one Hajjah already knew and liked. She linked it to her Femteditian's home. Soon other Pakistani children from the class crowded up behind her to listen to the music. More and more children gathered, and a queue formed of children waiting for their turn to try on the headphones. An ethnic Danish boy exclaimed: "Oh it's real Uzma music." Uzma was a girl in the class who mostly dressed in traditional Pakistani clothing and in other ways seemed to represent Pakistani culture to the ethnic Danish eye. This could easily have been meant as derogatory, but it wasn't. Another boy smiled, looked a little puzzled, and said with surprise in his voice: "It is actually good." (Field note 1115_2–7)

The odyssey ending with Pakistani music becoming part of the online 3D virtual environment creates a pattern of a heterogeneous collection of humans and things spreading widely beyond the computer lab. Various people and things were mobilized: first Hajjah, the virtual environment, and me; then Hajjah's cousin; then Pakistani pop music websites; then a few older boys, writing in India ink on Hajjah's forearm; and then a porn website, the linking in the virtual environment, headphones, classmates, and puzzling musical experiences. The linking feature of the virtual environment made it possible to involve participants that were otherwise not associated with Femtedit, and indeed Femtedit was formed though the involvement of the variety of things and people that were previously external to Femtedit.

The Lack of Communal Knowledge in Fluid Space

Because it seemingly created an extended web of people and things, we might want to conclude that the virtual environment contributed to performing a communal form of knowledge, just as the bed-loft did in the classroom. A gathering was even formed in the computer lab of children wanting to "witness" the music Hajjah had added to her Femteditian's house. There are however crucial differences. The Pakistani music was not large, spectacular, and nailed to walls, as was the bed-loft. Neither was it a collective product of the class. It could probably have drawn Hajjah's parents to the class, but it was unlikely that other parents would show up to witness the Pakistani song. It did not act as a magnet, as did the bed-loft. Materiality allowing the Pakistani song to establish a link to an inaugural ceremony, which could reinforce its "magnetism," was not available. Without such an event, the music also lacked the ability to create or sustain a community to spread communal knowledge.

Like resonance space, the formation established by the Pakistani song was a result of heterogeneous participants spread beyond a central place. The participants involved were, however, different than those involved in the communal knowledge of the classroom, and their materiality did not qualify for a resonance space. In order to examine this further, I return to Boyle and the witnesses involved in establishing communal knowledge of the experiment.

Shapin and Schaffer (1985) describe how the witnesses of Boyle's experiment were carefully selected following the taken-for-granted convention that Oxford professors were more reliable witnesses than Oxfordshire peasants. Just as it was important to make the experiment a public space by engaging witnesses, it was also crucial to let only "reliable" and "credible" people witness the experiment (p. 336). Haraway (1997) notes that Boyle sometimes conducted experiments late at night in order to exclude women from witnessing. He feared that women might interrupt the experiment, as had happened once, when a small bird was suffocating in the glass globe and an attending woman had demanded him to let air in to rescue the bird.

I argue that the Femtedit schoolchildren shared the fate of the Oxfordshire peasants and women, which rendered them worthless as witnesses. Oxford professors were reliable and credible because their interrelations and the assemblage of people and things that constituted their life were stable. They were interdependent and woven into a resonance that kept each of them in place, and thus the way in which they would spread their experiences from the laboratory was predictable and stable. Oxfordshire peasants could not perform the same societal stability, and hence they did not have the same immutable reliability and credibility.[13] The schoolchildren shared this fate. Knowledge did not become communal simply because it was spread among many people. It had to be spread in a stable assemblage with stable interrelations among the participants. Hajjah's cousin, her older friends, the India ink on her forearm, the porn site, and Hajjah's classmates did not constitute a stable resonance. Neither Hajjah's cousin nor her friends or classmates held stable positions, and their relations to one another varied. This lack of stable resonance meant that they did not account for one another, which made available undisciplined perceptions and accounts. The example of Hajjah's friends teasing her by writing a porn URL on her forearm shows their unreliability. She – and I – thought they would give her a link to a Pakistani song, but instead it was a porn site. It is unlikely that parents and the school principal would do something like that. These adults formed a formal resonance space with stable positions and stable relations to one another, featuring unambiguous mutual accountabilities. This stability disciplined their perceptions and accounts. They formed good witnesses to the class work. The knowledge of the bed-loft would credibly and reliably spread from them beyond the classroom and after the inaugural ceremony. One cannot expect the same from children. Therefore, even though the cousin, the older boys, and a porn site from beyond the virtual environment became involved in Femtedit, they formed neither resonance space nor communal knowledge.

Although Latour (1993) celebrates Shapin and Schaffer's book for taking the socio-material practice of knowledge production into account, I think at this point they relapse into a social, non-material thinking, referring to the convention that rendered some social groups more reliable and credible than others. My analysis, on the other hand, takes the socio-material space into account and shows that it is much more than socially

---

[13] The ability to display stability is achieved through power and wealth, both of which have to do with being bound up in a network of humans and things.

agreed-upon or collectively enacted conventions that make some persons (and, with them, a socio-material assemblage) suitable as witnesses and others not. The varying, preliminary way in which children were involved in the virtual environment did not perform the required stability. Who is or is not an appropriate witness is thus determined by the difference between the stable resonance pattern and the loose and unstable fluid space.[14]

Communal knowledge was not performed through the children involved, because they lacked the materiality necessary to become witnesses. Could communal knowledge have been performed by involving parents and the principal as witnesses to the virtual environment, as had been the case in the inaugural ceremony? Parents were involved as witnesses even before the project began. During the planning of the Femtedit project with the teachers of the fourth-grade class, the teachers asked us to present the project at a parent-teacher meeting. It seemed logical to me to present to the parents what their children were going to do in school. I did not think of this as already part of the knowledge of the virtual environment, but indeed it was. After the parent-teacher meeting, the project, which had not even started, had enrolled parents who, similar to the adults involved in the inaugural ceremony, would contribute to forming communal knowledge of Femtedit. Through the parent-teacher meeting, parents came to witness the Femtedit project, and a resonance space and communal knowledge

---

[14] Haraway (1997) appreciates Shapin and Schaffer's descriptions of how "proper knowledge" could only be produced by excluding a vast majority of the population as potential witnesses, but she criticizes their account for overlooking that this procedure produced a knowledge that was European, white, and male; this knowledge gives all attention to the observed object "out there," to the "nature" distant from the body of the observer, to which critical attention was minimized. By excluding women, people of non-white color, and people of non-European nationality, clashes of gender, ethnicity, or nationality could not emerge, and hence gender, ethnicity, and nationality were rendered invisible in the laboratory and in producing knowledge.

Haraway's commentary is sharp and important. But her emphasis on nationality, ethnicity, and gender overlooks a just-as-important social category: namely, age. Children were also excluded as witnesses, and by their exclusion they were involved in performing "proper knowledge" just as much as a European white male adult form of knowledge, a knowledge that rendered age invisible, that concealed the fact that the perceiving eye must be of a certain age in order to view the proceedings in a disciplined manner that renders its observations reliable and credible. Surely, the presence of children as witnesses in Boyle's new experiments would have contributed to forming knowledge and the experimental way of life in a way that was quite different from how it came to be. This is parallel to how we saw women challenging the experiment and causing it to become something different than what it became after they were banned. The form of knowledge and the way of life performed through Boyle's experiments were detached from the attributes of nation, color, gender, and age.

of Femtedit was initiated. Contrary to the inaugural ceremony, which completed the bed-loft, the parent-teacher meeting preceded Femtedit, and it thus created expectation, which had to be confirmed by Femtedit and through further witnessing of the virtual environment.

As I explained through Boyle's experiments, a material arrangement had to be carefully set up and calibrated in order for it to be possible to witness the arrangement. The globe had to be transparent for witnesses to be able to see the suffocating animals. Did Femtedit have something analogous to the glass globe? It had the researchers' accounts, which were delivered at the parent-teacher meeting. And thereafter? As Boyle presented the glass globe to Oxford professors, we gave parents access to the virtual environment. We sent the children home with notes that provided the URL of the web page from which parents could download the Eduverse platform and through this witness Femtedit from their home computers. However, probably due to the relative immaturity of digital technology at the time, this overstretched both parents and children. Downloading and installing Eduverse at home was not an easily accessible way for parents to witness the environment. Nor was visiting the school and entering the environment from there. Several parents who entered the Femtedit environment complained about its messiness, just as the teacher complained about the mixed-up jumble. Newcomers usually only move around in the environment without clicking on or bumping into building blocks to activate animations, sounds, web pages, and teleports. They do not hear the Pakistani song. They miss a lot of what is built. Furthermore, the Femtedit environment was intimately related to the frame story, the blog, and the Femtedit website, as well as the ongoing chats and dialogues, which the parents missed if they exclusively moved the avatar around in the environment. Apart from this special spatial arrangement, which was difficult to access for newcomers, the temporal ongoing transforming character of the environment made it difficult during a short visit to get a picture of what was going on and thus to establish a pattern with the virtual environment – or the Pakistani song – at its center. It would be like trying to understand a film by looking at the film poster. In these ways, Femtedit made witnessing unavailable to parents, and obstructed the creation of communal knowledge.

Translating Fluid Space into Regionality

Direct witnessing was not an option in Femtedit. One potential solution was virtual witnessing: a translation of what happened in the virtual environment into a materiality that could connect to parents or other significant figures. Because of the teachers' complaint that children did not learn anything, we – the researchers – decided to include in our field notes remarks on what each individual child had learned during each Femtedit session. We would then have these descriptions ready whenever somebody asked us to account for Femtedit. Thus, Tine wrote about Tvia's helpers Michael, Tim, and Pete:

Michael/Tim learned:

> Building
> How to use the codebook[15]
> Joining[16]
> Privilege password[17]
> How to log in to the Fifth Dimension server space[18]

Pete learned:

> How to build and use the codebook (found a bed, a toilet, etc.)
> Privilege password
> How to turn objects
> How to make a warp (almost)[19] (Tine's field note 1113_4)

Tine's learning remarks took the same form as those of the rest of us. These accounts neglected the fluid pattern. They did not include the complexity of parts entangling and disentangling over time, but instead described a space of generalized skills that the individual achieved and subsequently possessed, and to which the materials were genuinely irrelevant, belonging to another sphere beyond the individual. We see not a

---

[15] The codebook was a stapled stack of printed papers that listed the filenames of each of the more than 2,000 building blocks available in the Fifth Dimension. When inserting a building block, it was necessary to type in this filename.

[16] An avatar can "join" another avatar by completing a dialogue box, whereby the joining avatar is beamed directly to the location of the joined avatar.

[17] A user can grant another user the privilege of manipulating the objects that she has built. This is practical when collaborating, because without sharing privileges, only the one who has built an object can move it, change it, or delete it.

[18] On the Fifth Dimension server space, images, sounds, and objects were saved. If a user wanted to insert an image or sound in Femtedit that was not directly available on the web – for instance, a photo that he took – it was necessary first to store this image or sound on the Fifth Dimension server.

[19] Any object could be turned into a warp. When an avatar bumped into or clicked on the object, the avatar would be beamed to a new location, specified by the warp, in Femtedit or in other worlds in Eduverse.

pattern of mutation but a stable shape to which skills were added without the shape changing. We see immutable immobility. We see regional space.

The teacher had criticized that we did not teach children collectively. So we decided to make a building lesson. We realized that the children would probably learn from it, and even if they did not, it would allow us to confirm that we had indeed taught the children specific skills. I took on the task and went home to prepare. I drew a sequence of pictures of the building dialogue boxes of Active Worlds, and the following Tuesday I placed myself by the whiteboard in the computer lab, raised my voice, and asked everyone to listen to me for a while. Hands were removed from keyboards, and chairs were moved out into the middle aisle between the two rows of computers to get a clear view of the whiteboard. I drew the pictures I had prepared on the whiteboard. I asked what the next step was, I looked out over the pupils, I got answers, and I rehearsed the steps with the whole class. The teacher was very pleased. She told me I had good teaching skills, and I was proud of myself and relieved that now we seemed to be back on track with the teacher. It was not until later that I realized that, without being aware of it, I had created a regional space in which I was in one location, the pupils were in another location, and the knowledge in me was transferred collectively to the individual pupils, with the effect that I – in person – got the credit for the unfolding of the situation, black boxing the rearranging of chairs and bodies and the ability of the whiteboard to fixate gazes.

Liquid Knowledge

Examining the forms of knowledge performed in the classroom and by and through Boyle's experiment has helped us to understand how they differ from the form of knowledge performed with the virtual environment. I noted that single parts came together one after the other, continually transforming their relations, which were accordingly unstable. Indeed, the involved parts were optional and exchangeable. I showed how this fluid pattern of relations lacked the regional characteristics of representational knowledge and that single components coming together gradually did not make available a stable reality, standard, or model that could be referenced, that no infrastructure of references was in place. What took place with the virtual environment built on and involved external parts; it did not mirror external components. In addition, I showed that the assemblages of children and their socio-material relations lacked the stability necessary for performing communal knowledge.

With inspiration from Law and Mol's metaphor of fluidity, I call the form of knowledge performed with the virtual environment a *liquid form of knowledge*. Like Thrift's (1996, 2000) *nonrepresentational* knowledge, liquid knowledge is characterized by *"effectivity* rather than representation; not the *what* but the *how"* (Thrift 2000, p. 216). Thrift emphasizes the interest in invention rather than reflection, because invention is about adding to the world without adding *up*. Furthermore, his nonrepresentational style implies a selection principle that is concerned not with whether there is a link between account and reality but with whether or not "one travels," that is, whether or not an effort makes a difference. What Thrift says about his nonrepresentational style can be said about the form of knowledge performed with the online 3D virtual environment: It created or invented something; it did not refer; and its ongoing involvement with new parts resulted not in representation but in change, in making differences. This form of knowledge was effective: it produced effects. The stories of the "Twin Towers" and of the Pakistani song were both chains of effects in which one link resulted in another, resulting in a third, and so on. And even though the boys were focused on building something big, the ongoing process was primarily important, a process in which the wish of building something big was a participant rather than a guide or a motor. Likewise, the process of finding the Pakistani song through the enrollment of a number of human and nonhuman participants, rather than the end result, was the focus. This resonates with the computer game culture, in which the process of playing the game – rather than the object or goal of the game – is decisive. On the contrary, reaching the goal or target is usually experienced as an anticlimax, because it indicates that the game is over (Sørensen 1998). It is the *how* – rather than the *what* – that is vital for the liquid form of knowledge, in other words, the process, not the goal.

This implies that liquid knowledge is *processual*. "There is no last word; [only] infinite becoming and constant reactivation" (Thrift 2000, p. 217). The mobility of liquid knowledge, unlike the extension of communal knowledge, consists of reactivation or continuation; that is, mobility is created by drawing in new parts that make the process move and alter. Consider the way in which my colleague Tine Jensen participated when confronted with the "bashing Osama Bin Laden" site. She offered a personal, partial view as a resource for the continuing process, which could be absorbed and mutated by the process and which led to further forming and mutating. Contrary to this, the teacher provided a "view from beyond." With reference to an external standard, she reprimanded Pete for the worthlessness of what he was doing and contributed thereby a regional

spatiality in which knowledge can be evaluated in definitive and dichoto-
mous terms – as valuable or worthless. Assessments consequently come in
general terms, as universal, not as partial. As in Boyle's experiment, the
teacher's agency was thereby factored out of the knowledge/value claim. As
a result, it created a region – a measurement or standard against which
quality could be judged. Such a judgment is total in character; it is either
accepted or rejected as a value scheme for the entire space, which is contrary to the processual character of Tine's partial involvement in the
ongoing mutating process of fluid space.

The researchers however were not consequently – or not only – contributing to performing liquid knowledge. We for instance translated the
fluid experiences into regional accounts, which I exemplified in the field
note excerpt, presented in the previous section, about what Michael, Tim,
and Pete learned through Femtedit. Compared to the story of Tvia's
helpers, the list appears quite odd. What does the list have in common with
the field note report on the building of the "Twin Towers"? Where are all
the efforts, the conflicts, and the interrelations among objects, talk, and
thoughts? They are gone; they are narrated away. This is the problem of
virtual witnessing, of translating what happened in fluid space into a form
of knowledge that represents it. We need Thrift's help again in order to
understand this. Thrift opens his article "Afterwords" (2000) by contem-
plating on how to honor his late father:

> I feel a need to write the event and yet . . . I am not at all sure that this is
> what I want to do. In a sense, I believe that this writing down is a part of the
> problem. I do not want to take over my father's being by making him into
> fodder for yet more interpretation, by colonising his traces. (p. 213)

Thrift had experienced his father through interactions with him, and the
problem arose when he tried to produce a written account of his father.
A representation would colonize his father, causing him to recede into the
background of the formal, solemn ritual of an obituary, which was very
unlike the "small sayings and large generosities" of the late Mr. Thrift.
Representational knowledge would narrate him away.

In scientific discussions, this problem – or similar ones – is often
conceptualized as a problem of reductionism; that is, representations
supposedly simplify and miss out on the details and mess of practice.
I would like to emphasize that we are not dealing with a problem of
reductionism or of achieving a more or less correct or exhaustive representation. Critiques of reductionism miss the crucial point: accounts
of knowledge as liquid or "practical" are not less or more "reduced"

conceptualizations of knowledge than "theoretical," "abstract," or representational conceptualizations. The conception of the interrelation between "reality" and knowledge that is implied in the critique of reductionism establishes a regional space of more or less reduced accounts of a distant reality, which limits the imaginary of thinking about different forms of knowledge. Consider this story told by a character in Lewis Carroll's *Sylvie and Bruno Concluded* from 1894:

> "That's another thing we've learned from *your* Nation," said Mein Herr, "map-making. But we've carried it much further than you. What do you consider the *largest* map that would be really useful?" "About six inches to a mile." "Only *six inches!*" exclaimed Mein Herr. "We very soon got to six *yards* to the mile. Then we tried a *hundred* yards to the mile. And then came the grandest idea of all! We actually made a map of the country, on the scale of a *mile to the mile!*" "Have you used it much?" I enquired. "It has never been spread out, yet," said Mein Herr: "the farmers objected: They said it would cover the whole country, and shut out the sunlight! So we now use the country itself, as its own map, and I assure you it does nearly as well." (Carroll 1894, p. 524, ref. Smith 2003, p. 75)

We have to abandon the idea that knowledge necessarily takes the shape of a map. Several authors have stressed that "map" is a widespread but inadequate metaphor for a theory of knowledge (e.g., Smith 2003; Turnbull 1993). Representational knowledge fits the imaginary of a map quite well. But other forms of knowledge do not. Liquid knowledge of the virtual environment is not a knowledge that maps the practice to the environment "on the scale of a mile to a mile." It is not about making a representation that is not a reduction. Liquid knowledge is not a map. It is not regional.

Scholar of computer interaction and identity Sherry Turkle (1997) has described a new style of thinking that has evolved along with the proliferation of personal computers. She calls it *tinkering*, and by relating it to Lévi-Strauss's notion of bricolage she emphasizes that tinkering problem solvers proceed from the bottom up by trying one thing and then another, by making connections and bringing disparate components together. They learn by playful exploration and manipulation of the object by being "immersed in its cadences" (p. 61). And Turkle defines tinkering very much in contrast to abstract thinking, which she describes as characterized by following rules. My description of liquid knowledge resonates on several points with Turkle's tinkering. An important difference, however, is that Turkle keeps to a regional imaginary that describes tinkering as a skill, a way of working, thinking, and acting with the world, just as abstract thinking is a way of thinking about the world. Contrary to this, I describe liquid knowledge not as located in the individual but as a pattern of relations that varies, as shifting discontinuities, and as mutating connections and links that are transformed. A crucial characteristic of liquid knowledge is that it is performed as part of the flow of the ongoing mutation, not as a human possession or ability.

Developmental psychologist and activity theorist Lev Vygotsky's (1978) notion of the *zone of proximal development* (ZPD) for assessing children's developmental stage is useful for thinking about liquid knowledge as a flow of socio-material practice that, contrary to representational knowledge, does not make a distinction between the human and the world. Whereas psychologists and educators usually assess children's abilities independently, Vygotsky recommended we approach children in collaboration with an adult or with more capable peers. Such situations reveal the child's ZPD, in which it is "as though he were a head taller than himself" (Vygotsky 1978, p. 102) and thus capable of performing what he could not do on his own. Thereby the ZPD "contains all developmental tendencies in a condensed form and is itself a major source of development" (ibid., p. 102). The ZPD does not display a child's developmental stage as a given fixed facility, but shows the child's developmental motion; what he or she is about to achieve. Vygotsky considered this more relevant for learning how to support a child's development than information about the child's position on a developmental scale. Because it has the characteristics of a flow of potentialities, of ongoing, dependent variation, we may think of a ZPD as a fluid space.

It has become common to interpret the ZPD as a "scaffolding" of the child (e.g., Rogoff & Wertsch 1984): The child has certain abilities that she can carry out independently, but, when scaffolded by the adult or more capable peers, the child can do better than that. Philosopher Fred Newman and developmental psychologist Lois Holzman (1997) disagree with this interpretation and suggest an unconventional reading of Vygotsky. They find it more accurate to describe the ZPD as "an historical performance space or stage than a societal scaffold. In the ZPD, children perform 'a head taller than they are,'" which means that "human beings become who we 'are' by continuously 'being who we are not'" (Newman & Holzman 1997, p. 110). Newman and Holzman's version presents the child as a becoming in the ZPD, as a creature in progress through its immersion in a space of flow with other humans and things. This description better captures the motion Vygotsky implied with the notion of ZPD, which is contrary to the quite structurally immutable imaginary of the scaffold.

Furthermore, the scaffold creates a separation between the knowledgeable child and the scaffold. The knowledge created with the virtual environment did not speak about Femtedit or represent it. It lay in the buildings, links, chats, and dialogues, created by and through the environment, or, rather, in the continual mutation of buildings, links, chats, dialogues, and children. The liquid knowledge was this continual mutation. There was no point or place that one could isolate and point to, saying, "There it is, the knowledge." Liquid knowledge was all over, embedded in the socio-material practice; it was becoming.

Conclusion: Knowledge and Learning

We can start thinking about learning after this long odyssey through spaces of knowledge. Learning can be defined minimally as growth in knowledge. Due to the different spatial formations knowledges take, growth must necessarily also take different forms, which are contingent on the space by and through which it is formed. Growth in regional space is an accumulation of elements within a region. Representational knowledge is made up of a region located in the individual that relates to a reference in a region that is beyond the individual. Growth in representational knowledge thus implies an increase in relations between the individual and references "in the world." Accordingly, learning in regional space is an increase in the individual's connectability to references beyond the regional boundaries of the individual.

This understanding of representational knowledge as emerging out of the relation between dispersed references and as circulating around humans differs from Latour's (1999b) description of knowledge as emerging out of circulating references: samples, researchers, diagrams, maps, and reports circulate, and through this circulation knowledge becomes more and more true. We need to keep in mind the difference between the scientific knowledge that Latour discusses and the representational knowledge that is appropriated by pupils in schools: scientific knowledge is new in the sense that it is not yet established, whereas representational knowledge is already established and only new to the pupils. Scientific knowledge has to circulate in order to become known (and thus to become knowledge), as was the case for Boyle's experimental knowledge. Contrary to this, the references that are part of making representational school knowledge are already in place, and the effort needed to complete this knowledge is that of connecting people to these references.

Communal learning is an extension of relations in resonance space. Learning happens every time a new human or nonhuman participant is attached to the resonance. An effect of the growth of this resonance is that the communal knowledge becomes more and more a matter of course; it becomes more and more robust, more and more true (Latour 1999b). Communal learning cannot be reduced to an individual level. The extension of the resonance affects each participant in the space, and each participant then partakes in the more and more robust knowledge.

Liquid knowledge is inseparable from learning. Representational knowledge can be stagnant. It is not dependent on learning taking place, and it is indifferent to whether or not learning takes place. Communal knowledge can endure without learning, but, when learning happens, the communal knowledge is affected. The ongoing mutation that characterizes liquid knowledge is the epitome of learning. Liquid knowledge cannot exist without a gradual, ongoing mutation of knowledge, which we may – even though this is a genuinely alien concept to fluid space – conceptualize as "growth," simply because it does not stop. Fluid growth cannot be expressed in quantitative measures, but must be understood in terms of the changes taking place, in other words, how it is different from what it was before. As was the case for communal learning, fluid learning does not belong to the human individual; instead, each participant is affected by mutation of the space, not in terms of "more or less" but "qualitatively" in terms of differences.

Just as we have been talking about forms of technology and forms of knowledge, we must talk about forms of learning. Each different form of learning is contingent on a form of knowledge. Growth in representational knowledge is an accumulative form of learning, growth in communal knowledge is an extension form of learning, and growth in liquid knowledge is a mutation form of learning. Characterizing learning like this places us between and at the same time entirely beyond the disputes between rationalist and empiricist learning philosophy on the one hand and situated learning theory on the other. The proponents of the latter refuse to believe that knowledge is individual. The proponents of the former reject an understanding of forms of knowledge as socio-materially emergent. Analyzing learning as performed spatially shows us that being situated in practice and in the mind is in no way contradictory. Learning is individual if it is performed as such. But whether learning is accumulative or different can be established only through empirical analysis of particular spatial formations. Learning is performed through socio-material assemblages, and if the assemblage making up learning shapes it as in the mind, then the form and ontology of that learning, of that growth in knowledge, is in the mind. But as we have seen there are other forms. Forms of knowledge and forms of learning are multiple.

We need to add a specification to the conceptualizing of the knowledge aspect of learning in terms of growth in knowledge. "Growth" is a descriptive notion, not a normative, and learning is necessarily normative. Learning is a certain, desired growth, and not every growth in knowledge can be characterized as learning. Again, the criteria for desired growth, for learning, and for the methods for assessing learning necessarily differ from one spatial formation to the other. Each has different criteria for how to evaluate learning, that is, for how to identify whether learning has taken place and how much has been achieved or how well it was achieved. Representational knowledge that finds no points of connection beyond the classroom or computer lab has no validity. Such knowledge is radical individual. When the teacher from St. Marc Street School complained about Femtedit's lack of resemblance, she also mentioned that she would have preferred that the children build a virtual Viking village. The representational knowledge thus produced would have had widespread connection points, and thus high validity. History book pictures would have been represented in the virtual world, the open-air museum south of Copenhagen, which features a reconstructed Viking village, could have been visited. As I have shown in the analyses of the classroom and virtual environment, communal and liquid knowledge also imply extended patterns of relations among a large number of components. The validity of learning has less to do with whether and to what extent it establishes connections between the school and beyond, and more to do with how these connections are arranged.

Whether the extension of relations and inclusion of more components in communal knowledge can be characterized as learning depends on the level of consensus in the resonance. Communal knowledge is not valid and does not create learning if the people and things included in the resonance do not contribute to a closure of the knowledge. The participants need to stick together. If accounts or stories diverge too much or contradict one another, or if they start disregarding the object of concern (a bed-loft, for instance), then the communal knowledge looses its center and its closure, and thus its validity.

John Langshaw Austin's (1962) discussion of the difference between constatives and performatives may help us understand the criteria for evaluating different forms of knowledge. We may approach constatives in a way that is analogous to representational knowledge and performatives as

Table 5. *Forms of knowledge and learning.*

	Communal Knowledge	Representational Knowledge	Liquid Knowledge
Form of Learning	Extension of relations and inclusion of more participants	Accumulation of individual's ability to connect to references "in the world"	Continuous gradual mutation
Validation Criteria	Consensus	Truth	Felicitousness
Validation Method	Witnessing	Testing	Withnessing

similar to liquid knowledge. Like constatives, representational knowledge can be true or false, and it can be verified. Representations can be compared to references, which again can be compared to other references and representations, following, for instance, the method of triangulation. The different references and representations have to correspond to one another, and if they do, the representational knowledge can be identified as true.

On the other hand, liquid knowledge, like performatives, cannot be evaluated on the axis of truth and fallacy. It cannot be verified. However, it can or cannot be felicitous. Whether liquid knowledge succeeds depends on the current fluid formation, on whether the exchange of parts and the ongoing mutation allow a desired change to happen. It makes no sense to talk about whether or not what was created with the virtual environment was true. "Truth" is a concept that belongs to representational knowledge and the logic of regional patterns of relations. (See Table 5.)

In addition to the diverging validation criteria, we may identify different validation methods for each of the three spatial formations of knowledge discussed. Witnessing is not only a way of producing communal knowledge; it is at the same time the method for evaluating communal learning. Because communal learning depends on the particular interaction, communication, and collaboration of a resonance space, it is not possible to test or measure its validity in a standardized way. By witnessing communal knowledge, it is possible to assess whether it has kept its center and whether the relations among participants are intact or dissolving.

Representational learning, on the other hand, can be validated through tests that check the relations between individual and reference. The regional arrangement of representational knowledge makes it easy to test children's knowledge, and it makes it relatively easy for future employers and institutions of further education to differentiate between proficient and incompetent candidates. Whether it is possible to find connection points between these candidates and their representational knowledge and the task to be solved in the company is another question. Tests are easy measures to compare individuals' representational knowledge, but this does not necessarily mean that the tests are relevant measures.

Liquid learning provides us with a quite different scenario. As I described, Thrift (2000) wanted to honor his late father but refused to let an obituary colonize him. He continues: "We need a form of writing that can disclose and value his legacy – the somatic currency of body stances he passed on, the small sayings and large generosities, and, in general, his stance to the world – in such a way as to make it less important for him to be written" (p. 213). Thrift's solution is to disclose the *somatic currency* of his father, which, as discussed, could not be done through representation. In the article Thrift does not mention his father again after the first one and a half pages. His father stays in the text but as a ghost. We cannot evaluate whether his somatic currency is disclosed in the text, but I believe it is. I believe Thrift has done what he could to continue the "small sayings and large generosities," as well as other experiences of his father, in the text. With reference to Despret (2004b) I will call this *withness*, as a contrast to witnessing, and refer to this as the way of validating liquid learning. Whereas witnessing requires distance from the object that is witnessed, withnessing implies staying with the liquid knowledge in a way that discloses the somatic currency of this knowledge without making it a distant object. The way to evaluate – and at the same time cultivate – liquid learning in school is to participate carefully in the socio-material knowledge and contribute to its continuous gradual mutation, that is, to disclose its somatic currency.

Through empirical analyses of different spatial formations of knowledge, in this chapter I have shown that different materials contribute – due to their achieved materiality – to performing different spaces, and each gives rise to a different form of knowledge, a different form of learning, and a different validation method, as well as different criteria for validating learning. The conclusion to this discussion is simple: Due to the expanded and contingent effect of learning materials, it is no surprise that implementation of new learning materials in school so often fails to meet the criteria for learning set in advance. Learning criteria change with the learning material, and if we want to work constructively with learning materials, we must thus stop beginning our study with learning criteria and stop hanging on to the same criteria throughout the process of implementing new learning materials. Approaching learning materials spatially provides us with a much more subtle understanding of the potentially widespread consequences of implementing new learning materials with respect to the form of knowledge performed, the effect these materials have on pupils' eventual transition to the workplace or to higher education, and the interrelations among school and beyond. And it gives us a chance to understand how much of adjustment is required in order to completely integrate a learning material.

The Methodology of the Materiality of Learning
Lesson 4: Knowledge

I have discussed materiality and spatiality, and I can now start approaching learning. I have defined learning as growth in knowledge. Approaching learning as such has been heavily criticized on the basis of the argument that there is much more to knowledge than simply the accumulation of information. Indeed there is: My spatial analyses of knowledge have suggested that knowledge may take several forms, and, in each form, growth is different. What knowledge is, what growth is, and what learning is must be determined empirically. To do so, we must approach knowledge spatially, studying the patterns in which the variety of human and nonhuman participants relate. And we must describe the forms that knowledge takes in these patterns. This approach has much in common with the situated learning approach. It takes a practice approach to learning in which learning and knowledge are inseparable from practice. But instead of studying practice in place and time, the spatial approach studies the spatiality and temporality of practice. This allows us to take into account how materials contribute to the formation of practice, and thus to the formation of knowledge – how, for instance, the materials that represent are crucial for performing representational knowledge. Through this understanding of the materiality of knowledge, I have come to appreciate the rationalist and empiricist description of knowledge in the mind. I have discovered that there are patterns in which knowledge is performed that take the form of knowledge in the mind. Contrary to these approaches, however, I take this to be an empirically emerging ontology of knowledge. Representational knowledge is one ontology among many; I have also described two other ontologies: communal knowledge and liquid knowledge. Communal knowledge spreads with the extension of the resonance space, and liquid knowledge is an ongoing process of mutation of parts and relations. None of these latter two forms of knowledge perform boundaries between the human individual and other participants of the space. Thus, the knowledge of these spaces is not individual. Being individual does not mean that representational knowledge is isolated in the mind. On the contrary, this form of knowledge, like the others, is spatially formed and exists as that particular form of knowledge only because and as long as the space through which it is performed is upheld.

Approaching learning spatially as growth in knowledge and thus understanding how materials are involved in performing different forms of learning teaches us how changes in learning material can have wide-reaching consequences. A learning material contributes to performing a certain space, which gives rise to a certain form of knowledge, a certain form of learning, and a certain validation method, as well as certain criteria for validating learning. By following the spatial analyses of the learning that arises with different learning materials, we understand that each has implications beyond the learning situation and beyond the school. When digital technology is implemented in schools, it is usually expected to enhance the production of a certain form of learning, which is known from and performed by and through other learning materials. Having learned that the criteria for validating learning changes with the learning materials, it is thus no surprise that such technology fails to deliver the expected learning effects. When implementing new technology, we must decenter from the question of what we want to achieve with this technology. We should ask how this technology may change learning, what form of knowledge it may contribute to performing, what the methods of validation will be, and, by the end, what are the criteria?

5   Forms of Presence

Whereas we usually accept straightaway that knowledge has to do with learning – even though the discussion of how knowledge and learning are related is an issue of concern – the question of the relation between presence and learning more often needs to be explicated. Lave and Wenger (1991) note that cognitive approaches promote a non-personal understanding of learning as universal mechanisms of acquisition and assimilation. On the basis of their theory of situated learning, Lave and Wenger emphasize that learning always takes place as activity by specific people in specific circumstances. Like Lave and Wenger, Dreier points to the fact that most approaches to learning view learning on par with teaching and overlook thereby that these imply two entirely different perspectives on learning and that understanding the former requires that we take the learner's perspective into account. Dreier emphasizes the *first-person perspective* (1993, 2008) and defines learning as changes in personal participation in social contexts (Dreier 1999). The person in Dreier's theory is not an isolated individual, but is embedded in social practice. I have in the previous chapters been careful not to approach socio-material arrangements from a humanist perspective that a priori defines humans as actors and things and structures and other nonhuman entities as passive tools or constrains for action. This chapter does not diverge from this perspective, but we focus on the human in our analysis and ask how humans are enacted in the spatial arrangements. We may come to the conclusion that humans are central actors, but from the outset of the analysis we are receptive to the possibility that humans take different forms. By the end of the chapter I return to a discussion of Dreier's definition of learning and of how we, with the goal of understanding the materiality of learning, can deal with humans in spatial arrangements.

Before beginning these more fundamental discussions, the chapter investigates human participants in socio-material practices in the classroom and with the online 3D virtual environment. Like in the previous chapters, it focuses on interactions and asks how the presence of the participating humans is performed in socio-material interactions. Goffman (1959) introduces his *The Presentation of Self in Everyday Life* by discussing the sources of information about a person that people draw on when interacting with him. Many of these lie beyond the immediate interaction, but during the period in which the individuals are in the immediate presence of others, they will have to rely widely on the expressions given and impressions shaped as part of the interaction. Goffman investigates how people present themselves and how this presentation is inferred by others in interaction. He emphasizes the interaction as the entity in which the presentation is composed through performance and inference. Like Goffman, my focus of analysis is the interaction, and broadly I share Goffman's interest in question of how people come to be through interaction. Whereas Goffman focuses on how the individual presents himself and how *presentations* are perceived by the individual members of the audience, I turn to *presence* as a term that refers to the spatial arrangement of social and material entities through which certain ways of participating are made available. As discussed in Chapter 3, this spatial term turns our focus from the entities – in this case humans – relating in practice to the pattern of relations of a practice through which humans are performed. Whereas Goffman investigates how people present themselves in interaction with audiences on the basis of a given ontology of humans as beings of presented selves, I study how the ontology of humans comes to be with the world.

Another – related – difference between Goffman's approach and discussions of subjectivities in educational literature, on the one hand, and the discussions presented in this chapter, on the other, is the emphasis on materials and how these contribute to performing presences. Many authors have been absorbed by discussions of the ways in which computers and Internet may influence our selves and our identities. Turkle (1997) emphasizes that the computer is a new tool for thinking about identity and that the Internet and simulation software are especially useful for playing with the plurality of postmodern identities. My approach to human presence is different. Like Hans Gumbrecht (2004) and other contemporary scholars of the humanities, suggesting the notion of presence is an attempt to reach beyond meaning, beyond interpretation. Analyzing in terms of presence makes it possible to engage in the way in which humans are with materials, contrary to how humans make sense of materials – or how they make sense of themselves with the help of materials. This chapter does not deal with how humans may come to think about or understand themselves differently through interaction with computers. I ask about the materialities of humans and about the ways in which humans come to connect to other entities – technical, non-technical, human, or nonhuman – due to the involvement of the particular materials taking part in practice. As I have argued previously, technology should be studied with its social aspects. Likewise, humans should be studied with their technological or material aspects, as a result of socio-material practice. Thus, studying human presence is just as much about studying socio-material assemblages as were the studies of forms of technology and of forms of knowledge. The only difference is that now human presence is in focus as the performative effect of these assemblages. Socio-material practices are multiple, I have argued. Thus, understanding presence as an effect of socio-material practices implies that, as practices vary, so do presences. The focus of this chapter is to describe how different learning materials contribute to performing different forms of presence.

Whereas in Chapter 4 I named the forms of knowledge "liquid," "communal," and "representational" without any conceptual reference to other theorists of knowledge, I apply in this chapter the notions of subject (*Althusser*), collective (*Asplund*), and agent (*Giddens*), which are widely used terms concerning human presence. Each of these refers to a different macro-theoretical description of human beings, and their application may thus seem contradictory to my micro-analytical approach. My application of these terms refers not to the three different theoretical constructions, but to the pattern of relations each of these notions implies, which is indifferent to whether we deal with levels of micro or macro analyses. Another important difference between the three authors' applications of these concepts and mine is that I take each of them to be forms of presence that are performed in interaction and that may change from moment to moment, and I do not – as the fathers of these notions do – see them as explaining general (more or less historical) ontologies of human beings. With these reservations I apply these notions not only to depict the characteristics of the forms of presence I discuss, but also to clarify the differences among them.

Presence became of interest as I observed the teachers being restless in the computer lab. Because they did not seem restless in the classroom, this led me to question what made them restless while working with the virtual environment. We will attempt to solve this puzzle in this chapter through a comparison between presences constituted in the classroom and presences emerging with the virtual environment. Even though it is the teachers' presence I am investigating, we need to decenter from the teachers and look at the patterns in which materials and humans were related in the classroom. Because the teachers' and the pupils' forms of presence were co-constructed, I discuss not only the teachers' presence but also the presence of the pupils.

Blackboard and Songs, Regions and Collectives

We start with a field note excerpt from a lesson on the Danish language in the fourth-grade class at St. Marc Street School. I was seated in the back of the classroom with a notebook on my lap and a pencil in my hand. The teacher had arrived a few minutes beforehand, assisted by a teacher from the neighboring class, each carrying a pile of dictionaries.

> The dictionaries are distributed while the teacher explains that today they are going to learn how to use a dictionary. A necessary qualification for using a dictionary, she adds, is being familiar with the alphabet. "Let's sing the alphabet song," the teacher says, and picks up the chalk pencil from her desk. She turns to the blackboard and raises her hand with the chalk to the blackboard. With her body facing the blackboard, she turns her face toward the class and asks, "Are you ready?" This makes me curious. Ready for what? Everyone apparently knows what is going to happen. Except for me. The teacher takes a deep demonstrative breath and starts the song: "A, B, C, D . . ." Already at "A" the children join in and, with their eyes fixed on the blackboard, they sing the song out loud and clear. On the blackboard the teacher writes the letters one-by-one as they are mentioned in the song. It doesn't look easy to keep up with the pace of the song. By the end of the song the twenty-eight letters of the Danish alphabet are on the blackboard. The teacher turns around and, facing the pupils, she says with a smile: "I made it." (Field note 2509_40)

All pupils were seated at their desks. The teacher was at the blackboard, writing. The pupils were carefully watching the teacher's writing. Or, more precisely, they were watching the letters appear on the blackboard. The visual materiality of the letters appearing on the blackboard consti-tuted a geographic place to which each child's gaze was fixed. Vicky O'Day and colleagues (1998) note that the blackboard (or whiteboard, in their study) works as a "focusing feature." This was the case in the fourth-grade classroom as well not only because the letters had a visual materiality, but also because they were emerging in the very situation: They were at risk. The whole assemblage was a game in which the teacher, to the amusement of the pupils, put at risk her ability to write the letters at the same pace as they were mentioned in the song. The possibility of the teacher failing made the children carefully monitor the letters appearing on the blackboard.

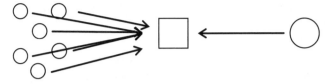

Figure 6. A depiction of children paying attention to the emerging letters on the blackboard that the teacher is writing.

Figure 6 is an attempt to sketch the assemblage of children (o), letters on the blackboard (□) and the teacher (O).[1] The letters on the blackboard were the center of attention. The teacher and the emerging visual materiality of the letters she was writing on the blackboard co-constituted one single and central geographic place to which the pupils' attention was drawn. The pupils were all seated. Due to the layout of the desks in the classroom, their gazes were easily directed toward the blackboard. This geographic place positioned the teacher opposite the pupils, with the teacher writing letters on the blackboard at one side and the pupils' gazes on the other. It was a *one-to-many relationship*: one teacher opposite many pupils. I return to this arrangement in the following discussion and discuss the forms of presence performed by and through it.

To emphasize the point that the visual materiality of the letters emerging on the blackboard was involved in constituting this one-to-many relationship, I contrast the occurrence with other occurrences of singing that I witnessed in the classroom, in which the visual blackboard was not involved. Here is a video transcript of one of them:

> It is the last lesson on the timetable. The class has been working with the exercise books. All pupils are seated at their desks. Standing at the blackboard, the teacher has told the pupils to pack their things, and she has said that she wants the class to sing a song when finished packing. Two minutes later, all desks are cleared, chairs are pushed under the desks, and the pupils are standing behind their chairs with their backpacks on their backs.
>
> The teacher's voice is heard again: "You need to put the desks back in place." Desks are pushed in place, while the teacher continues: "I badly need to hear some beautiful . . . some really beautiful song . . . Quiet!! . . .

---

[1] Representing humans with circles and materials with a square may be misleading, reproducing a stereotypical Western symbolism. It runs the risk of oversimplification and reduction caused by representing a complex activity with such a basic figure. However, I here need to appeal to the goodwill of the reader to read this figure as a partial element for discussing the pattern of relations rather than seeing it as attempting to accurately correspond to the activity discussed.

Pete!! . . . I dream about us being able to remember one of those we learned down at . . . eh . . ."

"Greenland," a pupil suggests.

"No, not that one, not the one from Greenland, the one down from . . . eh . . . Bulgaria." Several children suggest songs. "Which one do you say?" One child repeats the name [inaudible]. "Yes, that one!! Should we sing that one?" Children start chatting. The teacher says in high voice, "Let's try . . . hush-hush . . . remember [inaudible] . . . one, two, three . . ."

The teacher and pupils start singing. The pupils' bodies are swinging from side to side. Some put their hands on the backrests of the chairs, some have turned around and are leaning on the backs of the chairs, while others have stepped back from the chairs and stand in the open room. Keeping their feet in place, most of them swing their upper bodies slightly from side to side. Their faces move slowly from one side to the other. Gazes travel from face to face. Several times a child smiles when his or her eyes meet those of another child.

"Well done!!" the teacher says once the song is over. "Have a safe trip home, and don't forget the textbook tomorrow." Pupils start chatting while moving toward the door that has already been opened. (Video transcript 2510_2_37–40)

It is the singing that interests me – the way pupils' bodies swayed and the way their faces turned to look around the classroom. Calmly, pupils let their gazes travel and made eye contact with one another. The relations among them were constituted through the common singing and through letting their eyes and bodies meet. Sometimes, the mutuality was emphasized with a smile. Whereas the video highlights the visible bodies, it is important also to note the ubiquitous character of the sounds of the song. The song was present in the muscles and bodily vibrations involved in producing the song, and at the same time it filled the room and was everywhere between the four walls of the classroom. Looking at the bodily movements, we note that the pupils' visual attention followed the ubiquity of the sounds, letting their gazes travel around in the classroom. The ubiquitous sounds of the song, the continuously traveling gazes, the eye contact, and the smiles performed connections among pupils. They drew the singing together. By mutually drawing one another together, the song, traveling gazes, eye contact, swaying bodies, and smiles performed a *collective*.

Sociologist Johan Asplund (1985) defines the collective as a social formation of the medieval peasant society in which collectives and collective beings were characterized by being immersed in the present without any expectation of progress or change. A collective was directed toward itself, not toward something apart from it in either time or space. As a member of a collective, people shared their life and activities with others. They were not feathering their own nests – as is the case in the collective's counterpart, the individual – because no nest was isolated from the collective. There was no clear boundary between the one and the collective, and hence no individual stood out from the crowd. Not that there were no criminals, witches, and other "Others." Indeed, there were, but these were part of the collective (as Foucault [1979] also emphasizes). Criminals were collectively punished because crime was neither a personal business nor a business between a person and the authority; it was everybody's business. Everyone was mutually related in a collective. Inspired by the patterns of relation that the description of the collective depicts, I bracket the understanding of the collective as associated with a specific historical period. The mutuality of the gazes and swinging bodies created a form of presence in which humans were directed toward one another and the song. There was no external focal place, no goal or target to which the activity was headed. There was only the song and the bodies and gazes continuously performing mutuality among humans. It was here and now, and in this moment all humans were part of the song. The pupils were not acting differently nor was anyone standing out among the rest. They were connected collectively through the song.

We are all familiar with the ability of songs to contribute to performing collectives: from family gatherings and parties to religious ceremonies and national celebrations. Songs can indeed be crucial glue in sticking humans together in collectives. Returning to the occurrence in which the letters emerged on the blackboard, we notice that no collective was formed. The letters appearing on the blackboard absorbed the visual attention of the pupils and directed all gazes toward the same geographical place. Hence, children's gazes were parallel and directed toward an external place, contrary to their gazes and bodies during the Bulgarian song, which confronted one another. During the alphabet song the bodies and gazes of the pupils did not confront one another. They all confronted a geographical place in which the teacher was positioned opposite the pupils. Furthermore, the pupils were related to the emerging letters not only through their gazes but also through their voices and the song, whose rhythm matched that of the emerging letters on the blackboard. Due to the coordination of the rhythm of the song and the emerging letters on the blackboard, a rather strong one-to-many relationship was performed in which several elements were precisely calibrated to contribute to the same pattern of relations. Whereas I have already characterized the form of presence during the Bulgarian song as a collective, I hesitate to charac-terize the presence during the alphabet song. Before I return to this, we need to discuss this complex pattern of relations in more detail.

Through these two examples we learn how a one-to-many relationship and a collective were performed differently in the classroom. With and without the visual materiality of emerging letters on the blackboard, different interpersonal relations were performed. From focusing on the relationship among persons, I turn to focus on how *separations* were per-formed in the first but not in the latter. The occurrence with the Bulgarian song performed one gathered pattern without any internal separations. A pattern was formed that was held in shape by the mutuality of all par-ticipating elements. The occurrence with the emerging letters on the blackboard performed an assemblage with an internal separation: the writing teacher at the blackboard was separated from the singing and reading pupils. At the blackboard the teacher was writing and actively trying to keep up with the pace of the song, while, apart from her, the pupils were reading the emerging letters and reacting to whether or not she kept up the pace. As I have visualized in Figure 6, the teacher and children were placed on either side of the letters on the blackboard, whereas in the other example the pupils and the teacher were all within the Bulgarian song. The pattern of relations performed with the emerging letters on the blackboard created a central place at the blackboard and also a place from which this place was observed. Two separate regions were performed, one with the teacher and one with the pupils.

Regional Presence in the Classroom

A regional pattern of relations was performed that had two regions: one in which the teacher was writing and actively trying to keep up with the pace of the song and one in which the pupils were reading and reacting to the teacher's writing. During my classroom observations and especially when trying to describe and characterize the materials in the classroom, the blackboard appeared to me to be a pivotal material of the classroom. I realized, as I discuss in the following, that the blackboard was a regional technology. Or to put it more precisely: It was a technology that in its specific form in the classroom setting contributed to performing regional patterns of relations.

The blackboard contributed to creating a place in the classroom to which attention was drawn, as illustrated previously in the description of the emerging letters. The blackboard was a pivotal material in the performing of attention in the classroom because it took up a large part of the visual field of all pupils, seeing as their desks all faced it. This was not particular to when the alphabet song was sung. In almost all lessons I attended at St. Marc Street School, the blackboard played this role. At times the teacher put carefully prepared texts and images on the blackboard. At other times the teacher wrote words and signs on the blackboard to support her explanations of different spellings. One put numbers on the blackboard to make everyone focus on a specific calculation, and another drew a map to help children formulate sentences in English about directions and locations. During all these occurrences nearly all pupils' attention was directed toward the blackboard.

The pattern of relations depicted in Figure 6 was recurrently performed in the classroom, with the blackboard as the material involved in gathering attention at one geographic place. It created a place separate from the pupils to which attention could be directed. When the class sang the Bulgarian song, the materiality to which the pupils' attention was directed – the song – was not clearly delimited from the pupils. It was inside and among them. Contrary to this, the blackboard clearly established a place outside the children, whereby a "here" and "there" was established – a geographical "here" and "there." Here was the blackboard, there were the pupils (or vice versa). Not only was a geographical place performed at the blackboard, but through this a geographical "counter" place was performed opposite to the blackboard, from which the children could attend to the blackboard.

There were also words ("orientational metaphors" as Lakoff and Johnson [1980] call them) involved in performing these two places. "Laila, please come up to the blackboard," the teacher could say, and when the pupil had done what she was asked to at the blackboard she would be asked to "go down to your seat." There were two distinct places – "up here" at the blackboard and "down there" by the pupils. As clearly delimited places separate from each other, they contributed to performing a regional space. Two regions were performed by and through the assemblage around the blackboard.

While the blackboard anchored the pupils' gazes to its visual region, the lines of attention also separated pupils and the blackboard. Pupils were "here" attending to the blackboard "there." The lines of attention created a distance between pupils and blackboard. Pupils were connected to the blackboard, which was however distant and separate from them. The Bulgarian song was not distant from the pupils and hence did not have the ability to draw the pupils' attention to one single place. The Bulgarian song was ubiquitously among the children. It did not create any "here" and "there," any distances, any separations. The assemblage involving the visual materiality on the blackboard created distance and separations between the region of the blackboard and the region of the pupils. I characterize this separation further in the following text.

Meanwhile I take a closer look at each region. The blackboard region was the teachers' home. This was especially noticeable when those not "at home" in this region visited it. Even though the teachers were the most frequent writers on the blackboard, they were not the only ones. Sometimes, a pupil was called to the blackboard, which however did not necessarily mean she was going to write on the blackboard. "Going up to the blackboard" meant going to the area of the blackboard, not necessarily to write on the blackboard, as the following field note exemplifies:

> It is the library lesson in which pupils can either go to the school library to take out books, stay in the classroom and read, or write book reviews either at their desks or in the computer lab. When a book is finished, a review has to be written. After half an hour in which some pupils have been in the library, others have gone to the computer lab, and some have stayed in the classroom, all pupils and the teacher are again gathered in the classroom. The teacher has corrected a few book reviews, which she holds in her hand. Standing in front of the blackboard, she asks: "Who would like to read their review out loud"? Three children raise their hands. Johanna is one of them. "Johanna, please come up," the teacher says. Johanna goes to the blackboard. While seated, the teacher hands Johanna her review, saying loudly: "Johanna liked this book very much, so pay close attention. Maybe others might want to read it."
>
> Johanna has taken the review out of the plastic folder. She stands next to the seated teacher, in front of the blackboard, facing the rest of the class. She reads the review. When finished, the teacher says, "Very good, Johanna," and the pupils applaud. (Field note 2910_86)

By moving her body from the pupils' region to the blackboard to read a text out loud, Johanna's voice gained all the pupils' attention in quite the same way as did writing on the blackboard. It happened often that a pupil's presentation at the blackboard was followed by applause. This never happened as a reaction to a presentation given from a pupil's desk. The different reactions to similar presentations at different places contribute to performing a boundary between the region of the pupils and the region of the blackboard.

Even though pupils could cross the boundary to the blackboard region, they were clearly "guests" there: They only entered this region when they were explicitly permitted access. Teachers were mistresses of the black-board region, and they were the ones who regulated who could enter the region and when. Applause frequently followed pupils' presentations at the blackboard. Teachers were never applauded. They were not guests; they were at home. Consequently, what they did in the blackboard region was ordinary, whereas what the pupils did there was extraordinary. Indeed, the ordinary presence of the teacher was at the blackboard, whereas the pupils' ordinary presence was in the region of the rest of the classroom.

As the latter field note indicates, the blackboard region was not limited to the activity of writing on the blackboard. It was an area around the blackboard that had a particular identity in contrast to the region of the rest of the classroom. But writing was a crucial activity associated with the blackboard, and this writing was much more frequently done by the teacher than by the pupils. Teachers had chalk pencils with their names engraved on them. These pencils protected the skin of their fingers from drying out as a consequence of holding the chalk for so many hours every day. And the chalk pencils contributed to performing the difference between teachers and pupils. No pupil had chalk pencils. Because they rarely wrote on the blackboard, they had no need for a chalk pencil.

The blackboard region and the region of the pupils were separated by a boundary. The boundary separated the teacher from the pupils and created two distinct regions with different rules of conduct. There were, moreover, different norms for how long anyone would stay in the region. The pupils as well as the teacher always stayed only briefly in the "Other" region, as if a rubber band was attached to them, always pulling them back to their "own" region. While fast-forwarding the videotape from my classroom observations I realized that the teacher always went down to one, two, or three pupils to talk to them individually when they were working on their own with the exercise books. Then she walked back to the blackboard, stood there for a while, returned to talk to one or two pupils, and went back to the blackboard again. Sometimes she would write notes on the blackboard to remind herself of things to be explained later, but most often she would just stand next to the blackboard for a minute or two before she went "down" again to another pupil.

Even though the "inhabitants" of one region could visit the other, they were clearly performed as outsiders there. Each region was different from the other, and each region was homogeneous; that is, each region consisted of either the teacher or the pupils. The boundary, the distance between the regions, and the homogeneity of each region allowed the one-to-many relationship. Only as long as the pupils were all "the same" could the teacher instruct all of them at the same time, as one. She could teach in a broadcasting mode because of the performance of homogeneous regions separated by a boundary.

Authority and Subjects

Writing on the blackboard created a visual field that attracted the attention of pupils to what was happening on it. As described, the blackboard let the teacher hold all pupils' gazes – the whole class – in her hand, much like a puppeteer controls his puppets with slight wrist movements, or like a child controls her avatar in an online 3D virtual environment, as we see later. The geographical place at the blackboard, the distance, and the boundary that performed two regions made available a one-to-many relationship in which the teacher held the class in her hand; similarly, these elements also performed a broadcasting mode of interaction. By understanding authority as a superior power to influence or command the thoughts or acts of others, we can describe the blackboard as contributing to performing the teacher's presence as that of an authority vis-à-vis the pupils.

This relationship was further reinforced by the fact that what was written on the blackboard could be seen and witnessed by all pupils at the same time. This made it important:

> *T*: David, will you read out your speech for us?
> *D*: I didn't know I had to bring it
> *T*: But it was written on the blackboard! (Field note 2509_53)

The writing on the blackboard was official and could be referred to as such. Contradicting the statement about what was written on the blackboard meant turning against the perception of everyone else in the class. Through the blackboard and the arrangement in parallel directing all children's gazes toward the blackboard, the teacher was allied with all of the pupils' perceptions. Contradicting the statement implied not only contradicting the teacher but contradicting the whole arrangement of the interaction. Due to the blackboard, the alliance between the teacher and the pupils' perceptions contributed to performing the teacher's presence as an authority. The region of the blackboard was saturated with authority, with drawing attention to what was said and done, and to the individual who said and did. In the region of the rest of the classroom, it was possible to say and do a lot without anyone paying particular attention to it, without it gaining authority.

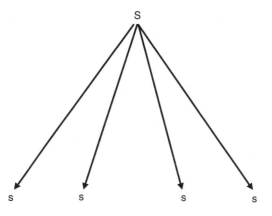

Figure 7. Højrup's depiction of interpellation of the subject (s) by the state Subject (S). (Based on: Højrup 2003, figure 24a, p. 162)

The previous discussion attempts to isolate the teacher's form of presence from that of the pupils. This has clearly not been entirely possible because the presence of the teacher and the presence of the pupils are co-produced, just as one region is co-produced with the other. The pattern of relation implied by Marxist philosopher Louis Althusser's (1971) notion of *interpellation* helps us understand this. Althusser discusses how ideology works to reproduce state power. The subject, he explains, comes into being through interpellation. Interpellation happens in moments when we recognize ourselves because we have been addressed, called out to: "Hey, you there!!" someone calls, and the hailed individual turns around: "By this mere one-hundred-and-eighty-degree physical conversion, he becomes a *subject*" (p. 163). When confronted with an authority – this may very well be a teacher – we become subjects because we are subjected to a state Subject with a capital *S*. Figure 7 is a reproduction of how ethnologist Thomas Højrup (2003, p. 162) depicts Althusser's relationship between the subject and the state Subject. Apart from the emerging letters in the center of Figure 6, Højrup's figure is similar to the way I have depicted the relations between the pupils and the teacher in the example of the emerging letters. Both have to do with a one-to-many relationship. Højrup's figure is however upright, with the state Subject on the top, which depicts well the region of the state Subject as "up there" and the subjects' (e.g., pupils') region as "down there." Althusser's notion of interpellation describes a pattern of two opposite and confronting forms of presence of authority and subjects. I follow this imaginary, referring to the pupils' form of presence as that of *subjects* in the alphabet song example and during

Johanna's presentation – in both situations they were interpellated as such by the teacher, the authority.

I would like to apply Althusser's discussion of the subject-authority relationship to draw attention to three crucial points about this form of presence. The first point concerns materiality. As is apparent in Højrup's illustration in Figure 7, Althusser does not involve any nonhuman materials in the direct interaction between the subject and the Subject. The interaction described consists of two individuals, the hailing, the turning, and the recognition. Althusser (1971) however clarifies that the interpellation is done not by a person but by an ideology, which "always exists in an apparatus, and its practice, or practices. This existence is material" (p. 156). Retaining the notion of materiality and the material basis of ideology on this highly abstract level, Althusser describes the emergence of subjects through interpellation by an authority as a generalized phenomenon. If we however turn to an analysis of the particular, detailed patterns of relations, as I have done, we realize that quite specific spatial – regional – arrangements of humans and nonhumans have to be in place in order for subjects and authority to be enacted.

Though founded on very different theories than Althusser's, social psychology has produced much literature on authority. One of the most quoted is T. W. Adorno and colleagues' *The Authoritarian Personality* (Adorno et al. 1950), which argues that authority is exercised due to a specific personality developed through early childhood. The work is still popular and standard content of social psychology textbooks. It is however also challenged. Cultural approaches see authority as a product of an authoritarian culture, whereas cognitive approaches have pointed to the human's limited information-processing abilities as the source for authority (Sabini 1992, p. 126*ff.*). Even though they diverge, these schools of thought share the implicit understanding that authority is located in the individual – either formed in early childhood, influenced by culture, or due to cognitive abilities. In discussing the nature of social psychology, Asplund (1985) notes about *The Authoritarian Personality* that rarely has such an untenable work had such an influence. His critique of the book as well as of the approaches critical to it is that none of them understand the historically variable qualities of social spaces, and consequently, their explanations are reduced to an individual level. I do appreciate Asplund's emphasis on the social (and hence historically variable) qualities of space, and thus on the emerging quality of authority, but I must on the basis of the previous analyses criticize him, along with Althusser and the general social psychology community, for their tendency to leave out any account of the practical contribution of particular materials in constituting authority.

The second point I'd like to make about the subject-authority relationship concerns the specificity of materials in enacting subjects and authority. In Foucault's (1979) discussion of discipline, he teaches us how the voices of teachers become a signal to which the disciplined bodies of pupils react instinctively. This was not the reality I experienced in the classroom. There was no doubt that the pupils were disciplined to listen to the voices of the teachers differently than to other voices. In addition, panoptic powers were performed when, for instance, one teacher unexpectedly, frequently, and individually reprimanded not only pupils disturbing the lesson but also pupils quietly doing what they were supposed to. This indeed resembled the random punishment crucial to the disciplining powers described by Foucault. We however learn little about the particularity of the materialities in Foucault: could the teacher's voice be replaced by the teacher clapping his hands or snapping his fingers? Are the materials arbitrary, or do they – as I have argued – have different achieved materialities that allow them to relate differently to other materialities, and thus to contribute better or worse to the cultivation of discipline? Through my analyses it has become clear that the materialities are not arbitrary. Not just any material can be formed to work as an instrument for discipline or authority.

Discussing play, Vygotsky (1978) observes that some things can be used as substitutes for "real things" in children's play and some cannot (p. 98*ff*.). The different materialities make different actions and presences available. Vygotsky moreover discusses how drawn figures need to have certain properties in order to be able to stand for specific things like a bucket or a bench when evaluated by children (p. 47*ff*.). Similarly, Thomas Hatch and Howard Gardner (1993) describe how the materiality of sand in a sandbox allows children to play "baking," which they do not play in the drama corner. Especially, they note, the sand is good for "baking" in October. In November the children dig tunnels because then the sand is wet. Just as these different materialities make available different activities and presences, it became clear through my observations in the classroom that the different materialities of the classroom gained different strengths and weakness in regard to attracting children's attention. Although teachers' voices were good at attracting the attention of individual pupils who were busy with something else, the blackboard was far superior when it came to attracting and keeping the whole class' attention, and therefore it was crucial for the performance of the pupils' and teacher's form of presence as subjects and authority.

The second point of discussion in relation to Althusser's notion of interpellation is directly derived from the former. Based on the conclusion that subjects and authority only result out of quite specific spatial arrangements, it follows that other forms of presence are possible, as I have shown. Indeed, forms of presence are multiple. I have discussed three forms of presence, but there is no reason to see these as exhaustive.

The third point concerning interpellation is the reciprocal character of this interaction. Whereas the subject needs recognition from the state Subject to become a subject, the state Subject also needs the subjects. Althusser (1971) describes this in quite abstract terms through the example of God duplicating himself and sending his Son to earth as a subject-Subject because he "needs to 'make himself' a man, the Subject needs to become a subject" (p. 167). As an empirical theorist I am hesitant to accept such abstract speculations. It is however possible through detailed description of classroom interaction to show how the authority is also dependent on the recognition of the subjects. Before closing the discussion of forms of presence in the classroom I turn to look at how the pupils contributed to the teacher's authority even when directed away from the region of the blackboard. Look at these field note excerpts:

> The teacher is going through common errors from this week's dictation. I notice Steven is carefully drilling his pencil into his eraser. He puts the eraser on the desk. The pencil stands like a flagpole in its eraser base. He takes a little ball out of the pencil case and carefully rolls it toward the flagpole. The flagpole sways as it is hit by the ball. Steven looks at Ariane next to him and smiles. He rolls the ball again. This time the flagpole tips over as the ball hits it. With his left hand, which has been lying behind the flagpole this whole time as a shield, he silently saves the pencil from landing with a clack on the desk. He hunches down in his chair, drawing up his shoulders, and smiles at Ariane again, whose eyes flicker quickly between the teacher and Steven's face. (Field note 2509_ 35)

> The English teacher is pointing at a drawing of roads, houses, shops, a school, and a church on the blackboard. He practices prepositions with the children. Just in front of me, in the opposite end of the classroom from the blackboard, Lana carefully tears out the corner of a sheet in the notebook in which she has just been writing. She folds the note gently and puts it under the desks with her hand. She carefully nudges Thomas's knee with her own under the desk. He looks at her. While passing the note to him under the desk, she whispers "Johanna." Thomas takes the note and passes

it to Johanna next to him. Johanna looks stiffly at the blackboard while receiving the note from Thomas, moving the hand with the note casually up from under the desk, opening the note with both hands, and waiting a while until she quickly glances down at the note and back up at the blackboard. Only a moment later Johanna looks at Lana, nods, and looks back at the blackboard. (Field note 2409_25)

The teacher is rehearsing the multiplication tables with the children. One after the other, pupils are asked to recite a multiplication table. Susanna sits next to me. While attending to the teacher and pupils reciting the tables, Susanna opens the hair clip in her hair. She shakes her long hair and puts the clip on the desk. She fumbles a bit with her necklace, lifts it over her chin, and puts it in her mouth. She plays with it a bit with her tongue. Her fingers find the hair clip on the desk and open it. For a while she closes and opens the clip. Then she raises it to her hair again, combs her fingers through her hair a few times, and attaches the clip. She rests her head on her hand while the other hand fumbles with her bracelet. At no time does her gaze deviate from those reciting the multiplication tables. (Field note 2709_85)

Although most of the field note excerpts in this book are related to educational activities in the classroom, there were many other things going on. The previous three field note excerpts show some of what went on apart from the educational activities. Much may be said about such activities, which were taking place all the time, parallel to the educational classroom activities. For instance, I can't help mentioning how I noticed again and again that girls, with their jewelry, long hair, hair clips, and elastics, had available many more materials than boys to keep their hands busy without the teacher noticing and thus many more opportunities to perform docility while at the same time being engaged in extra-educational activities.[2] Apart from the gender issue, it is interesting to note that these alternative activities generally involved materials whose alternative character was invisible (Star & Strauss 1999) in the educational practice. These were mainly either writing utensils or other contents of the pencil case or personal ornaments. Such materials were a legitimate part of the children's presence in the classroom, contrary to, for instance, mobile phones, toys, magazines, or comic books. As legitimate materials of the classroom or personal jewelry, they were inconspicuous and could therefore be involved

---

[2] In her discussion on rebellion and resistance in secondary school, Brenda Simpson (2000) shows similarly how dresses, hair colors, and adornments for boys and girls are available in different ways as a means for resistance.

in activities alternative to the educational activities without being sanctioned. Furthermore, as the excerpts show, pupils exercised these activities
with such skilful caution that they were not noticed by the teacher. As a
parallel alternative, these forms of presence did not confront or challenge
the authority. On the contrary, the cautiousness with which the alternative
activities were exercised contributed to performing the authority of the
teacher. The cautiously hidden character of the activities showed recognition of the authority of the activities the teacher was directing, as this
caution enabled the alternative activities to take place without disturbing
the educational activities. By creating the region of the pupils as alternative, they contributed to performing the authority of the blackboard region. The identity and norms of the pupil's region were performed as
different from the identity and norms of the blackboard region, altogether
confirming the regional pattern of relations. In other words, it is not only
the subject that emerges by recognizing itself as subjected to the state
Subject. The existence of the authority is dependent on the subject's recognition of it as such. And this mutual recognition is dependent on the
socio-material assemblage in which its elements are entangled.

Finally, I feel the need to mention that this does not mean that all
activities went smoothly without being challenged, with everyone contributing all the time to the singular agenda of performing the activities as a
regional space. As it appears, especially from the video transcripts, the
teachers invested a lot of effort into repeatedly calling for silence and
correcting and sanctioning different kinds of behavior. Often the teacher
would open the door to the hallway, mentioning that other teachers, the
headmaster, or parents might pass by, and that they would hear if pupils
were not behaving themselves. Sometimes, the teacher even left the
classroom with the door open, noting that when she came back, she wanted
to find the pupils quiet and busily working. The class was never as quiet as
in those occurrences.

Restlessness and One-to-One Relationships in the
Virtual Environment

Let's close the classroom door behind us and address the question of how
teachers' and children's forms of presence were performed with the online
3D virtual environment. Remember, the discussion of presence was
motivated by the teacher's restlessness in the computer lab. Let me start
out with a video transcript from the computer lab. It is the third session of
Femtedit. The children had arrived a little while beforehand, and everyone

is busy in Femtedit. The camera is positioned in the corner of the computer lab such that it covers two-thirds of the room, and it produces the following sequence:

> Most of the researchers are seated and turn from side to side to address the children next to them. They look at the computer screen to the right, talking to the child at that computer. Then, turning to the other side, they talk to the child at the computer there. Some researchers spend more time at one side before turning to the other. Others move at a higher frequency, as if they are trying to be in both places at the same time. The teacher moves around differently. He is rarely seated. He wanders around among children. He looks restless. His head and upper body move in staccato rhythms. He looks around uneasily. He bends down over a child, looks at his screen, and talks to him. After a while he gets up and goes to another child, just because she was in his way, or so it appears. He squats down and talks to her. He gets up and looks around. He walks to another computer, stands behind a child, and looks at the screen for two minutes. He points at something on the screen and talks to the child. He straightens his back. His eyes quickly scan the room. He turns around and scans the room again. He goes to an available computer, sits down, and works at the computer for four minutes. Then he gets up again, goes to a child, and looks at her screen while bending over her from the side. (Video transcript 2711_2_24–39)

The way the researchers shuttle between two computers makes them look restless. But they are seated, anchored between two computers, which makes the unrest less apparent. The most apparent restlessness on the video belongs to the teacher. I discuss this restlessness by studying the moments when the teacher interacted with the children and the moments when breaks in the interaction occurred, before I return to the restlessness of the teacher.

Two ways of interacting are shown in the video transcript: Either the teacher was offline, looking at the computer screen of the online child while talking to him or her, or he was logged on to the virtual environment and was interacting with children online. In the following, I analyze and compare such situations. Due to the character of my data, the interactions analyzed involved researchers and not teachers. I venture however to treat teachers and researchers equally, because it is the patterns of relations – which are the same for both teachers and researches – that we are interested in, rather than personal or professional characteristics.

The following field note involves offline as well as online interaction between child and researcher, which are the same two ways of interacting as we saw in the preceding video transcript. It was Tuesday morning. Half of the fourth-grade class of St. Marc Street School was in the computer lab with four researchers and a teacher. They were already logged into Femtedit. The field note reports:

> I was sitting on a chair between two computers. At my left-hand side Claus was busy, and on the other was Alena. Claus had read the message from his Femteditian Duni: "I can sense that a picture has been added to my home. A picture of a sweet little girl. This gives me energy. But the picture is so far away. If only you could bring it closer to my home. Then I can absorb its energy. Then, oh, I hope, I will be soon reanimated." Claus logged into Femtedit.
>
> Sitting behind Claus, off to one side, I asked him if he knew where the picture was that he was supposed move to Duni's place. He said yes. He hit the arrow keys and his avatar, Dunidk, hastened ahead inside the virtual world. The landscapes passed by quickly, and I couldn't see where he was heading, only that it wasn't to where the picture was.
>
> I turned to the computer next to him and logged into Femtedit. I searched around with my avatar, Estroide, until it faced Dunidk. I posted in the chat field that we could help each other move the picture. We (our avatars) went together to the location of the picture. Claus clicked on the picture and dragged it a little. He hadn't moved it very far, though, before it disappeared from his visual field on the screen. I saw his avatar fading into the distance. I ran after him. I stopped to write in the chat: "Where are you? Let's move the picture." I got no answer. And because I had stopped my avatar while writing the chat message, I had lost track of Dunidk in the virtual world. (Field note 2011_7)

The field note excerpt consists of three paragraphs. The first mainly sets the scene and provides the context for the following two paragraphs. I do not discuss that paragraph further. The second paragraph is about inter-action between the offline researcher and the online child, whereas the last paragraph is about interaction between the child and the researcher when they were both online. I discuss each of these two latter paragraphs in the following sections.

Offline Researcher Interacting with Online Child

The interaction between Claus and the researcher started with the researcher asking Claus a *pseudo-question* about whether he knew where a specific picture was. According to Sverker Lindblad and Fritjof Sahlström (1998), it is common for teachers to communicate with pupils in class by asking so-called pseudo-questions. Pseudo-questions do not follow a question-answer format (Goffman 1981, p. 6*ff.*). The query is not supposed to be followed by a reply that provides the inquirer with information she does not already have. On the contrary, the question is posed because the inquirer *does* know the answer, and the subsequent reply is expected to provide exactly the information the inquirer already knows.

Because the researcher enters the virtual environment later in the field note and tries to make Claus move the picture, it is reasonable to suggest that the researcher's question did not imply the expectation that Claus would give her an already-known verbal answer; rather, it indicated the expectation that Claus would find the picture and move it. Claus was expected to act in accordance with the question instead of answering it. With reference to John Sinclair and Malcolm Coulthard, Lindblad and Sahlström (1998) describe how a phrase that is literally a question – such as "Isn't it a bit chilly in here?" – may in practice work as an order, for example, "Shut the window." Even though it is literally a question, this phrase does not expect a verbal answer. Rather, it expects an action in response. In the computer lab, the researcher asked, "Do you know where the picture is that you are supposed to move to Duni's place?" which, according to the same principle, meant, "Find the picture and move it to Duni's place." However, Claus answered "yes" and thereby performed the dialogue in a question-answer format and not as a request for action.

Conversation is often taken to be the most important element of social interaction, and consequently it is often relied on as the only data for studies of social interaction in schools. However important conversation may be for performing spaces, it is only one component among a heterogeneity of components. An isolated focus on conversation not only overlooks other important constituents of a space; it also over-exaggerates the importance of conversation in spatial performance.

Apart from conversation, the visual materiality of Claus's avatar, Dunidk, was involved in the field note. Having configured the settings of the Active Worlds browser to show the "first-person view mode," Claus could not see his avatar on the screen. Instead the avatar's visual field appeared on the screen. With the arrow keys Claus moved the imagined avatar around; he visually experienced this movement as the avatar's visual field moved in relation to the pressing of the arrow keys.

Compare this to the visual materiality of the emerging letters on the blackboard that I described previously. I showed how the visual materiality as an effect of the assemblage was distant and separate from the pupils singing the alphabet song. In contrast, Claus literally had the avatar in his hand. By punching the arrow keys or moving the mouse, he moved the

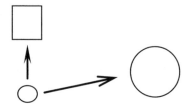

Figure 8. A depiction of two lines of attention reaching out from Claus.

avatar around and made it make gestures. His relation to the avatar was rather comparable to the classroom teacher's relation to the emerging letters on the blackboard. Just as she wrote the letters on the blackboard, Claus controlled the avatar in the online environment. And just as the chalk and the letters on the blackboard were an extension of the teacher in the classroom, the avatar was an extension of Claus. Whereas the pupils in the classroom were separate from the letters on the blackboard, no clear separation was performed between Claus and the avatar. The observation that the children usually talked about their avatars in the first person adds to this impression – "I am running as fast as I can," "I am over here," and so on.

The description of the conversation, the avatar Dunidk, and Claus provides an image of two lines reaching out from Claus (o) as shown in Figure 8. In one direction there was a line of attention toward Dunidk (□) as an extension of Claus, partly through the arrow keys on the keyboard and partly through the screen displaying the avatar's visual field. In the other direction was a line of attention toward the researcher's question (O). The two lines of attention did not meet. Along one line Claus moved around with his avatar, and along the other he answered the researcher's question. The conversational line of attention toward the question was not aligned with the visual and motor line of attention to the virtual environment. In the classroom the rhythm of the alphabet song was closely coordinated with the emerging letters on the blackboard, which provided the pupils with a strong bond of attention toward the blackboard. In the computer lab the attention was split in two between the virtual environment and the researcher. I will characterize this pattern of relations as *one-to-a-half*: one researcher relating to a half-child. Claus's attention was divided between the researcher's question and the virtual environment. The researcher looked at Claus's computer screen and tried to interact with Claus, but she succeeded only partly. Because he was allied with his avatar, Claus soon gave her the slip. Because she was related only to the listening Claus and not to the material he was working with – the virtual environment – she didn't succeed in creating a very strong bond with him.

Figure 9. A depiction of Claus/Dunidk in serial relation with Estroide/the researcher.

Online Interaction Between Researcher and Child

I now turn to the last paragraph of the preceding field note excerpt. The researcher logged into the virtual world, and in the shape of the avatar Estroide she approached the avatar Dunidk. Claus could now see Estroide opposite his own (not visible) avatar on the computer screen. Whereas Dunidk was not clearly separated from Claus and pressing of the arrow keys, Estroide indeed was separated from Claus. Claus, the avatars, and the researcher entered a line of relations in which Claus/Dunidk was on one side and Estroide/researcher was on the other. Whereas in the preceding sequence Claus was a bifurcation point of two diverging lines of attention, now there are two sets of elements connected with one single link, as depicted in Figure 9.

Interestingly, a change in verbal style occurred simultaneously with this shift from offline talk to visual presence online. Estroide approached Dunidk and posted, "Let's help each other with the picture," in the chat. This utterance points to collaboration, whereas the verbal request in the preceding sequence was a kind of order, or at least a request for Claus to act on his own. When Dunidk and Estroide moved together toward the picture, their actions were coordinated with the utterance, similar to how the emerging letters on the blackboard were coordinated with the singing of the alphabet song.

However, this coordination broke shortly after Dunidk ran off. The researcher tried but was unable to follow him and had no idea where he might be. This would never happen in the classroom. The classroom was enclosed by walls, which made it possible to always have an overview of all children.[3] Compared to this, the virtual environment was large, and the avatars were fast. At one moment the researcher was in contact with Dunidk and chatting with Claus, and at the next moment Dunidk was gone and out of sight.

---

[3] Lee (2001, p. 132) describes how the walls of the classroom "protect" children against undesirable influences. Keeping out undesirable influences is another important component of performing an overview.

Before the researcher lost track of Claus, they were connected through the mutually confronting visual materialities of their avatars. Compared to the one-to-a-half relationship I described when the researcher interacted offline with Claus, who was online, we can call this a *one-to-one relationship*, remembering that each "one" is (at least) a human and an avatar. In both cases the researcher and Claus were separate entities connecting. Compared to the Bulgarian song in the classroom, in which all elements were mutually related and acting collectively rather than standing out as individual participants, Claus and the researcher were present as separate but cooperating participants. CSCL scholars distinguish between collaboration and cooperation (Dillenbourg 2000; Lehtinen et al. 2000). The former refers to participants working together on the same task with a common goal, whereas cooperation describes a process in which each member works on his or her own part of a bigger task, whose product is a compound of the individual tasks. In this sense the Bulgarian song as well as Claus's and the researcher's interaction offline and online were collaboration. Even though both were collaboration, seen as a continuum rather than two entirely separate forms of presence, the two CSCL terms can help us differentiate between the interaction between Claus online and the researcher offline, which was closer to the pattern described by cooperation, and the Bulgarian song, which was pure collaboration. In the former the presences of the humans were more separate than in the latter.

The video transcript of the restless teacher showed how he moved from one child to the next. After each one-to-one relationship came another. The one-to-one relationships were temporary and sequential. The field note describing the interaction between the researcher and Claus depicts a similar sequence of connections and breaks: the researcher connected (offline), separated, connected again (online), and finally separated from Claus when Dunidk disappeared from the visual field of the researcher's screen. Note, that Claus was continuously connected to the virtual environment through his avatar, while the researcher alternated between connecting to and disconnecting from Claus and the virtual environment. Claus was involved in a continuous process in which the researcher was involved only temporarily but repeatedly. As such, the pattern of relation had characteristics described by the fluid metaphor. The researcher was an exchangeable and optional part of the process. Similarly, the teacher in the video transcript was an exchangeable and optional part of the children's ongoing processes.

Separating with Discontinuities

Separation in the Virtual Environment

Separations were performed as socio-material boundaries in the classroom, and these boundaries contributed to performing particular forms of presence. As a background for discussing the forms of presence performed with the online 3D virtual environment, I look in this section at how separations were performed with the online software.

The researcher lost track of Claus in the virtual environment and thus was separated from him. I compared this to the classroom and pointed to the extent of the virtual environment as a constituent of this separation – the extent of the space was performed differently in the classroom due to its walls. Loosing track of a pupil was one way in which the extent of Femtedit created separation in the virtual environment.

The extent of Femtedit furthermore made it impossible for the teacher to relate to many children simultaneously. There were only two ways of accessing what children were doing in the virtual environment – either by being offline and looking at the child's computer screen or by logging into the virtual environment. Neither of the two methods, however, provided the teacher with an overview of what all children were doing. Children were dispersed over an area far bigger than that which could be seen on the computer screen at one time, and the teacher could usually only follow what one avatar was doing. Sometimes she could follow a few children, due to the ruins in Femtedit where avatars gathered to collaborate. But getting an overview of twelve children logged on at St. Marc Street School was an insurmountable task. It was even more impossible to observe how they collaborated with the ten children logged on at Pine Valley School in Sweden. This separation, or rather limited access, was due partly to the large size of the virtual environment in comparison to what the visual field of the computer screen displayed and partly to the dispersed nature of the places in the virtual environment in which the children worked.

Was this different, one may ask, from when pupils worked individually in the classroom with exercise books? Did the teacher not have similar problems following the children there? The teacher often wandered around, among pupils in the classroom, attending to one after the other. In order to compare the teacher's ability to follow the children's work in the two places, we need to look at more than the teachers' behavior in the room. We need to take the exercise books into account as an extension of the classroom, just as the virtual environment was an extension of the computer lab. Two crucial differences appear: First, by glancing down at a page in a pupil's exercise book, the teacher got an immediate impression of what the child was doing and how far he had progressed in the book. It was lying open on the desk, and the pupil would not jump, for example, from page four to page twenty-three, and then to page sixteen. The exercise books defined a clear standard for the sequence of the children's work. Second, all pupils' exercise books were in principle identical.[4] Thereby, the teacher knew not just what one pupil was doing but what all pupils were doing. Because the exercise books were identical, the class set performed one homogeneous region, even though each child had his or her own book. This homogeneity limited the degree to which the exercise books formed an extension of the classroom. All pupils were active in the same region of the exercise books, so to speak, and thus the teacher could keep a one-to-many relationship with the children, even when they were working individually and even when she was relating to them one-to-one. The virtual environment could not be limited in the same way as the classroom. Simply because of the extension of the virtual environment, the teacher could not relate to more than one – or a few – children at a time.

Another separation between teacher and child was performed that had to do with extent. The preceding field note excerpt mentioned a picture from Cartoon Network that Claus had put into the virtual environment. Similarly, children linked to several other elements from outside of Femtedit and thereby added these to Femtedit. These entities extended the virtual environment: Pakistani music, the "Twin Towers," and satiric anti-terrorist web pages, among others. As time went on, and as more and more entities were involved in Femtedit, it got increasingly difficult to tell the

---

[4] When I went to school in the 1970s, our exercise books were all identical. Since then a new aspect has come into the center of educational politics in Denmark. It is referred to as "differentiation of education," which means that learning has to support an all-around and personal development for the individual pupil. This is inscribed in the Primary Education Act, it is emphasized in curricula, and it has changed learning materials. In today's exercise books, the "differentiation of education" is implemented by varying the level of difficulty of the exercises. In the exercise books used for lessons on the Danish language in the fourth-grade class in which I did my fieldwork, the structure and content of the exercise books were the same. The tasks were to fill in words on empty spaces in the printed sentences. For instance: "This ice cream is large and tasty, but that one is even larger and even tastier." The underlined words were missing, replaced by blank lines, and the pupil would have to fill in the right words on the blank lines. In some exercise books – for the most skillful pupils – both words were missing, whereas in the exercise books for the less skilled, only one word was missing.

"inside" from the "outside" of Femtedit. The online software was extended to involve elements that were out of the reach of the teacher, and thereby the extent of Femtedit as a result of the involvement of URLs was a further point hampering the teacher's overview.

In addition to the separations performed through the extent of the virtual environment, the teacher was disconnected due to the unpredictability of the children's activities. Not only did the children involve links to web pages out of the reach of the teacher; they do so continuously. Thereby, Femtedit gradually transformed, and it did so in unpredictable directions. The teacher had no idea what the next building blocks would be or which hyperlinks the children would attach to the homes of the Femteditians.

When comparing Femtedit to the classroom use of exercise books in regards to predictability, we see again two important differences. First, the teacher knew the content of the exercise books, and second, the exercise books did not change. Because she knew the content of the exercise books, the teacher could quite precisely predict what a pupil would be doing next, even after turning away from the pupil she had just been helping. This was not possible in the virtual environment, due to its gradual mutation.

Furthermore, imagine that the exercise books in some fantastic way suddenly changed. If new questions and instructions suddenly appeared, accompanied by blank lines, pictures, and video clips, the teacher would not know what the pupils would be doing when she turned away from them. It was only because the exercise books were immutable that the teacher could calmly turn her back on the pupils, well aware of what they would be doing next. By being allied with known and immutable exercise books, the teacher could at any time predict the pupils' activities. The possibility of surprises was reduced, due to the predefined content of the lesson through the immutable exercise books and textbooks.

The virtual environment did not allow the teacher to predict what new things children built, what new hyperlinks they added, or in which new ways they interrelated with other avatars. While the teacher was watching the screen of a child or when he was online in the virtual environment, he could see what the child was doing. But as soon as he got up and went somewhere else, he was completely incapable of predicting the continuation. The fluid pattern of relations of the virtual environment allowed the activities to turn in all sorts of directions. Whereas the activities in the exercise book in the classroom were predictable due to the immutability of the exercise books, the virtual environment was mutable. It was continuously changing, which rendered predictability impossible.

Discontinuities and Agents in Fluid Patterns of Relations

As described by Mol and Law (Law 2002b; Law & Mol 2001; Mol & Law 1994), fluid space does not necessarily perform boundaries. I have however described several ways in which the fluid pattern of relations constituted with the online software did perform separations. The teachers connected and disconnected from the children and the virtual environment. They were kept out not by a boundary, as in a regional pattern of relations; instead their connection to the children was limited to instances in which a teacher's course of action crossed the course of action of a child. They were connected by the streams or flows they took. And it was the same flows that separated them. Each child or group of children was flowing along a stream that involved the virtual environment. The teacher followed another stream, which at times crossed the child's flow or followed the flow for a time, and at other times flowed elsewhere.

"*Discontinuity*" is an appropriate term to characterize the kinds of separations performed in the fluid pattern of relations. In the classroom the pupils and teacher were separated by a boundary, which kept them at a distance from each other, while at the same time they constantly and dynamically co-performed each other as subjects and authority. In the virtual environment, the children and teacher were sometimes connected, sometimes separated. When connected, they were intimately connected. The teacher logged on to the virtual environment and collaborated with the child. In the regional pattern of relations of the classroom, the teacher and pupils did not collaborate. Each had their tasks and each their form of presence. They cooperated about the common task of educating the pupils, but they did not collaborate. In the virtual environment, however, the teacher and child met at eye level, so to speak.

When meeting at eye level and collaborating in the computer lab, the teacher and children had a symmetric relationship, contrary to that of the classroom. Referring to sociologist and structuration theorist Anthony Giddens (1984), I characterize the children's as well as the teachers' form of presence as that of *agents* (Kaspersen 1995; Mørk 1994). Giddens (1984) states: "[T]o be an agent is to be able to deploy . . . a range of causal powers, including that of influencing those deployed by others. Action depends upon the capability of the individual to make a difference, that is, to exercise some sort of power" (p. 14). In order to describe the performance of Claus and the researcher as agents, it is crucial that this term describe a pattern of relations of equal and powerful characters. This is indeed different than the presence of a subject. A subject is opposite the authority. An agent is not performed through opposition. Agents are placed side-by-side and have, in principle, equal ability to make a difference. This was very much what went on in the computer lab. Claus acted on his own, engaged with his own process. The researcher did so as well and tried to engage with Claus, to make a difference. Claus did collaborate with her to a certain extent, but he also had the power to stop doing so.

The active, knowledgeable, and equal character of agents does not mean that they are "free" in the sense of "not constrained." The agent always acts in a context to which she must adapt, a context of other agents, for instance. This was indeed the case in the pattern of relations with the virtual environment. The researcher had to adapt her way and means of communicating with Claus to his activities. And he turned away from what he was doing to collaborate with her. This fits well with the characteristics of fluidity. It is flexible, it mutates to fit to new elements involved, and it transforms as elements are exchanged and replaced.

In their discussion of the Zimbabwe Bush Pump as a fluid technology, de Laet and Mol (2000) talk about Dr. Peter Morgan. Morgan is the maker of the Bush Pump. Or so, at least, some say. Morgan himself insists that the engineer, local communities, the Swiss visitors, and many other people are involved in making the Bush Pump. He doesn't claim ownership of the pump. He regularly visits the pumps, not to monitor their functioning but to learn about them in their village environments. He has turned into a mere "facilitator," a "peripheral agent," de Laet and Mol write. It is crucial in their description of Morgan that he does not control, he does not claim ownership, and he does not exercise authority (pp. 521–522). Law (2002b, p. 101) describes him as a *fluid subject*. Considering the associations of the concept of "subject" with regions, interpellation, and authority, "subject" is the wrong term to assign to Morgan in the context of my analysis. He does not come into being as interpellated by an authority. He comes into being by interacting with a lot of other changing and exchangeable elements in the fluid pattern of relations that make up the Zimbabwe Bush Pump.

In my terms – with Asplund's, Althusser's, and Giddens' help in differentiating among forms of presence – Morgan is an agent, as were Claus and the researcher. Morgan is not a strong actor, as is an authority. He is a weak actor, an agent who flows along. His flow crosses and meets with pumps, visitors, engineers, and others. He may be peripheral, but he is not more peripheral than any other part of the arrangement, because they are all peripheral. His acting makes a difference for the pattern of relations that makes up the Bush Pump, and he adapts to the pattern and to what

other agents do. The same characterizes Claus's and the researcher's form
of presence with the virtual environment.

Most contemporary scholars discussing presence do so in terms of
subjectivity and base their theorizing on regional patterns of relations – for
example, Althusser. Feminist philosopher Judith Butler (1997) states that
the subject is defined by its boundary between the interior "own" and the
exterior "Other": "[T]he subject is produced by a condition from which it
is, by definition, separated and differentiated" (p. 9). Mead (1932) describes
how "the others and the self arise in the social act together" (p. 169). His
symbolic interactionism has a strong concept of the self as inseparably
defined through others. He however did not leave space for the possibility
that human presence could be constituted through other patterns of
relations than that of relatively stable opposite regions of self and other. All
three authors theorize that the subject is performed within regional space.
The possibility that presence may be something other than regional is one
important point to draw from my discussion of presence as agential.

Fluid Authority

I have characterized the researcher's and the children's form of presence as
that of agents, and I have described the separations performed with the
virtual environment as discontinuities, contrary to the boundaries performed in the classroom. This was indeed a restless form of presence for
the teacher. Due to the fluid pattern of relations, she had to flow along. She
had no rest, as she did at the blackboard in the classroom. The agent had
no place, no region to call home, as she had in the classroom. I noted that
the teachers' and children's forms of presence were equal when interacting
with the virtual environment. However, the teachers did not interact with
the children all the time, and when they did not, they were not equal with
the children. They were suspended from the fluid process. Their own form
of presence was fluid. They were not in the center of the stream. Instead
they were like a rivulet of water that diverged from the stream and formed
a small pond along the riverbank, and as the stream rushed by, the water
in the pond lay still. There is no center in fluid space, Mol and Law
repeatedly state (Law 2002b; Law & Mol 2001; Mol & Law 1994). This,
I think, is right from the perspective of the flow, but, when focusing on
separations, the distress of single parts in the peripheral position stands
out. The teacher was one such single optional and exchangeable part, a
part that was sometimes involved in the fluid process and sometimes not.
For such a component, there was a center in relation to which it was

peripheral. This was the awkward position of the teacher in the fluid pattern of relations performed with the virtual environment. This was the character of her restlessness – being sometimes part of a flow and sometimes peripheral or even suspended.

No boundaries were performed with the virtual environment; there was no region and no focal place toward which attention could be directed. Due to the lack of these characteristics, no authority was performed. Scholar of childhood studies David Buckingham (2000) presents the common argument that information technology provides children with access to information and to cultural and social worlds that are inaccessible, even incomprehensible, to their parents. Parents are not the focus here, but, obviously, teachers share the fate of parents on this point, and in the context of information technology the authority that parents and teachers normally exercise is no longer possible, or so the argument goes.

The authority being referred to here, however, is regional authority, that is, authority performed as a clear separation between the authority figure and the subjected, featuring clear boundaries between the two. This is a pattern of relations in which authority is performed as having an overview of and being capable of predicting others' behavior. But can there be another form of authority? Is it possible to think of authority in fluid patterns of relations? A fluid form of authority could be the authority of the preceding step. Because a fluid pattern of relations transforms gradually, it always takes little steps, one at a time, away from the preceding ones. The virtual environment proceeded by adding a link, a building block, an image, or a sound to the existing ones. Therefore, the last step in the ongoing gradual mutation of the fluid pattern of relations can be seen as having authority over the next. One step in the process is always indebted to the former. The former will always make possible and restrain the next.

Thinking in fluid terms frees the notion of authority from being bound to a regional space. The question of authority is thus no longer a matter of more or less power that resides in the region of the authority and is exercised over subjects. It is now – in spatial terms – a matter of different forms of authority. When restlessness is experienced by teachers working with computers, the solution is usually to compromise the fluid characteristics of the design and create a region that can contribute to performing regional authority. Another solution, however, is to improve and develop the materials to be better at connecting to the teacher, using a process of performing *fluid authority*. Creating fluid authority could involve supporting the teacher in giving feedback to the children in the blog and through the virtual environment in a way that better feeds into the fluid processes. Such feedback should connect in a fluid pattern to what children are doing in such a way that they pick up on it and integrate it as a part of an ongoing transformative process of fluidity. This authority would still be a superior power to influence or command the thoughts or behavior of others (without which the notion of teaching would not make much sense), but it would be constituted in a fluid pattern instead of as a regional space, which implies that the notions of "self" and "others" and their interrelations are variable and discontinuous but (potentially) recurrent. Focusing on the spatial differences, the descriptions have made available an analysis of how authority may be other than regional. Fluid technology in a (regional) elementary school setting could hence contribute to new – fluid – ways of performing authority.

The Power of Interactivity, the Power of Fluidity

Before concluding the chapter, I would like to mention sociologist of technology Andrew Barry's (2001) sharp analysis of interactivity. Barry analyzes the change in the setup of museum exhibitions. Museum exhibitions used to consist of objects that spoke for themselves; they were carefully ordered in showcases for the public to observe at a distance. Placed behind glass, the objects presented in themselves an almost sacred, indefeasible authority. The museum visitors could observe them, accept them, or do neither. But they could not touch them, alter them, or interact with them. In the more recent decades this has changed. Museums of science, which are Barry's object of study, have increasingly involved hands-on interactive technologies with which museum visitors can interact and experiment. Such interactive technologies deploy a different kind of power than the disciplinary technologies described by Foucault, Barry states.

Foucault (1979) notes the importance of what he terms body-object articulation for the exercise of disciplinary power. Discipline defines each of the relations that the body must have with the object it manipulates. It operates by fixing the relations between body and object to form a unified apparatus. In comparison, interactive technologies imply a much looser bond between the body and the object. Interactive technology does not regiment the body; it turns it into a source of pleasure and experimentation:

> Whereas discipline is exhaustive in its application, interactivity is specific, instantaneous and intensive. Whereas disciplinary technology manipulates and manages the body in detail, interactive technology is intended to channel and excite the curiosity of the body and its senses . . . Whereas discipline is direct and authoritative, interactivity is intended to turn the

user (visitor, school child, citizen or consumer) into a more creative, participative or active subject without the imposition of a direct form of control. (Barry 2001, pp. 148–149)

It is striking how much Barry's description of the power of interactive technologies resonates with fluid space and the agential form of presence it contributes to performing. I used different words previously, but the relations between teacher and child performed with the virtual environment were indeed specific, instantaneous, and intensive.[5] The frame story attached to the virtual environment design was blank in order to excite the curiosity of the children. The form of presence they performed was certainly that of agents – creative, participative, and active, without the imposition of a direct form of control. The "natural journey" for children today, Kenneth Hultqvist (2001, 2004) notes, is about "being a motivated learner that is able to explore . . . The child has become an entrepreneur of him- or herself" (2001, p. 163). This description also resonates with what philosopher Gilles Deleuze (1995) terms "control society."

Discussing the introduction of information technology in education, researcher of education and technology David Shutkin (1998) remarks – also with reference to Foucault – that the "authority that this deployment constructs does not form an oppressive power that says NO. Rather, it is a modern, productive form of power that says YES" (p. 211). Like Barry and Hultqvist, Shutkin emphasizes that we are still dealing with power, even if it takes another form. I have characterized the form it takes as fluid – a power that makes available ongoing mutation and flexibility but that also creates discontinuities and unreliability. Hence, the debate about an *active learner* approach is a discussion not about more or less power or more or less authority, but about different forms of power and authority and, with this, different winners and different losers.

With these comments on fluidity I challenge Mol and Law's (Law 2002b; Law & Mol 2001; Mol & Law 1994) and de Laet and Mol's (2000) celebration of the fluid pattern of relations for being flexible, continuous, and inclusive and their dishonoring of the regional pattern of relations due to its boundaries, exclusion, and suppression of differences. I have noted that separations were indeed performed in the fluid pattern of relations, but they took the form of discontinuities, whereas separations in a regional pattern of relations take that of boundaries. Furthermore, I hesitate to

---

[5] I added that these relations were also easily discontinued, which Barry interestingly does not discuss, just as Law and Mol have not focused on the kinds of separations a fluid space performs. They describe only the connections fluidity contributes to performing.

dishonor regional boundaries. As described, the clear difference between the subjects' and the authority's forms of presence in the classroom was, among other things, due to the blackboard as a centralizing device, and to the homogeneity of the learning materials. "Boundary," "centralizing," and "homogeneity" are words scholars of the turn of the millennium tend to dislike. But notice that the homogeneity of the exercise books, the central place at the blackboard, and the boundary not only separated; they also established a strong connection between teacher and pupils, constituting reciprocal places, shared learning materials, and a shared boundary, which everyone could refer to. Probably, these parts also contributed to constituting a "we" in the classroom, a communality of the class. The strong duality performed by the clear boundary between teacher and pupils in the classroom constituted a mutuality in the relationship. Pupils and teachers were constituted as each other's opposite, and hence contributed to performing one another. They were interdependent. Pupils contributed to performing and hence to legitimizing the regional pattern of relations by secretly letting a note pass under the desks and by playing with legitimate materials such as erasers, pencils, and hair clips instead of with illegitimate toys. Teacher and pupils contributed mutually to performing their regional positions. They were in it together, so to speak. This doesn't mean that their relationship was symmetric. As I have described, materials were involved in the pattern of relations that positioned them differently.

In the computer lab the teachers were recurrently connected to and disconnected from the fluid process with the virtual environment. The relationship between teachers and children was much looser. So was the relationship among the children. They worked in groups, but because they did not share materials and had no common delimited place, components for performing communality for the whole class were scarce. The regional assemblage in the classroom did not simply create separation and difference. It also performed enduring connections, a feature that was scarce in the virtual environment.

Conclusion: Posthumanist Presence

Contemporary theorists of subjectivity commonly theorize in regional terms, without considering the spatial character of presence. Consequently any understanding of how presence could be different is limited to variations of regional spatiality, which usually means reallocating power across regional boundaries. By applying a spatial thinking, it is possible to imagine quite different forms of presence. I have shown that presence is not necessarily founded on a regional pattern of relations, which implies that presence does not necessarily perform a pattern of well-delimited subjects or individuals separated by clear boundaries. A blackboard, the visual field of an avatar, the extent of a virtual world, exercise books, hyperlinks, textbooks, songs, chat messages, bodies, and voices allowed me to reach this conclusion. Taking into account materials that are generally neglected as parts of the constitution of human presence shows that presence may be different from how it is most often imagined. Such materials contribute to performing human presences. The human is far from simply human. Human presence is formed through arrangements to which materials greatly contribute. I have shown how social and material parts – in particular spatially coordinated arrangements – contributed to performing particular forms of presence. For instance, the teacher was performed as an authority through the blackboard, chalk, gazes, and songs, in opposition to the subjects, who were co-performed in the same instance, as opposite to the authority. It is only possible to follow the social psychological approach to authority as a personal possession by adding a filter to the lens through which data is analyzed that sorts out any material entity involved in the interactions taking place in school. A *posthumanist* and spatial approach to presence and authority gives us a chance to understand how authority may take different forms and will thus make us able to start thinking about forms of presence that are not regional. By *not* beginning with the human, the subject, the individual, or the agent, I have studied presence empirically as a result of the involvement of different materials.

My spatial analyses of presence have made it obvious that it is not only technologies and knowledge that vary with the arrangement of the social and material entities that make up learning practices and with the variation of spatial formations; forms of presence do so as well. Table 6 summarizes and compares schematically the characteristics of six dimensions of the three forms of presence I have dealt with. I have described the human as immersed, independent or well-delimited, and active or well-delimited, respectively, for the three forms of presence. These are the concentrate of the human's achieved ability to relate to other people and thus a characteristic of the *materiality of the humans* performed with each of the forms of presence with respect to other humans. When we look at the interpersonal relations and power relations that these forms of presence embrace, we understand more about the materiality of the humans that are performed by and through these forms of presence. Likewise, we notice that different ways of learning are appropriate to each form of presence. We cannot define a form of learning on the basis of the description of a form of presence, because there is no direct connection between form of presence and form of learning, like we saw between form of knowledge and form of learning. We may hypothesize that an authority-subject form of presence may fit well with a representational form of knowledge because both are shaped in regional space. But we need to be careful and open to the possibility of multiple forms of knowledge and learning, even within one spatial formation. Thus we must leave this as a question to be settled empirically.

Let me in concluding the discussions of forms of presence return to the theory of situated learning and subject research, to which I owe much of my thinking but which also needs crucial revision to reach the approach presented in this book. Dreier (1999) argues that learning is change in personal participation in social contexts. We can understand this by remembering Lave and Wenger's (1991) description of how a West African tailor apprentice starts his learning trajectory by attaching buttons and thereby already being part of the production process. While doing this simple task, he observes the work of the more experienced tailors and the particular ways of participating in this community of practice. Next, he engages in sewing and thereby attaching different pieces of fabric together, which is followed by cutting the fabric, and a number of other activities, until he has been through the whole production process. This sequence is not just a matter of acquiring competences in sewing and cutting; it is just as much a matter of becoming a more and more integrated participant of the tailor community of practice. The apprentice moves through different positions in the organization of tailor's practice; this system forms a learning *trajectory*.

Conceptualizing learning as a trajectory implies an imaginary of the whole educational process, and on the basis of such an imaginary it is not surprising that humans come to be seen as more or less well-delimited entities that move through an educational system. When analyzing my empirical material, I did not find any practices in which the human was enacted as moving in a trajectory through the educational system. Indeed, learning *practices* are rarely concerned with the educational process as a whole, but rather directed toward continuing and completing the particular practice in question. With all their wisdom on how learning is produced through situated social practice and with their emphasis on the "first-person perspective," it is ironic that the approaches to situated learning conceptualize the human as necessarily participating in educational practice via a trajectory. Thereby they steer clear of dealing with the human as performed through the different forms of presence that emerge

Table 6. *Forms of presence.*

	Collective	Authority-Subject	Agent
Limitations	Blurred demarcation	Boundaries	Discontinuities
Characteristics of Humans	Immersed	Independent, well-delimited	Active, well-delimited
Interpersonal Relations	Symbiotic	Mutual	Shifting between intimacy and isolation
Power Relations	Entangled	Characterized by dominance and subjection, rejection, restriction	Characterized by equality, affirmation, allowances
Authority	No authority	Fundamental, ubiquitous	Procedural, last step influencing the next
Ways of Learning	Collective mutation	Imitation, transmission	Active collaboration, participation

out of the diverging socio-material constellations of practice, and thus they neglect an important characteristic of each learning practice, namely, that each practice performs a specific form of presence.

I have shown humans performed in different ways, varying with the spatial pattern of relations of which they were part. In some of these constellations – the regional and the fluid – human presence did take the form of well-delimited entities, as subjects and actors, respectively. In the collective form of presence, however, we did not find a well-delimited human or person – only swaying and mutually engaging bodies, gazes, and the resonance of the song, which altogether made up this form of presence. Such presence is not a theoretical option when the human is predefined as a coherent person moving through a trajectory.

It is important to emphasize that the spatial approach does not exclude the possibility that a human may be moving through trajectories of the educational system, and even across different spatial formations. This is an empirical question, which should be answered neither affirmatively nor negatively, but with a description of the spatial formation such a movement takes, and through an analysis of the relations among entities enacted by and through the space in question: of its temporality, its stability, its way of changing, and so on, as listed in Table 4.

Furthermore, it is only when we realize the particularities of the socio-material arrangements that make up different, sometimes matching, and sometimes incompatible forms of presence that it becomes possible to start rearranging practice in order to allow, for instance, a teacher to connect to a fluid space and exercise fluid authority. Imagining the pattern of relations that I described that showed how the regional spatial formation the teacher was part of clashed with the fluid space performed by and through the virtual environment is a crucial part of becoming able to point to ways of rearranging practice that turn the clash into an alliance.

Likewise, it is crucial that the forms of presence enacted in schools can connect to the spatial formations of which a child is part. Learners' spatially achieved ability to participate in a form of presence is fundamental to educational practices. Children who do not have the materiality to connect to a spatial formation that shapes an educational practice have altogether no access to the practice in question. Mark Warschauer (1998) emphasizes that the strong emphasis on collaborative, reflexive, and communicative participation in the implementation of interactive software in schools tends to exclude ethnic and language minority pupils from a great deal of the learning. The active learning paradigm is much more reachable for middle-class children. Warschauer underlines that a "critical awareness" among teachers and pupils may change this circumstance. Such a result is important but at the same time far too abstract, because it does not indicate how educational practice may be rearranged to shape "critical awareness" and thus to provide better access for non-middle-class children. When it is found that most teachers and children do not possess "critical awareness," a common practical solution is to return to a more transmissional model of teaching. The argument seems to be that at least we know that this model tends to provide an effective learning environment for non-middle-class children, even if we have no theory to explain this relationship. A spatial approach to educational practice can point to which practical details contribute to reconfiguring the educational practices to create better access for children that are part of certain spatial arrangements than for children that are part of certain other spatial arrangements.

Lee (2001) notes that the contemporary discussions of the *active learning child* in, for instance, CSCL are a repetition of the child-centered educational approach from the 1970s: "Debates still continue over the issue of how active and free children *should* be allowed to be in schools. The question of whether teachers *should* be authority figures, of whether education *needs* to be based on the dominance of an adult over a group of children is very much alive" (p. 82, emphasis added). Like I concluded in the previous chapter about knowledge, we have learned in this chapter to focus on a variety of forms of presence instead of more or less one form of presence, for instance, authority. The preceding quote shows very well the style of the current debate on forms of presence in schools. It concerns whether children should be active and how active they should be. It enacts a regional imaginary in which we can have a varied range of authority or no authority at all, but in which different forms of authority are not possible. From being a matter of cultural, moral, and ideological issues, forms of presence become a practical matter that points out that whether or not authority is performed is not related to whether or not we (humans) want it or are able to create it; instead, authority is performed through socio-material arrangements of school practices. A humanist account of authority like the social psychologist approach I have outlined is dominating in school debates, and authority and presence are almost exclusively discussed from a humanist point of view, and consequently the influence of materials is ignored. Applying instead a posthumanist approach allows us to realize how intimately technology contributes to performing forms of presence and to point to a way of dealing with problems of authority and other issues of presence in school by carrying through very practical rearrangements of educational practice.

The Methodology of the Materiality of Learning
Lesson 5: Presence
Unlike knowledge, presence is not a constituent part of learning. Presence is however necessarily performed when learning is performed. And, for a human, being part of the performing of a form of presence is an obligatory point of passage (Latour 1987) in order to take part in a learning practice. Only those who succeed in becoming a part of a spatial formation that shapes the particular form of presence of an educational practice can have any hope of learning. Understanding the materiality of learning means paying careful attention to the spatial formations in which humans need to become entangled in order to be part of an educational practice.

Because of our strong tradition and tendency to approach learning from a humanist perspective that a priori grants humans exceptional positions in practice, it is important for the study of the materiality of learning to postpone the analysis of human presence to the last step of the investigation. This makes it obvious that it is not only technologies and knowledge that vary

with learning practices and with the variation of spatial formations. So do the humans – the teachers and the learners – participating in practices of learning.

In order to grasp the materiality of learning, we must describe
a particular learning practice as a pattern of relations of human
and nonhuman components, and we must characterize the way
in which humans are present in this practice. We realize that
humans' forms of presence vary, that teachers and children move
through a variety of forms of presence in school, and that being
part of the performance of these presences is a condition for
learning. We may notice that some humans do not seem to fit
into the form of presence in question, and thus in this text we
must look for what spatial formations these humans are part of,
and which form of presence they are entangled in. The detailed
description of the patterns of relations constituting forms of
presence reveal where and how connection points exist and
where and how separations exist. Maybe we see a clash among
different forms of presence, which keeps a human away from the
presence in question. By analyzing the pattern of relations further, we can point to where and how a clash of presences can be
turned into an alliance by rearranging the spatial formations of
which it is made up. Such a rearrangement may require material
investments and have material consequences, because a spatial
formation is always already entangled in patterns of relations that
do not remain unaffected.

But forms of presence are not only responsible for access to
educational practice. The analysis of forms of presence teaches us
that learning varies when presence varies and that mutation,
transmission, and participation (among others) are different
forms of learning achieved with different forms of presence.

Humans are not simply humans in learning practices. Their
forms of presence have materialities achieved through their
interrelation with other human and nonhuman entities of the
practice. The form of learning varies with forms of presence. In
order to understand the materiality of learning, we need to take
the performance of human presence into account. And in order
to understand the human, we need to establish a posthumanist
sensitivity.

6   The Materiality of Learning

We cannot learn what we already know. Therefore, I have been hesitant to provide theoretical definitions. Definitions have the ability to produce clarity and the disadvantage of making us stop wondering about and investigating what we have defined. By avoiding a priori definitions, and by meticulously describing each pattern of relations until a spatial formation took shape that could be characterized as a spatial imaginary, I have throughout the past chapters been able to describe a variety of forms of technology, knowledge, and presence. One of the crucial advantages of this sensitivity is that it allows us to describe the specificities of the *how* of participation and the *what* of performance. It thereby provides us with a methodology that allows us to reimagine technology, knowledge, and presence.

The principle of hesitating to provide definitions does not imply that we should avoid definitions altogether, or that definitions necessarily restrain intellectual development. On the contrary, the clarity they provide often forms good grounds for critique and reconsiderations. The principle of being hesitant is important, but at some point it is time to venture a narrowing-down of the discussion, and to let it come to rest in a definition. On the basis of the past chapters' discussions of materiality, spatiality, knowledge, and presence, we can define the materiality of learning. I defined materiality as the achieved ability to connect to other entities, and learning was defined as growth in knowledge. The materiality of learning must thus be understood as *the achieved ability of a growth in knowledge to connect to other particular entities.*

It comes as a surprise, even to me: The materiality of learning concerns how learning connects to other entities. The materiality of learning is comparable to what is usually known as *learning transfer.* Transfer is a crucial problem in theories of learning. According to cognitive approaches, knowledge is located in the individual and is transferred across situations with the human body. When a person possesses a body of knowledge, this can in principle be applied at any time and any place. Knowledge is understood as mental, and practice is irrelevant for knowledge achievement as well as for what is understood as knowledge retrieval. Lave (1988) has however demonstrated that what I call representational knowledge cannot be performed at every location (see also Sørensen 1998). Knowledge achieved in one situated practice is not directly applicable to another; that is, it is not as if knowledge is coded into a mental program, which simply has to be executed. Lave argues that this is not simply a problem of retrieval, but a matter of knowledge being situated not in the mind but in practice, and accordingly there is nothing to retrieve. Learning implies becoming a participant of a particular practice, and skills and knowledge cannot be moved out of that practice and applied elsewhere independent of the practice of learning.

By situating knowledge and learning in practice and overcoming the understanding of learning as mental, situated learning theory however does not solve the problem of learning transfer. When she was confronted with a question of learning transfer at a lecture in Copenhagen in 2000, I remember Jean Lave's agile body jumping from side to side between imaginative "practices" while she argued that it was still a mystery to her how this transfer takes place, because indeed, leaning transfer could not take place in the jumping manner that she demonstrated in front of the audience.

Lave and Wenger made an important contribution toward accounting for learning transfer, but by taking a regional imaginary for granted in their understanding of situations and communities, they did not leave room for questions about how forms of learning were shaped that did not start from a situation. Situations were imagined as regions surrounded by boundaries, and the questions of how these regional boundaries were transgressed and of how connections could be made across practices went unanswered. From a spatial point of view, we can say that the questions went unanswered because they were wrongly posed. We should instead ask how the boundaries and distances between situations are created in the first place and how the regional space is shaped. When learning is understood as unquestionably situated in regional space, then we are dealing with a "space of no space." Following the spatial imaginaries developed in this book, we realize that learning situated in a regional space is a particular form of learning for which certain rules and characteristics apply, whereas other rules and characteristics apply for other forms of learning. When we analyze situations as regions without understanding the regionality, that is, without acknowledging that a region is one spatiality out of other possible spatialities, we do not ask how situations are created and what the specificities of the situations are (as regions or other), and thereby we miss an important level of analysis in the inquiry into what learning transfer may be and into what form of learning transfer we are dealing with. Theories of learning have difficulty accounting for learning transfer, because learning is always seen as being situated in some place: in the mind or in practice. Instead, we should ask about the particular space – indeed the spatiality – of a particular form of learning.

My suggestion is that the theory of knowledge as situated in time-and-place-bound practices must be revised. Situated learning theory dissolves the cognitivist divisions between mind and practice, but it preserves the regional imaginary on which cognitive theory is based, moving the division from its location between mind and practice to a place between time-and-place-bound situated practices. As long as the situated learning theorist stays within one practice in his analysis of learning, he can nicely describe how learning takes places as a trajectory from newcomer to old-timer. When confronted with the question of how transfer across practices takes place, his theory does not help him much. The notion of practices as located in a multitude of arenas next to one another in society performs a regional imaginary whose limitation necessarily is the understanding of transfer across practices.

Remember Ben's two-meter jump in the classroom, which I discussed in Chapter 4. How can we conceive of the transfer of the knowledge of the length of the two-meter jump from Kim's math textbook in the classroom practice to practices beyond the classroom differently than situated learning theory suggests? When acknowledging the materials involved in learning and taking the materiality of learning into account, a different imaginary of practice appears. The practice of jumping and measuring in the classroom comprises the one-meter standard, which is present not only in the classroom, represented by the one-meter ruler, but in many other places beyond the classroom to which the interaction in the classroom is connected. My spatial approach dismisses the situated learning theory's notion of practice as existing within the boundaries of a given place and time, and inquires instead about the spatiality (and thus temporality) of practice. The limits, discontinuities, or reduction of the extension of practice are thus investigated empirically, rather than being given in advance.

Due to this different understanding of practice, the question of transfer changes. Contrary to the description of knowledge as circulating among places, I describe representational knowledge as dispersed across places. As I have described representational knowledge, it is persons who travel among a scattered constellation of material (re)presentations of the metric standard to which they connect in a particular (regional) pattern, which at each place performs representational knowledge. The metric standard could be performed in the classroom because a one-meter ruler was available. Even though the metric standard contributed to constituting a regional pattern of relations in which it was positioned in a region beyond the classroom, it was also materially present in the classroom as the ruler, without which the metric standard could not be performed. Similarly, the metric standard could only be re-performed at other places where the standard in one way or the other was present as a ruler, a tape measure, or information about sizes.

Because knowledge does not move according to this spatial understanding of representational knowledge, the problem of transfer does not appear: there is nothing to be transferred. Knowledge emerges at different places as a result of the relation between circulating humans and immobile references. References are always already scattered across places. But there are other components of knowledge. The humans are not scattered across places. They have to circulate among places and connect to places. When this is the case, we understand how crucial it is to take forms of presence into account when accounting for learning transfer. As we learned in Chapter 5, humans need to be able to connect to and thereby take part in performing certain forms of presence in order to be part of learning or knowledge practices. Accordingly, the human has to be able to circulate, which means to connect to the particular form of presence necessary in order to re-perform the representational knowledge with references at different places.

This pattern is specifically the case for regional space. Communal and liquid knowledge both move: Communal knowledge extends its location, and liquid knowledge transforms over time. The mobility of knowledge is at the core of the problem of transfer. It is however a different form of mobility than those engendered by and through resonance and fluid spaces. The question of transfer implies an imaginary of an object of knowledge located in a place – mind or practice – and moved to another place beyond the boundaries of the first place. The question of transfer is a question for representational knowledge. Communal knowledge moves as the resonance spreads, and liquid knowledge moves with the mutation of the fluid space, but none of them cross boundaries, as implied by the imaginary of learning transfer. These are only indications of the form of learning transfer that is performed with these different forms of knowledge. It is necessary in each question about the materiality of learning to return to our empirical descriptions of forms of knowledge and forms of learning and to describe how a form of learning is able to connect to other entities: to other spaces, other persons, and other forms of knowledge. In order to characterize the materiality of learning, we must describe in detail which entities enter into which relations that form which patterns in order to be able to characterize precisely the ability of a form of learning to connect to other entities.

If the question of transfer became less urgent in the case of fluid and resonance space, it however reappears when we consider how knowledge may move from one spatial formation to another. How does fluid space move to regional space? I provided an example of this when discussing how the researchers in the Femtedit project noted in our field notes what the children had "learned" in each session. Through a procedure of bracketing the efforts, the conflicts, and the interrelations among objects, talk, and thoughts, the liquid knowledge was recorded by the researchers as representational knowledge about skills achieved by each individual. Categorizing this movement from fluid to regional space as transfer is however inappropriate. Transfer has the connotation of a well-delimited object of knowledge being moved from one place to another. This was not what happened. Rather, we were dealing with a *translation* from fluid space to regional space, which was achieved through a socio-material process of bracketing, of individualizing, of establishing boundaries, and of recording, which translated and thus changed the knowledge from liquid to representational. When understanding knowledge in spatial terms, we cannot overlook the material process involved in what is usually called transfer, and when doing this we realize that we are dealing not with transfer but with translation (for further discussion on translation, see Callon [1986] and Brown and Capdevilla [1999]).

Often, the process of translating among spaces is not linear, as in this case. I described previously how representational knowledge is dependent on resonance, which makes it possible to refer to this knowledge from different particular places. As I discussed in Chapter 3, spaces never singularly exist on their own but are co-performed with other spaces. I described how representational knowledge was entangled with communal knowledge in the example of Boyle's experiments. Similarly, Latour (1993) has demonstrated this extensively in terms of purification and hybridization. Because spaces are intimately entangled with one another and because they interrelate and parts are shared across spaces, relations involved in one form of knowledge may be involved in another as well, and thus parts and relations of one space can participate in another. Here, we are dealing with relocation between spaces without any movement.

Whereas transfer implies that a more or less well-delimited body of knowledge moves between places (or is re-performed in different places), and translation describes a movement of knowledge between spaces that implies a change of knowledge, we are now dealing with an understanding of how knowledge can relocate across spaces without even moving. Because the latter is a partial relocation between spatial forms, I call this process *transformation*.

Any form of learning transfer is contingent on a particular form of learning, which is dependent on a particular form of knowledge, which is shaped through a particular spatial formation. And with any of these spatial formations, a form of presence is shaped that makes available certain ways of participating.

Following these theoretical discussions of the materiality of learning, I close the chapter – and the book – by discussing some of the implications my spatial methodology can have for the approach to educational politics. I first examine the political steps taken in 2005 as a consequence of the latest PISA (Programme for International Student Assessment) reports, which assess how well qualified fifteen- to sixteen-year-olds in the OECD (Organization for Economic Co-operation and Development) member countries were to meet the demands of information society (OECD 2004). This discussion clarifies the difference between a widespread way of analyzing and reacting to analyses of education and the spatial approach developed in this book, just as it demonstrates the applicability of this book's approach when dealing with educational political questions. The analysis of the consequences drawn from the PISA surveys is followed by a suggestion about how to deal with the multiplicity of forms of learning, knowledge, presence, and technology and the tension among them. This is a question that has come up as a consequence of the comparison of educational practices with analog and digital technology. The value of such comparison is considered. Finally, I close the book by underlining the two core abilities made available by the spatial methodology developed in this text: the reimagining and the rearranging of educational practice.

PISA and the Multiplicity of Educational Practice

As I was doing the analyses of the previous chapters, OECD published their latest PISA reports. Denmark received an average position in the evaluation that was inconsistent with the expectations most Danes, Danish schools, and certainly Danish politicians had of their school system. Consequently, the Danish liberal government decided on two interventions as a follow-up to the disappointing results: Danish pupils should be tested more often and discipline should be reinforced in Danish schools. The Danish ministry of education assembled three consortiums who were assigned the task of producing tenders for a battery of national tests for each grade of elementary school except the first. The tests were introduced in 2006. It is important to note that Denmark has a long tradition of schooling without testing, and before 2006 the first formal exams taken by elementary school pupils were given in eighth grade, the same year that pupils' performances were marked for the first time. In first to seventh grade, pupils' performances were evaluated orally during parent-teacher meetings.

The intent of the new tests is to make it possible for teachers to monitor pupils' competences and thereby enable teachers to quickly intervene when a pupil is behind the current milestones of the age group. The tests were to be seen as a tool for the individual teacher in his or her planning of the teaching. As such they were in line with the already-formed strategy of the current educational politics in Denmark, which over the past years has focused on an increase in assessment and goal-directed teaching. Five years earlier, the government had introduced the Clear Goals program, which required that teachers ensure that pupils pass specified milestones every four months.

PISA emphasizes that what is required in contemporary society and the labor market is the ability to act under unpredictable circumstances, often with unclear goals and without standard methods (OECD 2004). The Danish government agreed with this analysis. The interventions I mentioned were supposed to better prepare children for these conditions of life. From a spatial point of view, it is important to ask what the practical effects of these interventions are: what is performed in practices in which these interventions take part?

National tests are instruments for measuring the accumulation of individual skills or representational knowledge, as discussed in Chapter 4. Connecting test results with the Clear Goal guidelines makes the demand for representational knowledge act directly on the planning of the particular educational practice, which in order to perform this knowledge must increasingly be arranged regionally. Chapter 4 taught us that representational knowledge relies on materials that are widespread in society: References to length in meters can be encountered in a great number of places in society, which makes it possible to re-perform this representational knowledge in many places. This is the case with length, with volume, with colors, and with names of geographical places. Accumulating connections to representational knowledge – through accumulative learning – allows children to draw connections to these stable referents across places – known or unknown – as long as the representational references are in place.[1]

Assuming that the dispersion of references across practices in which children are going to take part is maintained, we can on the basis of this analysis expect that national tests and their coupling with the Clear Goal guidelines – which will increase regional educational practice – will improve children's ability to act under uncertain circumstances, provided that these circumstances are arranged with a sufficient number of representational references. To this extent, national tests can be said to meet the intentions behind these interventions. It is however unlikely that an uncertain situation will be thoroughly equipped with references, because references are materials that tend to contribute to producing certainty. It is furthermore unlikely that the tests can contribute to fluid, communal, or other forms of knowledge. Tests contribute to making it possible for children to take part in performing representational knowledge. As I have described in Chapter 4, representational knowledge contributes to performing only regional practices and is able to connect to only these spatial formations. PISA's aim – preparing children to be able to act in unpredictable circumstances – must however be seen as an intent to make it possible for children to connect to a variety of different spatial formations. Children predominantly qualified for regional practices will not be able to connect to fluid, network, resonance, or other spatial formations. Due to its singular focus on the performance of regional spaces, the efficacy of PISA's intervention is questionable. Due its invariability, representational knowledge is not necessarily the best form for meeting uncertainty. Liquid knowledge, which has the capacity to connect to and continue the ongoing stream of gradual transformation, may be a good candidate for contributing to an individual's ability to act in uncertain circumstances. But more than that, the ability to take part in and to contribute to performing a multiplicity of different spatial formations must be the most crucial attribute when learning to deal with uncertainty.

---

[1] We think mainly of the accumulation of connections to representational referents as a question of creating connections from the individual. Accumulation of connections to representational referents can however also be achieved by creating referents in more places and by making these more accessible. Globalizing Western referents in terms of, for instance, measurement systems, methods, and styles is thus also a way in which Westerners accumulate the ability to connect to more practices in the world. Simultaneously, individuals who have accumulated connections to referents that are replaced are de-learning.

Whereas the first governmental intervention implemented as a reaction to the PISA results had to do with knowledge acquisition, the second had to do with presence. They felt that schools should reinforce discipline in order to create peace and quiet, which would help the pupils concentrate on learning. The Danish minister of education appointed the Udvalg om disciplin, god adfærd og mobning i folkeskolen (Committee for Discipline, Good Behavior and Bullying in Elementary School). In 2006 the committee created a booklet with discipline guidelines to help schools formulate their individual regulations (Rasmussen 2006). The booklet's point of departure is that all children in school should feel secure and be able to move outside the classroom during breaks without fear of other pupils. Furthermore, children should be able to work undisturbed during lessons. Discipline is the means to secure this, it is stated. It is emphasized that discipline has nothing to do with being caned or with robot-like obedience. Rather, explicit values and clear rules of conduct are, according to the committee, the fundamental measures for creating discipline in schools. It is important that pupils feel ownership of the rules of conduct, which should accordingly be formulated and implemented through a dialogic process that includes the pupils as a social group. Whereas the constitution of the rules should follow a process of inclusion, violation of the regulations should be sanctioned with exclusion of individuals. The examples of sanctions mentioned in the booklet include ordering the pupil who is causing the disturbance to follow the teacher on playground duty, sending him or her into the corridor, detention, temporary or permanent exclusion from the school, or temporary or permanent transfer to another class.

The program reflects a logic often seen in the social sciences: order is social or collective, whereas disorder is ascribed to the individual. In spatial terms we can reformulate this as a regional order. The pattern of relations is founded on a values and rules system that applies to everybody within the region of the school. Sameness lies within the region, which is surrounded by firm boundaries. Disturbance within the region is a threat to the homogeneity of the pattern of relation, and must thus be excluded. This is a matter of course when existing and thinking within a regional pattern of relations. But we can reimagine this form of presence. The principal characteristic of fluid space is that change in one entity leads to mutation of the pattern of relations. If we think of the issue in spatial terms, we can see the "disturbance" as a space being destabilized. Following the spatial logic of presence discussed in Chapter 5, we must understand "the disruptive presence" as constituted through a pattern of relations, not by a single

entity, not by an individual. Disturbance must accordingly be seen as in-
terference between two spaces, and the relevant question to ask concerns
what patterns the disruptive presence interferes with, which rearrangements it gives rise to in the socio-material patterns of relations, and which
entities are rearranged. How could the disruptive space and the disrupted
space be rearranged in order for the two spaces to coexist (in modified
forms)? This is not a plea to give in to the disruptive presence and to adjust
school practice accordingly. It is a suggestion to supplement the imaginary
of how to arrange educational practices with non-regional spatial imaginaries. From the perspective of this book and the variation of spatial
formations I have discussed – which are far from exhaustive – a perspective
on school presence that follows only the logic of regionality seems inadequate. And if we return to the aim of schooling described in PISA – to
prepare children to act in uncertain circumstances – it is clear that a uni-
lateral expansion of regional spaces is not the way to reach this. Instead of
this singularizing endeavor, in order to reach the goal formulated by PISA
it is crucial, from a spatial perspective, that we connect a variety of spaces
and forms of presence and translate among them.

Contrary to the singularity produced by PISA, in Helen Verran's
(1999) work we find a fine sensitivity to multiplicity. She reports her experience with a Yoruba teacher in Nigeria who taught length by letting
children measure an object with a string. The teacher subsequently wound
the string around a ten-centimeter card and counted the number of winds.
Multiplying the number of winds by ten told the children the length of the
object in centimeters. As the teacher's instructor, Verran had to laugh
when confronted with this method, which rendered extension incidental to
length, which was instead enacted as contingent on multiplication. She was
disconcerted by this method, which was in strong contrast to the standard
English conception of length that she had taught the Yoruba teacher.
According to this, extension is a crucial abstract component that cannot be
left out of the understanding of length. Two explanations of the clash
between the two methods are readily available, Verran emphasizes:

1. It is a story of failure, in which Verran had failed in imparting the
    "proper" knowledge of length to the teacher and in which the Africans
    were consequently adopting a "primitive" way of quantifying.
2. It is a story of resistance, explaining how the teacher resisted
    Western incursion and taught a Yoruba form of quantification.

Verran accentuates that both of these common ways of interpreting the
incidence imply a singular order: either the order of one proper knowledge

or the order of one supreme power. They both explain away Verran's laughter and thereby the disconcertment she felt due to the confrontation of the English and the Yoruba ways of quantifying. Verran tries to establish a very different conclusion. She rejects "deleting and hiding the messiness and lack of smooth fit between the 'ideal' and the actual of quantifying" (1999, p. 149), and she suggests we describe what she calls symbolic-material routines, repetitions, and rituals instead of applying an imaginary of one singular order – of either kind.

Describing the socio-material practices in this book as spatial formations has in a similar way enabled me to avoid describing Femtedit as either failing to provide "proper" knowledge or "functional" presences or as being resisted by the teacher. I have done this by going through two steps. First, I have avoided following one singular order or one singular principle that describes degrees of failure or more or less powerful forms of knowledge or presence, just as I argued that the reactions to PISA – partly as a consequence of the power of quantitative surveys – asking for *more* knowledge and *more* discipline are a mistake. Technologies and other measures are implemented to boost knowledge achievement and good conduct. It is hardly ever asked what form(s) of knowledge and what form(s) of presence we have and what form(s) of knowledge and presence we want. We take for granted what knowledge is and what presence is – in singular – and we accordingly neglect to realize that knowledge and presence take diverse forms, as I have shown. I described the multiplicity of forms of knowledge and the different forms of presence as different juxtaposed spaces. I have been sensitive to how patterns of relations were formed and to what was formed through these spaces. This made available descriptions of the coexistence of multiple forms of knowledge and the coexistence of multiple forms of presence. Likewise, reactions to PISA should not ask for more; they should ask what forms of knowledge and presence are performed through the interventions suggested.

Second, I compared these spatial formations. Comparing enabled me to describe the tensions among different patterns of relations: how different forms of knowledge and different forms of presence intertwined with, clashed with, or repulsed one another. Just as Verran succeeded in creating a description that taught us about the Yoruba form of quantifying, the English form of quantifying, and the tension between the two – the laughter – I have described forms of knowledge and forms of presence without explaining away on the one hand the teachers' critique of the lack of resemblance and on the other the teachers' restlessness.

The teachers' critique and restlessness are in my descriptions expressions of neither failure nor resistance. They are the tension that exists in school practices as a result of different technologies in use. If there was only the ruler, only the bed-loft, only the blackboard, or only the online 3D virtual environment, then the diversity in forms of knowledge and forms of presence might decrease in school practices and as a result tension would decrease. Verran's disconcertment arose due to the introduction of the technology of winding string around a card. The teachers' critique and restlessness arose in Femtedit due to the introduction of the virtual environment. New (that is, not previously integrated into the practice in question) technologies contribute to shaping spatial formations that will very likely interfere with the existing spaces. I have been able to keep the tension among the different socio-material practices because I have taken the multiple spaces into account in my descriptions of what the technologies participated in forming. This is what the reactions to PISA fail to do. They have the inveterate habit of thinking in terms of one single spatial imaginary and thus on one single form of knowledge and one single form of presence at the cost of other forms. Analyzing in terms of spatiality, as suggested throughout the past chapters, makes us able to reimagine spatial formations and accordingly to reimagine knowledge, technology, presence, and learning.

Different spatial arrangements do not always fit together smoothly. The most common solution to this observation is to understand this as a problem or paradox in which one part has to be explained away or practically removed, as the U.S. schools did with the pupils' laptops, as described in Chapter 1. The results of the analyses of this book point in another direction. They urge us to investigate the patterns of relations of the different spatial formations and to look for potential connection points – or bridges – that can be built among spatial formations and among forms of knowledge, presence, or learning. Chapter 5 described such a bridge in terms of establishing a new, fluid form of authority that connects the regional form of authority to the fluid spatial formation of the virtual environment. We must look for connection points in the spatial formations where bridges can be created, and we must connect diverse forms of knowledge or forms of presence while keeping the tension among them. Tension is not a problem; it is a necessary effect of engagement with technologies. Consequently, our task is to find artful[2] ways of dealing with

---

[2] To talk about dealing "artfully" with tensions is inspired by Suchman's (1999) notion and practice of *artful integration*.

these tensions, which involves building bridges and practicing translations. We should treat different forms of learning in ways that stay true to the different ways in which they are socio-materially performed, and that maintain the tensions among the forms of learning and deal with the reality of the coexistence of multiple patterns of relations, instead of trying to fit the different practices into one single order or one single spatial formation. If we succeed in staying true to multiplicity and the tensions this implies, Verran states, we can start training children in the routines of both Yoruba and English quantification, and we can train them to adopt routines that translate between the spaces. In addition, pupils, teachers, headmasters, and politicians could start engaging in different forms of knowledge and different forms of presence, as well as in building bridges and creating routines that translate among the forms of presence and knowledge.

Comparing Technologies

My point of departure was to study a 3D virtual environment, but the nature of the empirical field led me to ask questions about materials I thought I knew all to well: a blackboard, notebooks, pencils, chalk, even walls and doors. I was surprised to find how crucial and unexpected were the formations these materials contributed to performing. By comparing the ways in which digital software and established analog learning materials take part in school practices, it has been possible to show quite precisely how their ways of participating differ, and what different forms of knowledge, presence, and learning they perform, which teaches us not only about the already-established learning materials, but also about digital technology and where to look for bridges between the two. Research on educational technology hardly ever considers that various forms of knowledge, presence, and learning already exist in educational practice, as shown in Chapters 4 and 5, and thus the practices established by traditional learning materials are rarely examined. As soon as we do the comparison, we realize that different forms of knowledge, presence, and learning are performed and, consequently, that our question should no longer be about more or less knowledge and presence when implementing new technology, but about *which* of these forms we want "more" of. Such a question cultivates sensitivity in dealing with the specificities of educational practices and in understanding what is performed with different technologies.

Comparison between traditional and established learning materials and newly implemented computer technologies is an important method for studying technology in school practice. As computers were introduced in schools, the literature on educational technology significantly increased. Paper after paper describes different educational uses of new technology. Very few take into consideration learning materials that have been used in schools for centuries.[3] Thereby much literature on educational technology implicitly creates an image of school practices as having been devoid of technology until the arrival of the computer, and this literature provides an understanding of digital software as constituting new school practices as a matter of course. It is often argued that digital software overcomes the problematic transmission model of traditional classroom practice (e.g., Hewitt 2001), but it is rarely discussed how the transmission model is performed by way of the traditional learning materials of the classroom, and how the practicalities of this arrangement differ from the ways in which digital technologies participate in school practices, as I have done in Chapters 4 and 5. The practical ways in which school practices should be – and inevitably are – rearranged when different technologies are involved thus remain obscure.

I suggest that the reason for the lack of focus on traditional, analog technologies and the lack of comparison between these and digital technologies lies in the fact that educational scholars tend to focus on the desired aims of educational practice, and thus they tend to ask how new technologies can help achieve these aims. New technologies are usually implemented without any consideration of how the already-established learning materials – notebooks, blackboards, pencils, and erasers – contribute to forming the current educational practice. Accordingly, what happens to educational practice – as a consequence of not only inserting new technology but also removing traditional learning materials that up to that point had been in charge of part of the unfolding of educational practice – remains unobserved. Materials are removed from and inserted into educational practice on the basis of a simplified understanding of technology as an instrument for educational aims, and consequently teachers, headmasters, pupils, politicians, and others concerned with school practice are taken aback by the chaos and loose ends formed by the disruption of the relations within which the traditional materials were bound up and the lack of connection between the new technology and the current educational practice. When investing $30 billion into school computers, as in the example mentioned in Chapter 1, stakeholders should demand that such ends and connections be analyzed and taken care of. Many more comparative studies of how traditional and new technologies participate in

---

[3] Cuban's work is a notable exception (e.g., 1986).

educational practice and what spatial formations they contribute to shaping are needed. How new technologies contribute to forming new educational practices can only be fully understood on the basis of a detailed analysis of how contemporary or past materials shape such practices. Appreciation for such sensitivity requires that we approach technologies as contributing to forming educational practice through interaction. In order to reach symmetry between analog and digital technologies, we need to stop dealing with technologies exclusively as a means or foundation for educational aims. And, importantly, such a comparison also helps us understand and requires us to accept that when new technology is implemented, different forms of learning, knowledge, and presence will be shaped.

The Reality, Reimagining, and Rearranging of Educational Practice

Latour (2004c) notes that science studies have mainly been occupied with playing detective, that is, revealing what science actually is, and thereby deconstructing and destabilizing scientific facts. In learning theory we see the same tendency to reveal what learning actually is, and thereby to deconstruct and destabilize the cognitivist understanding of learning. But just as Latour emphasizes that this is a fruitless form of critique that only contributes to digging lines of trenches, I have realized through working with this book that we need to get beyond the tendency to demonstrate over and over again that learning is actually situated. The spatial analyses I have presented in this book have dealt a lot with regionality, with representational knowledge, and with regional authority. This is because such spatial formations are widespread. It is no wonder that the cognitivist approach to learning is so popular, because representational knowledge and accumulative learning are indeed the core forms performed in educational practice. Note that my analyses have not concluded that regionality is actually a network or a fluid. In spatial terms, this would make no sense. Regions are regional, period. And being regional implies being performed as such. When knowledge is performed as representational, then it is representational. This is important: The spatial analyses I have presented do not create different levels of reality, such as apparent and actual reality (see Despret 2004b; Latour 1999c). I do not conclude that regional knowledge is actually situated, and thus not in the mind. On the contrary, I conclude that regional knowledge is socio-materially performed and in the mind, because, indeed, it is performed as located in the mind, as I have described in Chapter 4. Likewise, authority is not solely a result of socio-material interaction, with only the appearance of authority. Rather, authority is a result of socio-material interaction, and thus it is authority – apparently and actually. A crucial difference between deconstructivist or critical attempts and this spatial approach is that the latter makes it possible to account for different spatial formations and the tensions among them without explaining away any of them. Knowledge "in the mind" does exist, because there are socio-material practices – regional practices – that perform such form of knowledge. The mistake of cognitivist learning theories is that they fail to acknowledge that knowledge in the mind is performed, rather than that they claim that knowledge in the mind exists, which social approaches to learning tend to point out.

A crucial result of the studies presented in this book is the idea that knowledge, presence, learning, and technology are performed in different ways as representations, liquids, agents, authorities, imitations, accumulations, and mutations. This is not only an argument of the multiplicity of educational practice. It furthermore creates a sensitivity that allows us to reimagine knowledge, presence, technology, and learning. Only by appreciating that different forms exist can we start asking the question of how these different forms are performed, and only then can we subsequently start reimagining spatial formations. Moreover, on the basis of reimagining spatial formations through detailed descriptions of the patterns of relations that shape them and through descriptions of the forms of knowledge, technology, presence, and learning, we can point to the particular patterns, relations, and entities that can be rearranged to create new forms, and to the places where entities and relations can be added to build bridges among different forms.

We may say that any discussion, theory, analysis, intervention, plan, or conversation follows a certain logic, frame, regime, routine, system, structure, paradigm, set of rules, or form. I have chosen "form," and the spatial methodology developed throughout this book is a methodology for challenging the forms that contribute to shaping our thoughts in particular patterns. It is a methodology that simultaneously examines an empirical field and challenges the habitual ways in which we imagine and deal with empirical fields – which are most often regional. By analyzing how materials and materialities participate in school practice, a wide range of different forms unfold that materials and materialities contribute to performing. Taking the materiality of learning seriously changes the form of our thinking and the forms of our practice, and it makes it possible to reimagine and rearrange educational practice, that is, to reimagine and rearrange technology, knowledge, presence, and learning.

The Methodology of the Materiality of Learning
Lesson 6: The Materiality of Learning
On the basis of the definition of materiality (Lesson 2) and of the definition of learning (Lesson 4), we can now define the materiality of learning as the achieved ability of a growth in knowledge to connect to other entities. In other words, the materiality of learning is comparable to learning transfer. As we learned to talk about forms of learning, we must talk about forms of learning transfer that differ according to the forms of knowledge and spatial formations through which the learning and thus the learning transfer is performed. We must apply the same core principle as we did when analyzing forms of learning; that is, we must first describe the practical details of patterns of relations, then characterize the spatial formation, followed by a meticulous description and characterization of forms of knowledge and forms of presence. Only then it is possible to start describing and characterizing first learning, then learning transfer.

Accounting for the materiality of learning is about asking the right questions – about creating sensitivity – which allows us to describe the spatial formations of our object of study. It is about following the forms in which relations create patterns, about the frame within or logic according to which the practices and thus knowledge, presence, and learning are spatially formed. It is also about reimagining and rearranging forms of knowledge, presence, and learning on the basis of the concrete connection points discovered through the spatial analysis. The ability to find connection points, to create bridges and translations between spatial formations, rests on five core sensitivities:

1. Sensitivity to materials and to materiality as performed, as emerging through the socio-material arrangement that the materials are part of, which is studied with a minimal methodology
2. Sensitivity to comparing well-established and new technologies, and thus to the variations in the ways in which materials take part in socio-material arrangements
3. Sensitivity to spatial patterns of relations instead of to entities, because knowledge, presence, and learning are shaped spatially

4. Sensitivity to multiplicity, because only through appreciation of a multiplicity of forms is it possible to start reimagining the spatial formations of educational practices and of knowledge, presence, and learning
5. Sensitivity to particularity, because it is the particularities of educational practices that show us which entities and relations to rearrange in order to create new forms of learning, knowledge, and presence, and to build bridges or translate between different spatial formations

The methodology of the materiality of learning is sensitive to forms of educational practices, and it can thus help us challenge, reimagine, and rearrange these forms.

Reference List

Adorno, Theodor W.; Frenkel-Brunswick, Else; Levinson, Daniel J.; and Sanford, Newitt. 1950. *The Authoritarian Personality*. New York: Harper & Row.

Agalianos, Angelos; Whitty, Geoff; and Noss, Richard. 2006. "The Social Shaping of Logo," *Social Studies of Science* **16**, 2: 241–267.

Akrich, Madeleine. 1992. "The De-Scription of Technical Objects," in Bijker, Wiebe E., and Law, John (eds.) *Shaping Technology/Building Society: Studies in Sociotechnical Change*. Cambridge, MA: MIT Press, pp. 205–224.

Althusser, Louis. 1971. "Ideology and Ideological State Apparatuses: Notes Towards an Investigation," in Althusser, Louis, *Lenin and Philosophy and Other Essays*. London: NLB, pp. 123–173.

Amit, Vered (ed.). 2000. *Constructing the Field: Ethnographic Fieldwork in the Contemporary World*. New York: Routledge.

Asplund, Johan. 1985. *Tid, rum, individ och kollektiv* [Time, Space, Individual and Collective]. Stockholm: Liber Förlag.

Austin, John Langshaw. 1962. *How to Do Things with Words*. Oxford: Oxford University Press.

Barab, Sasha, and Plucker, Jonathan A. 2002. "Smart People or Smart Contexts? Cognition, Ability, and Talent Development in an Age of Situated Approaches to Knowing and Learning," *Educational Psychologist* **37**, 3: 165–182.

Barab, Sasha; Sadler, Troy D.; Heiselt, Conan; Hickey, Daniel; and Zuiker, Steven. 2006. "Relating Narrative, Inquiry, and Inscriptions: Supporting Consequential Play," *Journal of Science Education and Technology* **16**, 1: 59–82.

Barad, Karen. 1998. "Getting Real: Technoscientific Practices and the Materialization of Reality," *Differences: A Journal of Feminist Cultural Studies* **10**, 2: 87–128.

——— 2007. *Meeting the Universe Halfway: Quantum Physics and the Entanglement of Matter and Meaning*. Durham, NC, and London: Duke University Press.

Barry, Andrew. 2001. *Political Machines: Governing a Technological Society*. London: The Athlone Press.

Bingham, Nick, and Thrift, Nigel. 2000. "Some New Instructions for Travellers: The Geography of Bruno Latour and Michel Serres," in Crang, Mike, and Thrift, Nigel (eds.) *Thinking Space*. London: Routledge, pp. 281–301.

Bloor, David. 1976. *Knowledge and Social Imagery*. Chicago: University of Chicago Press.

Boyd, Sally. 2002. *Literature Review for the Evaluation of the Digital Opportunities Projects*. Wellington: New Zealand Council for Educational Research.

Brewster, Maria. 2001. *Supermanual: The Incomplete Guide to the Superchannel*. Liverpool: Foundation for Art and Creative Technology.

Brown, Steven D., and Capdevilla, Rose. 1999. "Perpetuum Mobile: Substance, Force and the Sociology of Translation," in Law, John, and Hassard, John (eds.) *Actor Network Theory and After*. Oxford: Blackwell, pp. 26–50.

Buckingham, David. 2000. *After the Death of Childhood: Growing Up in the Age of Electronic Media*. Cambridge: Polity Press.

Butler, Judith. 1993. *Bodies that Matter – on the Discursive Limits of "Sex."* New York: Routledge.

———— 1997. *The Psychic Life of Power: Theories of Subjection*. Stanford, CA: Stanford University Press.

Callon, Michel. 1986. "Some Elements of a Sociology of Translation: Domestication of the Scallops and the Fishermen at St. Brieuc Bay," in Law, John (ed.) *Power, Action and Belief*. London: Routledge and Keagan Paul, pp. 196–233.

———— 1998. *The Laws of the Markets*. London: Blackwell Publishers/Sociological Review.

Callon, Michel, and Law, John. 1997. "After the Individual in Society: Lessons on Collectivity from Science, Technology and Society," *Canadian Journal of Sociology* 22: 165–182.

Casey, Edward S. 1998. *The Fate of Place: A Philosophical History*. Berkeley: California University Press.

Christensen, Pia H., and James, Allison. 2000. *Research with Children: Perspectives and Practices*. London: Falmer Press.

Clarke, Adele E. 2005. *Situational Analysis: Grounded Theory after the Postmodern Turn*. Thousand Oaks, CA, London, and New Dehli: Sage.

Cole, Michael. 1996. *Cultural Psychology: A Once and Future Discipline*. Cambridge, MA: Belknap Press.

Colley, Helen; Hodkinson, Paul; and Malcom, Janice. 2002. *Non-Formal Learning: Mapping the Conceptual Terrain: A Consultation Report*. Leeds: University of Leeds Lifelong Learning Institute.

de Coninck-Smith, Ning, and Gutman, Marta. 2004. "Children and Youth in Public," *Childhood* 11, 2: 131–141.

Crang, Mike, and Thrift, Nigel. (eds.) 2000. *Thinking Space*. London: Routledge.

Cuban, Larry. 1986. *Teachers and Machines: The Classroom Use of Technology Since 1920*. New York: Teachers College, Columbia University.

Deleuze, Gilles. 1995. *Negotiations*. New York: Columbia University Press.

Despret, Vinciane. 2004a. *Our Emotional Makeup*. New York: Other Press.

———— 2004b. "The Body We Care For: Figures of Anthropo-Zoo-Genesis," *Body and Society [Special Issue on Bodies on Trial]* 10, 2–3: 111–134.

Dewey, John. 1929. *The Quest for Certainty: A Study of the Relation of Knowledge and Action*. New York: G. P. Putnam's Sons.

———— 1938. *Experience and Education*. New York: Macmillan.

Dillenbourg, Pierre. 2000. "Virtual Learning Environments." Paper presented at the EUN Conference 2000, Geneva.

Dreier, Ole. 1993. *Psykosocial Behandling – En teori om et praksisområde [Psycho-Social Treatment – A Theory of a Field of Practice]*. Copenhagen: Dansk psykologisk Forlag.

1999. "Personal Trajectories of Participation across Contexts of Social Practice," *Outlines – Critical Social Studies* **1**: 5–32.

2003. "Learning in Personal Trajectories of Participation," in Stephenson, Niamh; Radtke, H. Lorraine; Jorna, Rene; and Stam, Henderikus J. (eds.) *Theoretical Psychology: Critical Contributions*. Concord: Captus University Publications, pp. 20–29.

2008. *Psychotherapy in Everyday Life*. Cambridge, MA: Cambridge University Press.

Druin, Allison, and Solomon, Cynthia. 1996. *Designing Multimedia Environments for Children: Computers, Creativity, and Kids*. New York: John Wiley & Sons.

Ejlskov, Morten W.; Jensen, Kenneth H.; Jensen, Tine; and Sørensen, Estrid. 2001. "Situmanual – Incomplete Guide to the Superchannel," in FACT (ed.) *Situmanual – Incomplete Guide to the Superchannel*. Liverpool: FACT, pp. 3–35.

Elgaard Jensen, Torben. 2001. *Performing Social Work – Competence, Orderings, Spaces and Objects*. Copenhagen: University of Copenhagen.

2007. "Witnessing the Future," *Forum: Qualitative Social Research* **8**, 1: Art. 1.

Foucault, Michel. 1972. *The Archeology of Knowledge*. London: Tavistock.

1979. *Discipline and Punish: The Birth of the Prison*. Harmondsworth: Penguin.

Freud, Sigmund. 1994. *The Interpretations of Dreams*. New York: Modern Library Edition.

Gane, Nicholas, and Haraway, Donna. 2006. "When We Have Never Been Human, What Is to Be Done? Interview with Donna Haraway," *Theory, Culture & Society* **23**, 7–8: 135–158.

Garfinkle, Harold. 1967. *Studies in Ethnomethodology*. Cambridge: Polity Press.

Giddens, Anthony. 1984. *The Constitution of Society*. Cambridge: Polity Press.

von Glasersfeld, Ernst. 1985. "Reconstructing the Concept of Knowledge," *Archives de Psychologie* **53**: 91–101.

Goffman, Erving. 1959. *The Presentation of Self in Everyday Life*. Harmondsworth: Penguin.

1981. *Forms of Talk*. Philadelphia: University of Pennsylvania Press.

Gomart, Emile. 2004. "Surprised by Methadone: In Praise of Drug Substitution Treatment in a French Clinic," *Body and Society [Special Issue on Bodies on Trial]* **10**, 2–3: 85–110.

Goodwin, Charles. 1994. "Professional Vision," *American Anthropologist* **96**, 3: 606–633.

Griffin, Peg, and Cole, Michael. 1984. "Current Activity for the Future: The Zoped," in Rogoff, Barbara, and Wertsch, James (eds.) *Children's Learning in the "Zone of Proximal Development."* San Francisco: Jossey-Bass, pp. 45–64.

Gumbrecht, Hans Ulrich. 2004. *Production of Presence: What Meaning Cannot Convey*. Palo Alto, CA: Stanford University Press.

Hammersley, Martyn, and Atkinson, Paul. 1995. *Ethnography: Principles in Practice*. London: Routledge.

Haraway, Donna. 1991. "A Cyborg Manifesto: Science, Technology, and Socialist-Feminism in the Late Twentieth Century," in *Simians, Cyborgs, and Women: The Reinvention of Nature*. New York: Routledge, pp. 149–182.

1997. *Modest_Witness@Second_Millennium. Femaleman©_Meets_ OncoMouse™*. New York: Routledge.

2003. *The Companion Species Manifesto: Dogs, People, and Significant Otherness.* Chicago: Prickly Paradigm.

Haraway, Donna J. 2008. *When Species Meet.* Minneapolis: University of Minnesota Press.

Hastrup, Kirsten, and Ovesen, Jan. 1985. *Etnografisk grundbog: Metoder, teorier, resultater [Ethnographic primer: Methods, Theories, Results].* Copenhagen: Gyldendal.

Hatch, Thomas, and Gardner, Howard. 1993. "Finding Cognition in the Classroom: An Expanded View of Human Intelligence," in Salomon, Gavriel (ed.) *Distributed Cognitions: Psychological and Educational Considerations.* New York: Cambridge University Press, pp. 164–187.

Henriksen, Dixi Louise. 2003. *ProjectWeb as Practice: On the Relevance of Radical Localism for Information Systems Development Research.* Roskilde: Roskilde Universitetscenter.

Hetherington, John, and Lee, Nick. 2000. "Social Order and the Blank Figure," *Environment and Planning D: Society and Space* **18**, 2: 169–184.

Hewitt, Jim. 2001. "From a Focus on Tasks to a Focus on Understanding: The Cultural Transformation of a Toronto Classroom," in Koschmann, Timothy; Hall, Rogers P.; and Miyake, Naomi (eds.) *CSCL 2: Carrying Forward the Conversation.* Mahwah and London: Lawrence Erlbaum, pp. 11–42.

Hine, Christine. 2000. *Virtual Ethnography.* London: Sage.

Hine, Christine (ed.). 2005. *Virtual Methods: Issues in Social Research on the Internet.* Oxford: Berg.

Hirschauer, Stefan. 2004. "Praktiken und ihre Körper: Über materielle Partizipanden des Tuns" [Concerning Material Participants of Doing], in Hörning, Karl H., and Reuther, Julia (eds.) *Doing Culture: Neue Positionen zum Verhältnis von Kultur und sozialer Praxis.* Bielefeld: Transcript, pp. 73–91.

Højrup, Thomas. 2003. *State, Culture and Life-Modes: The Foundations of Life-Mode Analysis.* Hampshire: Ashgate.

Holzkamp, Klaus. 1995. *Lernen: Subjektwissenschaftliche Grundlegung [Learning: A Subjectivity Research Foundation].* Frankfurt am Main: Campus.

Hoppe, Ulrich H. 2007. "Educational Information Technologies and Collaborative Learning," in Hoppe, Ulrich H.; Ogata, Hiroaki; and Soller, Amy (eds.) *The Role of Technology in CSCL: Studies in Technology Enhanced Collaborative Learning.* New York: Springer, pp. 1–9.

Hudson-Smith, Andy. 2001. "30 Days in ActiveWorlds: Community, Design and Terrorism in a Virtual World," in Schroeder, Ralph (ed.) *The Social Life of Avatars: Presence and Interaction in Shared Virtual Environments.* Berlin, Springer-Verlag, pp. 77–89.

Hughes, Thomas P. 1989. "The Evolution of Large Technological Systems," in Bijker, Wiebe E.; Hughes, Thomas P.; and Pinch, Trevor J. (eds.) *The Social Construction of Technological Systems.* Cambridge, MA: MIT Press, pp. 51–82.

Hultqvist, Kenneth. 2001. "Bringing the Gods and the Angels Back? A Modern Pedagogical Saga about Excess in Moderation," Hultqvist, Kenneth, and

Dahlberg, Gunilla (eds.) *Governing the Child in the New Millennium.* New York: Routledge Falmer, pp. 143–171.

2004. "The Traveling State, the Nation and the Subject of Education," in Baker, Bernadette M., and Heyning, Katharina E. (eds.) *Dangerous Coagulations? The Uses of Foucault in the Study of Education.* New York: Peter Lang: pp. 153–188.

Hutchins, Edwin. 1995. *Cognition in the Wild.* Cambridge, MA: MIT Press.

Jasanoff, Sheila. 2007. "Making Order: Law and Science in Action," in Hackett, Edward J.; Amsterdamska, Olga; Lynch, Michael; and Wajcman, Judy (eds.) *The Handbook of Science and Technology Studies*, 3rd Edition. Cambridge, MA: MIT Press, pp. 761–786.

Jensen, Casper, and Lauritsen, Peter. 2005. "Qualitative Research as Partial Connection: Bypassing the Power-Knowledge Nexus," *Qualitative Research* **5**, 1: 59–77.

Jensen, Tine. 2005a. *Thinking about Competence and Subjectivity in the Fifth Dimension: Working on the Boundaries of Virtuality and Subjectivity in and out of School.* Roskilde: Roskilde University.

2005b. "When Faith and Good Will Is Not Enough: Researcher Positions in Interactive Research with School Children," *Annual Review of Critical Psychology* **4**, 4: 166–178.

Jensen, Tine; Jensen, Kenneth; and Morten, Jack. 2005. "Learning in Virtual and Physical Communities," in Nocon, Honorine, and Nilsson, Monica (eds.) *School of Tomorrow: Teaching and Technology in Local and Global Communities.* New York: Peter Lang, pp. 87–130.

Johnson, Jim (aka Bruno Latour). 1995. "Mixing Humans and Nonhumans Together: The Sociology of a Door-Closer," in Star, Susan Leigh (ed.) *Ecologies of Knowledge: Work and Politics in Science and Technology.* Albany, NY: SUNY Press, pp. 257–277.

Karsten, Lia. 2003. "Children's Use of Public Space: The Gendered World of the Playground," *Childhood* **10**, 4: 457–473.

Kaspersen, Lars Bo. 1995. *Anthony Giddens – introduktion til en samfundsteoretiker [Anthony Giddens – Introduction to a Social Theorist].* Copenhagen: Hans Reitzels Forlag.

Klette, Kirsti. 1998. "Introduksjon til klasseromsforskning som forskningsfelt" [Introduction to Classroom Research as a Research Field], in Klette, Kirsti (ed.) *Klasseromsforskning – på norsk.* Oslo: Ad Notam Gyldendal, pp. 13–35.

Knorr Cetina, Karin. 1999. *Epistemic Cultures: How the Sciences Make Knowledge.* Cambridge, MA: Harvard University Press.

Knorr Cetina, Karin, and Preda, Alex. 2004. *The Sociology of Financial Markets.* Oxford: Oxford University Press.

Koschmann, Timothy. 1996. *CSCL: Theory and Practice of an Emerging Paradigm.* Mahwah, NJ: Lawrence Erlbaum Associates.

Koschmann, Timothy; Hall, Rogers P.; and Miyake, Naomi (eds.). 2002. *CSCL 2: Carrying Forward the Conversation.* Mahwah and London: Lawrence Erlbaum.

Kuhn, Thomas. 1970. *The Structure of Scientific Revolutions.* Chicago: University of Chicago Press.

de Laet, Marianne, and Mol, Annemarie. 2000. "The Zimbabwe Bush Pump: Mechanics of a Fluid Technology," *Social Studies of Science* **30**, 2: 225–263.

Lakoff, George, and Johnson, Mark. 1980. _Metaphors We Live By_. Chicago: University of Chicago Press.

Latour, Bruno. 1987. _Science in Action_. Cambridge, MA: Harvard University Press.

1988. _The Pasteurization of France_. Cambridge, MA: Harvard University Press.

1990. "Drawing Things Together," in Lynch, Michael, and Woolgar, Steve (eds.) _Representation in Scientific Practice_. Cambridge, MA: MIT Press, pp. 19–68.

1993. _We Have Never Been Modern_. Hertfordshire: Harvester Wheatsheaf.

1999a. "A Collective of Humans and Nonhumans," in _Pandora's Hope – Essays on the Reality of Science Studies_. Cambridge, MA: Harvard University Press, pp. 174–215.

1999b. "Circulating References – Sampling the Soil in the Amazon Forest," in _Pandora's Hope – Essays on the Reality of Science Studies_. Cambridge, MA: Harvard University Press, pp. 24–79.

1999c. "Do You Believe in Reality" in _Pandora's Hope – Essays on the Reality of Science Studies_. Cambridge, MA: Harvard University Press, pp. 1–23.

1999d. "On Recalling ANT," in Law, John, and Hassard, John (eds.) _Actor Network Theory and After_. Oxford: Blackwell, pp. 15–25.

2004a. "How to Talk About the Body? The Normative Dimensions of Science Studies," _Body and Society [Special Issue on Bodies on Trial]_ **10**, 2–3: 205–229.

2004b. "Scientific Objects and Legal Objectivity," in Pottage, Alain, and Mundy, Martha (eds.) _Law, Anthropology and the Constitution of the Social: Making Persons and Things_. Cambridge: Cambridge University Press, pp. 73–113.

2004c. "Why Has Critique Run Out of Steam? From Matters of Fact to Matters of Concern," _Critical Inquiry_ **30**: 225–248.

Latour, Bruno, and Woolgar, Steve. 1986. _Laboratory Life: The Construction of Scientific Facts_. Princeton, NJ: Princeton University Press.

Lave, Jean. 1988. _Cognition in Practice_. New York: Cambridge University Press.

Lave, Jean, and Wenger, Etienne. 1991. _Situated Learning: Legitimate Peripheral Participation_. New York: Cambridge University Press.

Law, John. 1989. "Technology and Heterogeneous Engineering: The Case of Portuguese Expansion," in Bijker, Wiebe E.; Hughes, Thomas P.; and Pinch, Trevor P. (eds.) _The Social Construction of Technological Systems: New Directions in the Sociology and History of Technology_. Cambridge, MA: MIT Press, pp. 111–134.

1999. "After ANT: Complexity, Naming and Topology," in Law, John, and Hassard, John (eds.) _Actor Network Theory and After_. Oxford: Blackwell, pp. 1–14.

2002a. _Aircraft Stories – Decentering the Object in Technoscience_. Durham, NC: Duke University Press.

2002b. "Objects and Spaces," _Theory, Culture and Society_ **19**, 5/6: 91–105.

2004. _After Methods – Mess in Social Science Research_. Oxon: Routledge.

Law, John, and Hassard, John (eds.). 1999. _Actor Network Theory and After_. Oxford: Blackwell.

Law, John, and Mol, Annemarie. 2001. "Situating Technoscience: An Inquiry into Spatiality," _Environment and Planning D: Society and Space_ **19**: 609–621.

Law, John, and Singleton, Vicky. 2005. "Object Lessons," _Organization_ **12**, 3: 331–355.

Leander, Kevin M. 2002. "Silencing in Classroom Interaction: Producing and Relating Social Spaces," *Discourse Processes* **34**, 2: 193–235.

Lee, Nick. 2001. *Childhood and Society: Growing Up in an Age of Uncertainty.* Buckingham: Open University Press.

Lee, Nick, and Brown, Steven D. 1994. "Otherness and the Actor Network – The Undiscovered Continent," *The American Behavioral Scientist* **37**, 6: 772–790.

Lefebvre, Henri. 1991. *The Production of Space.* Oxford: Blackwell.

Lehtinen, Erno; Lipponen, Lasse; Hakkarainen, Kai; Rahikainen, Marjaana; and Muukkonen, Hanni. 2000. "Computer Supported Collaborative Learning: A Review," in de Jong, Frank; Simons, Robert-Jan; and Meijden, Henry (eds.) *Computer Supported Collaborative Learning in Primary and Secondary Education: A Final Report for the European Commission.* Nijmegen: University of Nijmegen, pp. 1–46.

Leontiev, Alexei Nikolajewitsch. 1978. *Activity, Consciousness and Personality.* New York and Englewood Cliffs: Prentice Hall.

Ligorio, Maria Beatrice, and van Veen, Klaas. 2006. "Constructing a Successful Cross-National Virtual Learning Environment in Primary and Secondary Education," *Association for the Advancement of Computing in Education Journal* **14**, 2: 103–128.

Lindblad, Sverker, and Sahlström, Fritjof. 1998. "Klasserumsforskning: En oversigt med fokus på interaktion og elever" [Classroom Research: An Overview with Focus on Interaction and Pupils], in Bjerg, Jens (ed.) *Pædagogik – en grundbog til et fag.* København: Hans Reitzels Forlag A/S, pp. 224–257.

Luhmann, Niklas. 2002. *Das Erziehungssystem der Gesellschaft* [The Educational System of Society]. Frankfurt am Main: Suhrkamp Verlag.

Lyotard, Jean François. 1984. *The Postmodern Condition: A Report on Knowledge.* Minneapolis: University of Minnesota Press.

Magnus, P. D. 2007. "Distributed Cognition and the Task of Science," *Social Studies of Science* **37**, 2: 297–310.

Marland, Michael. 1993. *The Craft of the Classroom: A Survival Guide.* Oxford: Heinemann Educational.

McCormick, Robert M., and Paechter, Carrie. 1999. *Learning and Knowledge.* London: Open University Press.

Mead, George Herbert. 1932. "The Objective Reality of Perspectives," in *The Philosophy of the Present.* Chicago: Chicago University Press: pp. 161–175.

1934. *Mind, Self, and Society.* Chicago: University of Chicago Press.

Medd, Will, and Marvin, Simon. 2007. "Making Water Work: Intermediating between Regional Strategy and Local Practice," *Environment and Planning D: Society and Space* (Advance Online Publication), http://www.envplan.com/abstract.cgi?id=d3205.

Merleau-Ponty, Maurice. 1962. *Phenomenology of Perception.* London: Routledge and Kegan Paul.

Merton, Robert K. 1973. *The Sociology of Science: Theoretical and Empirical Investigations.* Chicago: Chicago University Press.

Miller, Daniel, and Slater, Don. 2000. *The Internet: An Ethnographic Approach.* Oxford: Berg.

Mol, Annemarie. 1999. "Ontological Politics: A Word and Some Questions," in Law, John, and Hassard, John (eds.) *Actor Network Theory and After.* Oxford: Blackwell, pp. 74–89.

2002. *The Body Multiple: Ontology in Medical Practice.* Durham, NC: Duke University Press.

Mol, Annemarie, and Law, John. 1994. "Regions, Networks and Fluids: Anaemia and Social Topology," *Social Studies of Science* 24: 641–671.

Mørk, Sven. 1994. "Handlingsteorien" [The Action Theory], *Udkast – Dansk tidskrift for Kritisk Samfundsvidenskab* 22, 1: 3–47.

Newman, Fred, and Holzman, Lois. 1997. *The End of Knowing: A New Developmental Way of Learning.* New York: Routledge.

Nielsen, Klaus, and Kvale, Steinar. 1999. *Mesterlære: Læring som Social Praksis [Apprenticeship: Learning as Social Practice].* Copenhagen: Hans Reitzels Forlag.

Nocon, Honorine. 2005. "The Role of Network in the School of Tomorrow," in Nocon, Honorine, and Nilsson, Monica (eds.) *School of Tomorrow: Teaching and Technology in Local and Global Communities.* New York: Peter Lang, pp. 131–166.

O'Day, Vicky; Bobrow, Daniel; Bobrow, Kimberly; Shirley, Mark; Hughes, Billie; and Walters, Jim. 1998. "Moving Practice: From Classrooms to MOO Rooms," *Computer Supported Cooperative Work: The Journal of Collaborative Computing* 7, 1–2: pp. 9–45.

OECD. 2004. *Learning for Tomorrow's World: First Results from PISA 2003.* Paris: OECD.

Papert, Seymour. 1980. *Mindstorms: Children, Computers, and Powerful Ideas.* New York: Basic Books.

1993. *The Children's Machine: Rethinking School in the Age of the Computer.* New York: Basic Books.

Philo, Chris. 2000. "Foucault's Geography," in Crang, Mike, and Thrift, Nigel (eds.) *Thinking Space.* London: Routledge, pp. 205–238.

Piaget, Jean. 1972. "The Myth of the Sensory Origin of Scientific Knowledge," in Pickering, Andrew (ed.) *Psychology and Epistemology: Towards a Theory of Knowledge.* Harmondsworth: Penguin, pp. 45–62.

Pickering, Andrew. 1995. *The Mangle of Practice: Time, Agency & Science.* Chicago: University of Chicago Press.

Popper, Karl. 1963. *Conjectures and Refutations: The Growth of Scientific Knowledge.* London: Routledge and Kegan Paul.

Quinn, Naomi. 1991. "The Culture Basis of Metaphor," in Fernandez, James W. (ed.) *Beyond Metaphor: The Theory of Trope in Anthropology.* Stanford, CA: Stanford University Press, pp. 56–93.

Rasmussen, Kim. 2004. "Places for Children – Children's Places," *Childhood* 11, 2: 155–173.

Rasmussen, Lise Bagge. 2006. *Vejledning om disciplin, god adfærd og trivsel i folkeskolen – et inspirationshæfte [Guidance in Discipline, Good Behavior and Well-Being in Elementary School – an Inspiration Booklet].* Copenhagen: Undervisningsministerietsafdeling for grundskolen og folkeoplysning.

Rogoff, Barbara, and Wertsch, James. 1984. *Children's Learning in the "Zone of Proximal Development."* San Francisco: Jossey-Bass.

Roth, Wolff-Michael. 1999. "Authentic School Science: Intellectual Traditions," in McCormick, Robert M., and Paechter, Carrie (eds.) *Learning and Knowledge*. London: Open University Press, pp. 6–20.

Sabini, John. 1992. *Social Psychology*. New York: W.W. Norton.

Salomon, Gavriel. 1993. *Distributed Cognition – Psychological and Educational Considerations*. Cambridge: Cambridge University Press.

Scheffer, Thomas. 2003. "The Duality of Mobilisation: Following the Rise and Fall of an Alibi-Story on Its Way to Court," *Journal for the Theory of Social Behaviour* **33**, 3: 313–347.

Scheffler, Israel. 1999. "Epistemology and Education," in McCormick, Robert M., and Paechter, Carrie (eds.) *Learning and Knowledge*. London: Open University Press, pp. 1–5.

Schroeder, Ralph; Huxor, Avon; and Smith, Andy. 2001. "Activeworlds: Geography and Social Interaction in Virtual Reality," *Futures* **33**: 569–587.

Shapin, Steven, and Schaffer, Steven. 1985. *Leviathan and the Air-Pump: Hobbes, Boyle, and the Experimental Life*. Princeton, NJ: Princeton University Press.

Shutkin, David. 1998. "The Deployment of Information Technology in the Field of Education and the Augmentation of the Child," in Popkewitz, Thomas S., and Brennan, Marie (eds.) *Foucault's Challenge: Discourse, Knowledge, and Power in Education*. New York: Teachers College Press: pp. 205–230.

Simpson, Brenda. 2000. "The Body as a Site of Contestation in School," in Prout, Alan (ed.) *The Body, Childhood and Society*. London: Macmillian Press, pp. 60–78.

Sismondo, Sergio. 2004. *An Introduction to Science and Technology Studies*. Oxford: Blackwell.

Smith, Richard G. 2003. "Baudrillard's Nonrepresentational Theory: Burn the Signs and Journey without Maps," *Environment and Planning D: Society and Space* **21**: 67–84.

Sørensen, Estrid. 1998. "Computerspil – virkelighed eller fiktion?" [Computer Game – Reality or Fiction?], *Nordisk Psykologi* **50**, 2: 135–150.

2001. "Constituting Notions of Knowledge with Philosophy and Technology," *Outlines – Critical Social Studies* **29**, 1: 67–86.

2003. "From Research Result to Technological Development," EU-report for Fifth Frame Program project "5D, Local Learning in a Global World."

2005. "Lær af computerspil!" [Learn from Computer Games!], in Walther, Bo Kampmann, and Jessen, Carsten (eds.) *Spillets verden*. København: Danmarks Pædagogiske Universitets Forlag, pp. 283–295.

2007. "The Time of Materiality," *Forum Qualitative Social Research* **8**, 1: Art. 2.

Spradley, James P. 1979. *The Ethnographic Interview*. New York: Holt, Rinehart and Winston.

St. Pierre, Elizabeth Adams. 1997. "Methodology in the Fold and the Irruption of Transgressive Data," *International Journal of Qualitative Studies in Education* **10**, 2: 175–189.

Star, Susan Leigh. 1991. "Power, Technology and the Phenomenology of Conventions: On Being Allergic to Onions," in Law, John (ed.) *A Sociology of Monsters: Essays on Power, Technology and Domination*. Cambridge: Polity, pp. 26–56.

Star, Susan Leigh. 2002. "Infrastructure and Ethnographic Practice: Working on the Fringes," *Scandinavian Journal of Information Systems [Special Issue on Ethnography and Intervention]* **14**, 2: 107–123.

Star, Susan Leigh, and Strauss, Anselm. 1999. "Layers of Silence, Arenas of Voice: The Ecology of Visible and Invisible Work," *Computer Supported Cooperative Work: The Journal of Collaborative Computing* **8**: 9–30.

Steiner, Barbara. 2003. *Superflex/Tools*. Köln: Verlag der Buchhandling Walther König.

Stengers, Isabelle. 1997. *Power and Invention: Situating Science*. London: University of Minnesota Press.

2000. *The Invention of Modern Science*. Minneapolis and London: University of Minnesota Press.

Strathern, Marilyn. 1996. "Cutting the Network," *Journal of the Royal Anthropological Institute* **2**: 517–535.

Suchman, Lucy. 1987. *Plans and Situated Actions*. Cambridge, MA: Cambridge University Press.

Suchman, Lucy. 1999. "Working Relations of Technology Production and Use," in MacKenzie, Donald, and Wajcman, Judz (eds.) *The Social Shaping of Technology*. Buckingham and Philadelphia: Open University Press, pp. 258–268.

2007. *Human-Machine Reconfigurations: Plans and Situated Actions, 2nd Edition*. Cambridge, MA: Cambridge University Press.

Taylor, Charles. 1985. *Philosophy and the Human Sciences*. New York: Cambridge University Press.

Thrift, Nigel. 1996. *Spatial Formations*. London: Sage.

2000. "Afterwords," *Environment and Planning D: Society and Space* **18**: 213–255.

Traweek, Sharon. 1988. *Beamtimes and Lifetimes: The World of High Energy Physicists*. Cambridge, MA: Harvard University Press.

Turkle, Sherry. 1997. *Life on the Screen: Identity in the Age of the Internet*. London: Phoenix.

Turnbull, David. 1993. *Maps Are Territories: Science Is an Atlas*. Victoria: Deakin University Press.

Uni-C. 2007. *Computere i Skolen* [Computers in School]. Retrieved December 6, 2007, from http://cis.emi.dk.

U.S. Census Bureau. 2007. Administrative and Customer Services Division, Statistical Compendia Branch, Table 248. Retrieved December 6, 2007, from http://www.census.gov.

Varenne, Hervé, and McDermott, Ray. 1998. "Introduction," in Varenne, Hervé, and McDermott, Ray (eds.) *Successful Failure*. Oxford: Westview Press, pp. 1–24.

Verran, Helen. 1998. "Re-Imagining Land Ownership in Australia," *Postcolonial Studies* **1**, 2: 237–254.

1999. "Staying True to Laughter in Nigerian Classrooms," in Law, John, and Hassard, John (eds.) *Actor Network Theory and After*. Oxford: Blackwell, pp. 136–155.

Vygotsky, Lev S. 1978. *Mind in Society – The Development of Higher Psychological Processes*. Cambridge, MA: Harvard University Press.

Warschauer, Mark. 1998. "Online Learning in Sociocultural Context," *Anthropology & Education Quarterly* **29**, 1: 68–88.

Webster's New World Dictionary, and Thesaurus (Version 1.0). 1997. Accent Software International/Macmillan Publishers.

Winthereik, Brit Ross; de Bont, Antoniette; and Berg, Marc. 2002. "Accessing the World of Doctors and Their Computers: 'Making Available' Objects of Study and the Research Site through Ethnographic Engagement," *Scandinavian Journal of Information Systems [Special Issue on Ethnography and Intervention]* **14**, 2: 47–58.

Winthereik, Brit Ross, and Vikkelsø, Signe. 2005. "ICT and Integrated Care: Some Dilemmas of Standardising Inter-Organisational Communication," *Computer Supported Cooperative Work: The Journal of Collaborative Computing* **14**, 1: 43–67.

Index

Active Worlds. *See* 3D virtual
    environments
activity theory, 10, 37, 129
actor-network theory, 9
    after-ANT, 69–70, 86
    classic-ANT, 57, 67, 69–70, 71
    critique of, 66–68
Adorno, Theodor W., 150
after-ANT. *See* actor-network theory
agents, 164–166, 169, 173
    vs. subjects, 164
Althusser, Louis, 149–150, 152
ANT. *See* actor-network theory
arrangements. *See* assemblages,
    socio-material
Asplund, Johan, 142, 150
assemblages, socio-material, 16, 19, 53,
    57, 61, 70, 139
assessment, 127, 129, 132–134, 183
association, 36–38, 59
Austin, John Langshaw, 133
authority, 148–154, 164–175,
    191–192
    fluid authority, 166–168, 188
    regional authority, 167, 188, 191
avatars, 3

Barry, Andrew, 168–169
becoming, 13, 41, 51, 56, 126, 129, 130
blackboards, 140–141, 143–150,
    152–154, 158–159, 170
blank objects, 80
Blekinge Institute of Technology, 37, 46
blog, used in Femtedit project, 3, 24,
    42–46, 51, 54, 63, 113, 115–116,
    117, 167

boundaries. *See* separating
Boyle, Robert, 100–104, 107–108,
    109–112, 120–121

Callon, Michel, 66, 70
classic-ANT. *See* actor-network theory
classroom observation, 23–25
Cole, Michael, 37
collectives, 140–144, 173
comparison, of technologies, 25,
    190–191, 193
computer-supported collaborative
    learning, 5
contingency, 11, 35, 134, 182
CSCL. *See* computer-supported
    collaborative learning
Cuban, Larry, 6
cyborg, 60

decentering, 57, 136
design, 19, 22, 24
    designer expectations, 6, 7,
    34, 72
    design research, research design,
    33–34, 59
    and use, 23, 27
Despret, Vinciane, 82, 85, 134
discontinuity. *See* separating
dissociation, 37, 52, 59, 66
distributed cognition, 89–92
doing, 15, 18
Dreier, Ole, 18, 57, 137, 172

Eduverse. *See* 3D virtual environments
entanglement, 31, 39, 53
    vs. coordination, 84

ethnography, 3, 21, 25
    constructing the field, 30–61
    distance and immersion, 21
    and nomadic gaze, 25
euclidian space, 75, 84
evaluation. *See* assessment

failing, 7, 63, 78, 85, 187
FEMTEDIM, 19–23, 38–46, 83–84
Femtedit, 19–23, 30–61, 62–88
field notes, writing of, 22, 25
Fifth Dimension, 37–38
fluid space, 27, 56, 62–88, 115–131,
    164–170
    and network space, 81–85
    and regional space, 123–125
    vs. regional space, 117–118, 128–129,
    167–168, 169–175
forms, 27, 82, 187
Foucault, Michel, 72–73, 151, 168
frame story, 23, 24, 41, 45, 54, 80,
    117, 169

Giddens, Anthony, 164
Goffman, Erving, 17, 138
growth in knowledge,
    learning as, 130–132, 135–136, 177
    materiality of learning as, 193
Gumbrecht, Hans Ulrich, 138

Haraway, Donna J., 67, 68, 120, 122
heterogeneity, 34, 53, 60
heterogeneous engineering, 33–34,
    63–64
Hirschauer, Stefan, 18
Holzman, Lois, 129
humanist approach, 2, 6
hybrids, 38, 59, 60, 87

imaginaries, 13–15, 29. *See also*
    reimagining
    as formal descriptions, 26
    spatial imaginaries, 25–29, 56,
    73, 76
immutable mobiles, 54, 85
infrastructures, 36, 53, 110, 125
interpellation, 141, 149–150, 152

knowledge, 89–136
    communal knowledge, 108–112, 133
    liquid knowledge, 125–130,
    133, 180
    ontology of, 90–92, 135
    representational knowledge,
    102–104, 133

language games, 82
de Laet, Marianne, 77, 165, 169
Latour, Bruno, 35, 53, 54, 57, 66, 70,
    85, 90, 102, 121, 130, 181, 191
Lave, Jean, 18, 89, 92, 137, 172, 178
Law, John, 27, 33, 35, 36, 38, 51–52,
    54, 58, 62, 63, 68–70, 71, 82, 86,
    88, 97, 164, 165, 166, 169
learning, 5, 130–135
learning transfer, 177–182, 193
Lee, Nick, 67, 80, 159, 174
Lefebvre, Henri, 70, 71, 72

Magnus, P. D., 91
material, definition of, 61
materiality,
    definition of, 61
    of learning, definition of, 177, 193
methodology, 1, 3, 10–19, 25–29, 177,
    192, 194
    minimal methodology, 26, 28, 193
Mol, Annemarie, 27, 62, 69–70, 75–76,
    77, 82–83, 84–85, 86, 97, 164, 165,
    166, 169
multiplicity, 69, 81–87, 182–189, 194
    Femtedit as a multiple object, 86
    vs. pluralism, 82

network space, 27, 30–61, 62, 75
    critique of, 66–68
    and fluid space, 81–85
    vs. fluid space, 62–88
Newman, Fred, 129
nomadic gaze, 24
nonrepresentationalism, 126

observing participants, 21
online discussion forum, 4, 23, 24,
    44, 54

ontology, 13, 28, 32, 36, 42, 53, 60, 91, 132, 135, 138

participant observation, 22, 25
participation, 17–19, 28, 36
  and learning, 172
particularity, 18, 76, 173, 194
patterns of relations, 70–72, 76
performance, performativity, 15–17, 28, 133, 177, 191, 193
  performative research, 33
perspectivism, 71, 72, 82, 84, 85
Philo, Chris, 72
PISA (Programme for International Student Assessment), 182–188
place. *See* space, spatiality
posthumanism, 2, 3, 15, 170–175, 176
practice approach, 22, 135
presence, 137–176, 180. *See also* agent; authority; collectives
  and learning, 171
  reimagining presence, 190–194
prolonging, 16, 29, 82
purification, 31, 38, 61, 71, 181

reality, 16–17, 36, 82, 84, 99, 103, 118, 125, 126, 128, 191
reductionism, 127–128
regional space, 27, 56, 74, 75, 100, 103, 108, 127, 128, 130, 133, 144–150, 154, 166, 178–179, 180, 185
  and fluid space, 123–125
  vs. fluid space, 117–118, 128–129, 167–168, 169–175
  and inclusion/exclusion as a means of discipline, 185
  and network space, 191
  vs. network space, 109
reimagining, 14, 15, 177, 182, 185, 188, 191–194
relationality, 57, 75
  vs. spatiality, 70, 87
resonance space, 56, 106, 108, 120–123, 131, 133, 136, 180
  vs. network space, 106

Schaffer, Steven, 100–104, 108, 120, 121
science and technology studies, 7, 8, 9
separating, 144, 146, 161–164, 166, 176
  and connecting, 170
  of boundaries, 13, 97–98, 102–104, 136, 146–148, 169–171, 178–181
  of boundaries vs. discontinuity, 164–166, 169
  and discontinuity, 63, 129, 166, 168
Shapin, Steven, 100–104, 103, 108, 120, 121
singularity, 30, 68, 82, 86–88, 186–187
situated learning, 9, 90, 92, 131, 135, 137, 172, 178, 179
socio-materiality, 2, 5, 9, 10, 60, 121, 137, 187
somatic currency, 134
songs,
  Bulgarian song, 140–144
  Pakistani song, 118–120
space, spatiality, 26, 70–76, 87–88, 181–182, 185–189, 191–194.
    See also fluid space; network space;
  vs. place, 74
  regional space
  vs. relationality, 70, 87
spatial imaginaries. *See* imaginaries
spatial metaphors, 27, 71, 75
stability, 55, 85, 86
  fluid stability, 64, 65, 77
  network stability, 52, 58, 59, 67–68
  regional stability, 98, 99
  resonance stability, 121
Star, Susan Leigh, 66
Stengers, Isabelle, 34, 36
STS. *See* science and technology studies
subjects, subjectivity, 148–154, 166, 170, 173
  vs. agents, 164
  vs. collectives, 173
Suchman, Lucy, 14, 78, 114, 188
Superflex, 34
symmetry, 18, 59
  between analog and digital technologies, 25, 191

symmetry (*cont.*)
  between humans and nonhumans,
    5, 18, 58
  between inside and outside, 58
  between knowledge practices, 33
  between materials and discourse, 58
  between object and field, 58

technology, technologies, 58, 86, 88
  comparison of, 25, 190–191, 193
  as an instrument, 2, 7, 151
  as a means to an end, 5–8
  as separate from user, 30–32
  and theory, 31
textbooks,
  and blankness, 80
  and regional knowledge, 100
  and representational knowledge, 104
theoretical technology, 12, 15, 16,
    26, 29
3D virtual environments, 3, 30–61,
    62–88. *See also* FEMTEDIM;
    Femtedit
  Active Worlds, 3, 4, 30–32, 34
  Eduverse, 38
Thrift, Nigel, 17, 57, 126, 127, 134
time, temporality, 56, 67, 72–74, 76,
    83, 135
topology, 75

transfer. *See* learning, transfer of
transformation, 182
translation, 13, 16, 29, 123–125, 127,
    181, 193
  chains of, 70
  vs. transfer and vs. transfomation,
    181–182
transmission model, 174, 190
trials of strength, 51, 39–52, 58, 59, 63,
    70, 76, 83
  vs. ongoing trials, 65, 68
truth, 133
Turkle, Sherry, 128, 138

Verran, Helen, 13–14, 15, 16,
    186–188, 189
version, 16, 82
virtual environments. *See* 3D virtual
    environments
Vygotsky, Lev, 129, 151

weblog. *See* blog, used in Femtedit
    project
witnessing, 96, 100, 102, 106, 107, 109,
    120–123
  virtual witnessing, 108, 110, 123, 127
  vs. withnessing, 134

zone of proximal development, 129

Titles in the Series *(continued from page iii)*

Mind and Social Practice: Selected Writings of Sylvia Scribner
Ethel Tobach, Rachel Joffee Falmagne, Mary Brown Parlee, Laura
M. W. Martin, and Aggie Scribner Kapelman, Editors

Cognition and Tool Use: The Blacksmith at Work
Charles M. Keller and Janet Dixon Keller

Computation and Human Experience
Philip E. Agre

Situated Cognition: On Human Knowledge and Computer Representation
William J. Clancey

Communities of Practice: Learning, Meaning, and Identity
Etienne Wenger

Learning in Likely Places: Varieties of Apprenticeship in Japan
John Singleton, Editor

Talking Mathematics in School: Studies of Teaching and Learning
Magdalene Lampert and Merrie L. Blunk, Editors

Perspectives on Activity Theory
Yrjö Engeström, Reijo Miettinen, and Raija-Leena Punamäki, Editors

Dialogic Inquiry: Towards a Sociocultural Practice and Theory of Education
Gordon Wells

Vygotskian Perspectives on Literacy Research: Constructing Meaning Through Collaborative Inquiry
Carol D. Lee and Peter Smagorinsky, Editors

Technology in Action
Christian Heath and Paul Luff

Changing Classes: School Reform and the New Economy
Martin Packer

Building Virtual Communities: Learning and Change in Cyberspace
K. Ann Renninger and Wesley Shumar, Editors

Adult Learning and Technology in Working-Class Life
Peter Sawchuk

Vygotsky's Educational Theory in Cultural Context
Alex Kozulin, Boris Gindis, Vladimir S. Ageyev, and Suzanne M. Miller, Editors

Designing for Virtual Communities in the Service of Learning
Sasha A. Barab, Rob Kling, and James H. Gray, Editors

Bakhtinian Perspectives on Language, Literacy, and Learning
Arnetha F. Ball and Sarah Warshauer Freedman, Editors

Beyond Communities of Practice: Language, Power, and Social Context
David Barton and Karin Tusting, Editors

The Learning in Doing series was founded in 1987 by Roy Pea and John Seely Brown.